Modernism and Its Environments

NEW MODERNISMS SERIES

Bloomsbury's *New Modernisms* series introduces, explores, and extends the major topics and debates at the forefront of contemporary Modernist Studies.

Surveying new engagements with such topics as race, sexuality, technology, and material culture, and supported with authoritative further reading guides to the key works in contemporary scholarship, these books are essential guides for serious students and scholars of Modernism.

Published Titles

Modernism: Evolution of an Idea
Sean Latham and Gayle Rogers

Modernism and the Law
Robert Spoo

Modernism in a Global Context
Peter J. Kalliney

Modernism's Print Cultures
Faye Hammill and Mark Hussey

Modernism, Science, and Technology
Mark S. Morrisson

Modernism, Sex, and Gender
Celia Marshik and Allison Pease

Modernism, War, and Violence
Marina MacKay

Race and Modernisms
K. Merinda Simmons and James A. Crank

Forthcoming Titles

Modernism and Its Media
Chris Forster

Modernism and Its Environments

Michael Rubenstein and Justin Neuman

BLOOMSBURY ACADEMIC
LONDON • NEW YORK • OXFORD • NEW DELHI • SYDNEY

BLOOMSBURY ACADEMIC
Bloomsbury Publishing Plc
50 Bedford Square, London, WC1B 3DP, UK
1385 Broadway, New York, NY 10018, USA

BLOOMSBURY, BLOOMSBURY ACADEMIC and the Diana logo are trademarks of Bloomsbury Publishing Plc

First published in Great Britain 2020

Copyright © Michael Rubenstein and Justin Neuman, 2020

Michael Rubenstein and Justin Neuman have asserted their right under the Copyright, Designs and Patents Act, 1988, to be identified as Author of this work.

For legal purposes the Acknowledgments on pp. ix–x constitute an extension of this copyright page.

Cover design: Daniel Benneworth-Gray
Cover image: *The Weather Project*, 2003, by Olafur Eliasson, Installation in Turbine Hall, Tate Modern, London. Photo, October 24 2006. © Nathan Williams / www.simiant.com / Flickr

All rights reserved. No part of this publication may be reproduced or transmitted in any form or by any means, electronic or mechanical, including photocopying, recording, or any information storage or retrieval system, without prior permission in writing from the publishers.

Bloomsbury Publishing Plc does not have any control over, or responsibility for, any third-party websites referred to or in this book. All internet addresses given in this book were correct at the time of going to press. The author and publisher regret any inconvenience caused if addresses have changed or sites have ceased to exist, but can accept no responsibility for any such changes.

A catalogue record for this book is available from the British Library.

Library of Congress Control Number: 2020934297

ISBN: HB: 978-1-3500-7603-7
PB: 978-1-3500-7602-0
ePDF: 978-1-3500-7605-1
eBook: 978-1-3500-7604-4

Series: New Modernisms

Typeset by Deanta Global Publishing Services, Chennai, India

To find out more about our authors and books visit www.bloomsbury.com and sign up for our newsletters.

For Karen and Séamus; and for Walker, Alden, and Grayson

CONTENTS

List of Figures viii
Acknowledgments ix

Introduction: The New Modernist Studies, Environmentalism, and Ecocriticism 1

1 Modernism's Energy Environments 25

2 Modernism's Urban Environments 57

3 Modernism's Animals 89

4 Modernism in the Wilderness 115

5 The Climate of Modernism 143

Works Cited 175
Index 189

FIGURES

Cover Photo: *The Weather Project*, Olafur Eliasson
1 *Portrait of a Young American Girl in the State of Nudity*, Francis Picabia — 30
2 The city of the future, frame shot from *Metropolis* — 58
3 *Houses of Parliament in the Fog*, Claude Monet — 68
4 "The Three Magnets," from Ebenezer Howard's *Garden Cities of Tomorrow* — 80
5 *Unique Forms of Continuity in Space*, Umberto Boccioni — 91
6 Deborah Kerr's bird hat, frame shot from *The Life and Death of Colonel Blimp* — 102
7 *Electrocuting an Elephant*, frame shot — 111
8 Theodore Roosevelt and John Muir at Yosemite Falls — 127
9 *Spiral Jetty*, Robert Smithson — 159

ACKNOWLEDGMENTS

We wish to thank the editors of the New Modernisms series, Sean Latham and Gayle Rogers, who entrusted us with the work of writing this book, and whose suggestions for revision made it stronger. We also thank David Avital, senior publisher, and Lucy Brown, editor, at Bloomsbury Press, for their work in bringing this project to print. David Rodriguez was our most thorough reader, and he did a wonderful job in editing the manuscript—tracking down references, proofreading, and making critical interventions. We owe him a special debt of gratitude. Aaron Rosenberg graciously shared his panel paper from MSA 2016, "From Waste to World War: Fixations on Nitrogen," with us (we can't wait to see that work in print), and Imre Szeman shared a proof copy of his book *On Petrocultures: Globalization, Culture, and Energy* so that we could quote from it here.

Some of our early ideas for this project were presented in November of 2016 at the Modernist Studies Association annual conference in Pasadena, in a seminar we organized called Modernist Energy Regimes, and in March of 2018 at the American Comparative Literature Association annual conference in Los Angeles, in another seminar we organized called Modernism and Its Environments. In both seminars our colleagues offered ideas, research, and inspiration that have undoubtedly made this a better book.

Michael thanks those who volunteered to read portions of the manuscript as it was being written: Elyse Graham, Karen Lloyd, Drew Newman, and Mike Tondre. A faculty fellowship in spring 2017 funded by the Humanities Institute at Stony Brook University provided time and space to write. Ann Kaplan offered inspiration. Celia Marshik provided expert advice about writing a book like this one, along with an outstanding example in the one she wrote with Allison Pease, *Modernism, Sex and Gender*. Justin would like to thank William Spengemann, John Elder, Jennifer Wicke, Michael

Levenson, Jahan Ramazani, and Peter Brooks for their teaching and guidance over the years, as well as Elizabeth Tucker for her keen editorial eye and invaluable insights about the visual arts.

Finally, writing a book tends to be a rather solitary affair, if not a lonely one; in this case it was a joy. For their patience, intelligence, and the occasional strict deadline, we each owe our coauthor a debt of gratitude.

Introduction

The New Modernist Studies, Environmentalism, and Ecocriticism

A change in the weather is sufficient to create the world and oneself anew.

MARCEL PROUST, *THE GUERMANTES WAY* (1925)

Most people have seen a reproduction of the Norwegian artist Edvard Munch's painting *The Scream*, dated with some uncertainty between 1893 and 1910. This is true not because *The Scream* is a staple of modernist visual art, but because it has become a staple of dorm-room kitsch; reproductions are nearly as common as those of Van Gogh's *Starry Night*. The title of Munch's painting is generally taken to refer to the human figure in its center, holding its head between its hands with its mouth open and appearing, indeed, to be screaming. But Munch suggests in a journal entry from January 22, 1882, that the titular scream referred to something else entirely. While walking out "along the road with two friends" one evening in Kristiana (now Oslo), Munch describes an unsettling experience: "The sun was setting, I felt a wave of sadness, the Sky [*sic*] suddenly turned blood red.... My friends walked on, I stood there quaking with angst, and I felt as though a vast, endless scream passed through nature" (qtd. in Prata et al. 1379). So the scream doesn't refer to the human figure in the foreground after all; it refers to (and originates from) the bloodred sky of the background.

Art historians have often interpreted *The Scream*'s red sky, composed of wavy expressionistic brush strokes, as a motif symbolizing the figure's externalized "pain, morbid feelings, and angst," a version of the pathetic fallacy by which the figure's psychological state is projected onto the weather surrounding it (Prata et al. 1379). Then in 2004 a bold theory was put forth by a group of astronomers, based on Munch's journal entry in conjunction with his proven tendency to play fast and loose with dates: that the massive eruption of a volcano at Krakatoa on August 27, 1883, had caused the skies over Oslo to turn spectacularly red; and that Munch had observed this, imagined it as a scream from nature, and made it the subject of his painting (see Olson et al.). Another theory emerged in 2017 from the meteorologists Svein Fikke, Jón Kristjánsson, and Øyvind Nordli: that the red sky was produced by a rare formation of nacreous clouds, a "type of polar stratospheric clouds" that "generate very dramatic skies and are most noticeable as the sun sets" (Prata et al. 1382). But whether the sky in *The Scream* was inspired by a volcanic sunset or by a rare cloud formation, our point is that the sky is itself the main subject of the painting, not the human figure at its center. It is weather that determines the mood of the figure, not the figure's mood that determines the painting's representation of the sky; thus the style of the painting is less expressionistic, less symbolist, and far more mimetic than was previously thought. This is not to reduce Munch's painting to pure mimesis, but rather to open new avenues of interpretation for a work that the critical tradition had understood as almost pure modernist poesis, and that the market had reduced to kitsch.

The Scream stands in this book as an opening gesture because its critical history testifies to the kind of work that ecocriticism can do. Ecocriticism can reveal in modernist works a dialogue with nature where previously we saw a deep dive into human psychology or an experiment in painterly style; it can show us that our instincts about the relationship between foreground and background are often confused or even inverted; and it can help us to see new aspects of modernism's engagement with its environments. Moreover, *The Scream*'s recent critical reevaluation exemplifies a mode of interdisciplinary engagement made possible by an ecocritical approach to culture.

Modernism and Its Environments

The main question our book sets out to explore is this: What would it mean to present a cultural history of modernism under the banner of environmentalism? As we shall demonstrate, modernism has much more to say about the environment, and ecocriticism has much more to say about modernism, than has traditionally been understood in either modernist studies or the environmental humanities. To launch our inquiry, we start with one grounding assumption: that the urgency of applying ecocritical methods and concerns to modernist culture derives from our current environmental crisis, especially the discovery and scientific confirmation of anthropogenic climate change. In their *Environmental Humanities: A Critical Introduction*, Robert S. Emmet and David E. Nye similarly ground their work in a statement of its urgency:

> On the basis of the scientific evidence, we think global warming is taking place, and do not think it is an open question as to whether human beings have contributed to it or not. We believe that species extinction is occurring at an alarming rate, and we reject the notion that humanity has a special place in creation that legitimates the elimination of other forms of life. We believe that current consumption of the earth's resources is not sustainable. (1)

We share these convictions, and we understand them, like most scholars contributing to the environmental humanities, as statements of fact. This view separates us in crucial ways from the writers and artists we consider in this volume, who were, as we discuss in our chapter on energy, largely ignorant of the climatological effects of fossil fuel use.

As we will see, ecocritics did not initially take up modernism for the obvious reason—which turned out, as this book shows, to be superficial—that modernism was perceived as at its best indifferent, and at its worst hostile, to environmentalist conceptions of nature. Ecocritics did not look to the modernists at first because they saw in modernism a rejection of their own naturalist aesthetics and conservationist ethics. Modernist texts are often deliberately, even flagrantly, ecocidal, in thrall to what Hugh Kenner once called their "mechanic muse." But as the global climate emergency becomes more apparent, the modernists—as the cultural ambassadors of the war on nature—become anxiously relevant, since their works can now be analyzed for the epistemologies and ontologies that have led to the present crisis.

We hasten to add that the point of this book is not anachronistically to judge artists according to today's standards of sustainability. On the contrary, we are enthusiastic scholars of modernism who find a great deal more in modernist culture than ecocidal impulses to critique. Instead, the question is one of relevant archive: rather than searching for "green" pockets in modernism's wastelands, we set out to investigate both the green and the gritty manifestations of the modernist imagination. It is probably obvious to most of our readers that learning about the carbon cycle will be essential to meeting the challenge of climate change, but it is less intuitive that such knowledge will help us read the poetry of T. S. Eliot or the novels of Virginia Woolf. And yet, as we hope to demonstrate in this volume, the impetus for thinking about modernist environments is deeply woven into the fabric of modernism itself across a variety of its expressive modes.

From our grounding assumption we now move to an animating question: How does the cultural movement we've come to know as modernism—uneasily, as we shall see—conceive and represent what we've come to call the environment? On their own, both terms signify abstractions whose referents are far from being matters of settled certainty. If we were to be semantic sticklers, "modernism" and "environment" as we understand them today are both anachronisms when applied to the period between 1890 and 1930— the period traditionally understood to encompass modernism. It will prove instructive to unpack these anachronisms, but it will also prove expedient to stop worrying about them once we've marked their traces, returning to an informed, contemporary definition of each term in order to turn to particular cultural histories of specific concepts within modernism. We dedicate the subsequent chapters of this book to some of the most significant conceptual categories that shaped modernist thought about the environment: energy, the city, the animal, the wilderness, and the weather.

We call this book *Modernism and Its Environments*, but in fact ours is really a story about the shifting valences of these two terms and of the art we might productively associate with them. In a way, the only really suitable title for this book, one that would capture all our meanings at once, would be *Modernisms and Their Environments*, but that only succeeds by failing in a different way, flattening the narrative arc of the story we uncover here. That story in its most general form goes like this. For a few decades in the middle of the twentieth century, cultural critics imagined modernism as a grandly singular aesthetic vision, coherent unto and consistent with itself—a great wave of avant-gardism, abstraction, and experimentation cresting around 1922 or 1925. This was the tradition canonized as the so-called high modernism practiced by an international and highly interconnected coterie working across a panoply of artistic disciplines, a group whose luminaries included figures such as T. S. Eliot, Pablo Picasso, James Joyce, Marcel Proust, Henrik Ibsen, and Virginia Woolf, to name only a few.

At the time there was no popular concept of "the environment" like the one we know and use today. Instead, there were multiple local environments: the urban contrasted with the rural, parks with slums, factories with farms, mountains with plains, deserts with forests, and so on. To call these sites local environments, however, is already to use a language foreign to the moderns of the early twentieth century. As Joshua Schuster argues in *The Ecology of Modernism*, they thought instead in terms of plural environs rather than the singular environment (8). But by the last decade of the twentieth century, the conceptual relationship between modernism and the environment had reversed itself: modernism was in pieces, and came to be understood as multiple and diverse *modernisms*. And the diverse and multiple environs of high modernism were reimagined as one singular, interdependent, planetary, and ecological whole: *the* environment.

The monolithic understanding of modernism was an invention of the new critics who wrote and thought from the postwar university. The high modernists were far more factional than they have come to seem retrospectively, having thought of themselves not as a unified school or movement but as confrontational splinter groups— Symbolists or Dadaists or Surrealists or Vorticists or Futurists; turf-wars were real and the voices loud. The manifestos of Vorticism and Futurism, for example, explicitly celebrated the machine age and condemned the natural world, attaching a heroic, aggressive masculinity to the former and a weak, passive femininity to the latter. Before the Great War of 1914–18, few referred to modernism, and to be an "environmentalist" implied something very different from what we mean by it today. What the moderns did share was a sense of living in a time of acute social crisis and rapid technological transformation—amid what Marshall Berman memorably calls "the maelstrom of modern life," a storm driven by new developments in science, transportation, communications, and warfare (16). These changes precipitated a whole host of revolutionary movements in aesthetics. Looking back on this period in his memoir of modernism, *The World of Yesterday*, Austrian intellectual Stefan Zweig describes "a period of wild experimentation [that] began in all fields of art, in an attempt to overtake all that had ever been done in the past in a single mighty bound" (324). "Every page should explode," wrote Tristan Tzara, the Dadaist artist and revolutionary, epitomizing the shock and awe strategy of modernism's trademark transgressiveness (7). An ethos of transgression and innovation united the modernists in a general sense, even as they struggled to differentiate themselves from one another individually. Italian political theorist Antonio Gramsci makes this claim with unique force regarding the Futurists in particular: "They have destroyed, destroyed, destroyed, without worrying if the new creations produced by their activity were on the whole superior to those destroyed" (Kolocotroni et al. 215). Concern with the preservation of the natural environment from damage caused by human influence does not appear high on the modernists' priority list; causing destruction, creative or otherwise, was modernism's métier.

In the 1920s environmentalism did not connote, as it does today, "concern with the preservation of the natural environment, esp. from damage caused by human influence; the politics or policies associated with this" (OED). Environ, we learn from the *Oxford English Dictionary*, is a verb meaning "to form a ring round." We might say, following this definition, that the radii of the rings the moderns drew round their environments tended to be very small indeed, though Virginia Woolf's deep ecological sensibility, a subject we examine later in this chapter, is one stunning exception to this rule. The term's most common use was figurative, as a synonym for milieu, surrounding influences, or conditions—as William Carlos Williams uses it in *Spring and All* in reference to the "crudely repressive environment" that shaped the poet Edgar Allan Poe (198), or as in the completely misleading title—when reading with contemporary eyes—of F. R. Leavis and Denys Thompson's 1933 book *Culture and Environment: The Training of Critical Awareness*, in which "environment" had nothing to do with nature and meant something like a milieu of cultural influences, as one might find in a coterie like the Bloomsbury Group, for example. More troublingly, those who identified as "environmentalists" in the 1910s and 1920s were apt to subscribe to a species of climatic determinism premised on the belief that not only could one's institutional surroundings—family, school, work, state—shape one's character but so too could the prevailing weather. "Before the term was appropriated by the green movement," writes Peter Coates, environmentalism "was often allied to a racist view of history" (20). *Civilization and Climate*, which might easily be mistaken for a contemporary monograph discussing the threats of climate change, is in fact the title of a 1915 volume by Ellsworth Huntington, then a professor of geography at Yale University and subsequent president of the American Eugenics Society, that tries to explain social hierarchies and justify a wide array of prejudices by pointing to their supposed "environmental" causes. Instead of being predetermined by our genes, established by a higher power, or subject to social conditioning, "mental activity," Huntington maintains, "reaches a maximum when the outside temperature averages about 38 degrees [Fahrenheit], that is, when there are mild frosts at night" (8). Huntington was by no means the first writer to venture such theories, but his writings exemplify their rising popularity in the modernist period. Another prominent "environmentalist" in this sense was Henry Ford, whose assembly-line manufacturing process and the automobiles his company popularized have done so much to shape society that we might speak, without exaggeration, of driving into modernity. In addition to being an innovator and entrepreneur of deserved fame, however, Ford was also an ardent racist and anti-Semite, buttressing his views with pseudoscientific ideas about the influence of climate on human civilizations: "The thermometer is one of the staffs of authority which life wields over us. You will find within a certain belt around the world all the progress that is contained within the world, and the secret of that belt's prosperity, progress, morality and superiority is revealed to us by the thermometer" (425). Ford, to whom we return in our chapter on modernism's urban environments, like Huntington and many other "environmentalists" of the period, subscribed to a Goldilocks theory of the ideal climate—not too hot, not too cold—

in which "civilization," as he understood it, might flourish. There was a strong sense in the modernist period—a sense profoundly shaped by the racist discourses of imperialism—that local climates shaped people. There was, however, little sense, as emerged later in the twentieth century with the environmentalist movement, that people could shape the global climate. That shift is explored in detail in our final chapter.

Institutional History of Ecocriticism and the New Modernist Studies

In this book—and in keeping with Ezra Pound's now very old modernist injunction to "make it new"—we present the newest and most innovative ideas in modernist studies and in the environmental humanities; we survey the extant critical conjunctions of the two fields to the best of our knowledge; and we offer what we think might be promising new directions and connections between them. As William Carlos Williams once famously wrote in his 1927 poem *Paterson*, there are "no ideas but in things." As it happens, "modernism" as a coherent field of study emerged out of the postwar boom in state-funded universities in the United States around 1945–50. Environmentalism as a popular movement is usually dated to around 1962 with the publication of Rachel Carson's *Silent Spring* or, alternatively, to the first Earth Day in 1970—the same year, not coincidentally, which saw the foundation of the Environmental Protection Agency in the United States and the Ministries of Environment in the UK and France (Warde et al. 20).

No ideas—"modernism," "the environment"—but in things: institutions like universities, scholarly journals, publishing houses, and government agencies are where abstractions become concrete (paper and ink or bits and bytes; laws and norms; collaborative networks of people; not to mention steel and stone and wood and glass). So it is that we can trace the new decentered, centrifugal modernist studies to the foundation of Modernist Studies Association (MSA) in 1998. The MSA was founded and continues to thrive on the principle of rigorous revision of our notion of what, where, and when counts as modernism. By revision here we mean the opposite of refinement or restriction. In 2008 Douglas Mao and Rebecca Walkowitz looked back at the first ten years of new modernist studies and boiled it down to a single principle: "Were one seeking a single word to sum up transformations in modernist literary scholarship over the past decade or two one could do worse than light on *expansion*" (italics in original, 737). Similarly, Susan Stanford Friedman opens her *Planetary Modernisms* in an expansionary, and expansive, mood:

> The shift that *Planetary Modernisms* asks for is a fundamental rethinking of modernity that posits it as a geohistorical condition that is multiple, contradictory, interconnected, polycentric, and recurrent for millennia and across the globe. . . . Like the modernity of which it is a part, modernism is also multiple, polycentric, relational, and recurrent. Modernism, as I use the term in *Planetary Modernisms*, is not a single aesthetic period, a movement, or a style. Instead, the creative expressivities in all media constitute the modernisms of given modernities—on a planetary scale, across time, in the *longue durée*. (4)

With references to millennia and the *longue durée*, Stanford Friedman redefines modernism as a portable cultural contour that can be discovered well before and long after the temporal boundaries that traditionally define high modernism. Examples of modernism in this sense can be found throughout historical time and—as the "planetary" in her title indicates—across the globe. Moreover, the new modernist studies seeks explicitly to break out of its habitual eurocentrism in order to find, and to integrate into its expanding canon, previously neglected modernisms from all over the world.

Simultaneously with the rise of the new modernist studies in the 1990s, a robust environmentalist cultural criticism announced itself in 1992, with the foundation of the American Society for the Study of Literature and Environment (ASLE), and in 1993, when ASLE launched its academic journal, *Interdisciplinary Studies in Literature and Environment (ISLE)*. The year 1996 saw the publication of Cheryll Glotfelty and Harold Fromm's edited anthology *An Ecocriticism Reader*, which turned "ecocriticism," a term whose first use is credited to William Rueckert in 1978, into a rallying cry for scholars interested in the relationship between literature and the environment. As Glotfelty writes in her introduction to

An Ecocriticism Reader, ecocriticism didn't cohere in the 1970s. There were a few ecocritics, like Rueckert, but

> they did not organize themselves into an identifiable group; hence, their various efforts were not recognized as belonging to a distinct critical school or movement. . . . These critics rarely cited one another's work; they didn't know that it existed. In a sense, each critic was inventing an environmental approach to literature in isolation. Each was a single voice howling in the wilderness. (xvi–xvii)

The gathering momentum of ASLE, *ISLE*, and *An Ecocriticism Reader* united those voices "howling in the wilderness" into an intellectual and institutional force and, at the same time, cemented our now-commonsense notion of the—singular, planetary—environment.

An oft-quoted definition of ecocriticism proposed by Glotfelty in *An Ecocriticism Reader* appears to offer the elegance of simplicity: "Ecocriticism is the study of the relationship between literature and the physical environment" (xviii). This works as long as you are a literary critic and don't put too much pressure on the meaning of the "the physical environment." But as we've already pointed out, the concept of the environment has a history that is wrapped up in the history of modernism and modernity. Perhaps that is why other ecocritics have proposed other definitions that dispense with "the environment" altogether, like Greg Garrard's in his book *Ecocriticism*: "Ecocriticism is the study of the relationship of the human and the non-human, throughout human cultural history and entailing critical analysis of the term 'human' itself" (2004: 5). It is worth noting that Garrard broadens ecocriticism's purview from literature in particular to culture more generally. But what is fascinatingly counterintuitive about Garrard's definition is how "the human" grounds the entire project, as everything that is not human is sweepingly categorized in the negative as the nonhuman. Neither "nature" nor "the environment" intrudes upon this definition, which in effect leaves the relationship between ecocriticism and nature or the environment entirely open-ended. And there is much to recommend this approach, as it unsentimentally acknowledges the impossibility of escaping the necessary solipsism of embodied human consciousness. It is unlikely that we can know nature or the environment without conceiving them in relation to ourselves, simply because all of our human-knowing is inextricably wrapped up in our human-being. Ecocriticism, Garrard suggests, should accept that fact and perform its work while keeping vigilant watch over the uses and abuses of the concept of the human.

None of this history implies that there weren't critics participating in the shift of priorities in modernist studies and ecocritical studies before the decisive institutional developments of the 1990s. The emergence of MSA and ASLE in that time simply marks the era when the new modernist studies and ecocriticism went from being emergent discourses to being dominant discourses, at least within the restricted sphere of academic cultural criticism. While institutions like MSA and ASLE have profoundly changed how we think about modernism and environmentalist criticism, it is also true that institutions tend by their nature to consolidate orthodoxies. For example, the formation of ASLE and MSA at roughly the same time has meant, until fairly recently, that ecocritical scholarship and new modernist scholarship conducted themselves in relative isolation from one another, each in their institutional silo. Thus it is not until the twenty-first century that we begin to see real growth in the number of critical works dedicated to the intersection between modernism and ecocriticism, with new scholarship on Virginia Woolf leading the way, including books such as Christina Alt's *Virginia Woolf and the Study of Nature* (2010), Bonnie Kime Scott's *In the Hollow of the Wave: Virginia Woolf and Modernist Uses of Nature* (2012), J. Kostkowska's *Ecocriticism and Women Writers* (2013), and Kelly Sultzbach's *Ecocriticism in the Modernist Imagination: Forster, Woolf, and Auden* (2016) and numerous articles and book chapters such as Greg Garrard's "Worlds Without Us: Some Types of Disanthropy" (2012) and Bonnie Kime Scott's "Ecocritical Woolf" (2016). Joyce studies soon followed, with Robert Brazeau's and Derek Gladwin's edited collection *Eco-Joyce: The Environmental Imagination of James Joyce* (2014) and Alison Lacivita's *The Ecology of Finnegans Wake* (2015). Early monographs on modernist ecocriticism that go beyond the single-author study include Robin G. Schulze's *The Degenerate Muse: American Nature, Modernist Poetry, and the Problem of Cultural Hygiene* (2013), Joshua Schuster's *The Ecology of Modernism: American Environments and Avant-Garde Poetics* (2015), and Jeffrey McCarthy's *Green Modernism: Nature and the English Novel, 1900 to 1930* (2015).

As even this partial list demonstrates, modernist studies and ecocriticism are rapidly forming new connections, and our book is intended both to document and to contribute to the growing number of conversations between the new modernist studies and the environmental humanities. While we want to attend here to the new ideas generated at the points of convergence between these two important traditions, we also want to attend to the spaces covered by neither, to the wide-open vistas and the hidden valleys where new ideas and new connections between modernism and the environment might germinate.

One of the questions raised by the institutional history of the new modernist studies and ecocriticism is why they have developed in such a short time frame at the end of the twentieth century. A compelling answer is that both develop in the wake of the dominance and unraveling of postmodernism, understood multiply as an aesthetic category and as a mode of cultural inquiry whose key terms include "simulacra" (Baudrillard), "*différance*" (Derrida), and "*jouissance*" (Lacan). None of these terms point toward ecological thinking. Moreover, postmodernism's declarative end to what many of its proponents called metanarratives (Lyotard)—particularly modernist metanarratives like social, technological, and political progress or transcendent concepts like Nature and Truth—meant that assertions of the centrality and importance of nature coming from environmentalists were often seen as a category mistake or as theoretically unsophisticated from within the literature departments where postmodernism held sway.

As Ursula K. Heise points out, "The bulk of cultural criticism [from the 1960s to the 1990s] was premised on an overarching project of denaturalization" (2006: 505). When postmodernists thought about the environment—for example, in works like Gaston Bachelard's *The Poetics of Space* (1958) and Michel de Certeau's *The Practice of Everyday Life* (1980)—they tended to think almost exclusively in terms of the built environment, the architecture of cities, and the like. Ecocriticism "renaturalizes" the object of cultural criticism (even when that object is the city itself), and it confronts postmodernism with a new metanarrative: the limits of nature. By prematurely declaring the end of modernism and nature, postmodernism spring-loaded the energies that would give birth to both ecocriticism and the new modernist studies at the end of the twentieth century. This is not to suggest that the methodological toolkit of ecocriticism has no use for postmodernism, many of whose ideas—particularly about space, place, and the urban—persist in various strains of both the new modernist studies and ecocriticism. It is to suggest, however, that the waning institutional dominance of postmodernism has made new institutional space for ecocriticism and the new modernist studies.

It is important to note here the difference between environmentalism and ecocriticism, which operates similarly to the difference between modernity and modernism. Environmentalism is a politics, implying an ethics and a philosophy of human relationships to the natural world. It is not in itself a theory of culture or literature. A given cultural text can be motivated or inflected or influenced by an environmentalist ethic, and can thus be said to be "environmentalist," but that label does not in fact tell us much, if anything, about the formal elements of the text in question, in whatever medium and in whatever genre. Ecocriticism, on the other hand, names a methodology or protocol for reading cultural texts: it is a critical practice whose products are usually lectures, conferences, curricula, critical essays, articles, and books. Not everyone working in the field of environmental humanities agrees with this definition of ecocriticism. Lawrence Buell prefers "environmental criticism" but nevertheless concedes the convenience of "ecocriticism." Part of his objection, however, stems from the argument that ecocriticism has not yet attained the distinction of a method proper; it is rather more like a thematic orientation using methods borrowed from other literary-critical schools such as marxism, feminism, postmodernism, posthumanism, object-oriented ontology, or psychoanalysis. This may have been true for a time in ecocriticism's early years, but with the number and quality of scholars now working in the field, it is becoming less true with each new essay and monograph.

One can perform an ecocritical reading of a cultural text that involves nature writing—as Lawrence Buell does with Thoreau's essays in *The Environmental Imagination* (1996) or John Elder does for Robert Frost's poetry in *Reading the Mountains of Home* (1999), for example. But, as we have suggested, ecocritical readings are not limited to cultural texts that avow an environmentalist ethos. To theoretically inclined critics, as Dana Phillips argues, first-wave ecocriticism often seemed guilty of "confusing actual and fictional trees, or trying to conflate them," by insisting that "environmental literature [is] a kind of writing, in the narrow sense of *inscription*, which bears little of the freight associated with traditional genres and forms" (2003: 10, 15). "Once I thought it helpful to try to specify a subspecies of 'environmental text,'" Lawrence Buell reflects on the development of his own environmentalist thinking in *The Future of Environmental Criticism* (2005), "the first stipulation of which was that the nonhuman environment must be envisaged not merely as a framing device but as an active presence, suggesting human history's implication in natural history" (25). But Buell eventually came to the conclusion that the goal of ecocriticism was not exclusively to identify environmentalist texts, but rather to develop a methodology by which the environment could be discovered in texts that were not particularly aware of it, or that even actively repressed it. "Now, it seems to me more productive to think inclusively of environmentality as a property of any text—to maintain that all human artifacts bear such traces, and at several stages: in the composition, the embodiment, and the reception" (25). This kind of analysis is characteristic of a second wave of ecocriticism. In the case of cultural texts that are environmentally agnostic, ecocriticism now affords methods—inherited from third-wave feminism and Marxist formalism—to engage with, and to read them for clues about their deep, unstated, perhaps even unstateable relationship to their environment. Such a method might, for example, consist of reading, on the analogy to the *political unconscious* in Marxist formalism, for an *environmental unconscious*, even (and perhaps especially) in texts that seem to have little in the way of self-conscious environmentalism. In fact, ecocritical readings can be made of texts that are avowedly anti-environmentalist, a stance that would accurately characterize many modernist texts that were unapologetic in their desire to modify nature to suit human desires, and triumphant in their sense of having attained the technical capacity to do so.

Many first-wave ecocritics were willing to write the modernists off as an environmental lost cause, preferring instead to focus their scholarship on the nature-loving transcendentalists and romanticists of the early nineteenth century and on nature writers directly informed by environmentalist sensibilities in the contemporary moment, skipping the century between. "Modernism was never very green," concedes Joshua Schuster in *The Ecology of Modernism*, "if by green we mean an astute awareness of biodiversity, vigilance against pollution and overdevelopment, care for bioregional conservation, and earth-focused activism that goes beyond human-centered interests" (2). Meanwhile, the reverse is also true: with its traditional focus on urbanism, interiority, and aesthetics, modernist studies tended to assert the independence of the work of art from its environment under the aegis of aesthetic autonomy. As assertions of creative will, the "work of art . . . stands beside nature on equal terms" rather than representing the world, as Wilhelm Worringer wrote in his 1908 essay "Abstraction and Empathy" (Kolocotroni et al. 72). As Jeffrey Mathes McCarthy argues, "At the simplest level, to claim that nature is significant to modernism is to cut against the grain of a century of scholarship" dominated by a mode of "modernist studies [that] has largely rebuffed the insights of ecocriticsm thanks to the aesthetic armor of its autonomous, urban texts" (1–2).

One way to remedy this scholarly blind spot is to recuperate the more ecophilic strains of modernism muted by the canon's focus on urban, autonomous texts. Excellent examples can be found in the writing of Virginia Woolf, helping to account for the relatively early adoption of her work by ecocritics. In "A Sketch of the Past," for instance, Woolf recounts memories from her summer vacations in Cornwall, on a relatively remote spit of land at the southwest tip of England. She has a naturalist's sensibility, and writes of how, while walking in the gardens at St Ives, she "stopped; smelt; looked," and what she feels is "rapture" (66):

> I was looking at the flower bed by the front door; "That is the whole," I said. I was looking at a plant with a spread of leaves; and it seemed suddenly plain that the flower itself was a part of the earth; that a ring enclosed what was the flower; and that was the real flower; part earth; part flower. It was a thought I put away as being likely to be very useful to me later. (71)

Not only is this moment an essential one in Woolf's artistic self-fashioning—like Proust with his theory of involuntary memory and his madeleine, Woolf insists that the "shock-receiving capacity is what makes me a writer" (72)—it also contains some of the central lessons of more recent paradigms in ecological thinking. As the branch of science devoted to the reciprocal interactions between species and their environments (themselves understood as complex adaptive systems), ecology insists on the fundamental interconnection of all things; it is holistic rather than atomistic science. Woolf's environmental orientation steers her not to personified impressions of the natural world (though there is a strong tradition of reading these flowers as symbols of female sexuality), but to a sense of embeddedness and interconnection, a whole-earth perspective and sense of affective engagement that stands in stark contrast to the taxonomic rationalism that was characteristic of botanical science in her day, but one that resonates quite clearly with the rhetoric and sensibilities associated with the deep ecology movement begun by Norwegian philosopher Arne Naess in the 1970s.

The continuing critical project of modernist ecocriticism will weave other threads into what Gayle Rogers and Sean Latham call the cable of modernism, emphasizing the important role of artists like Isadora Duncan, the American dancer, teacher, and choreographer who veered away from classical ballet instruction and urged her pupils to seek inspiration "from the movements in Nature. The movements of the clouds in the wind, the swaying trees, the flight of a bird . . . for all the parts of their supple bodies, trained as they would be, would respond to the melody of Nature and sing with her" (Kolocotroni et al. 156). Modernist minimalism offers another example of a positive legacy awaiting recuperation. As Annelise Fleischmann, then a student at the German Bauhaus School, writes in a manifesto on "Economic Living" from 1924, the ideals of minimalism and aversion to ornamentation that define modernist design will conserve resources and reduce energy consumption: "maximum efficiency" is her motto, achieved by designing every machine to "require a minimum of energy" (Kolocotroni et al. 302).

Just as modernist studies has broadened, changing our understanding of what, where, and when a modernist text might be, so too has ecocriticism in its second wave, often motivated by questions of environmental justice. Though the field began by studying places beyond human culture—inspired by the work of men like Emerson, Thoreau, and John Muir, rugged individualists with a passion for wild lands and cultural isolation—ecocriticism today understands humans as a constitutive part of the environment and devotes much of its attention to studying ecological devastation, energy systems, or urban ecosystems. This shift in focus manifests itself in books like Rob Nixon's *Slow Violence and the Environmentalism of the Poor* (2011), which focuses on resource imperialism, deforestation, and oil spills; Imre Szeman's extensive writing on the energy humanities and petroculture; Timothy Mitchell's *Carbon Democracy: Political Power in the Age of Oil* (2011); or Imre Szeman, Jennifer Wenzel, and Patricia Yaeger's *Fueling Culture: 101 Words for Energy and Environment* (2017). Ecocriticism has even discovered its "bad" side, with Nicole Seymour's *Bad Environmentalism: Irony and Irreverence in The Ecological Age* (2018), a book whose title clearly echoes that of Douglas Mao and Rebecca Walkowitz's *Bad Modernisms* of 2006. For Seymour, "bad environmentalism" questions the basic assumption that love for nature or reverence for the environment are necessary for ecological thinking, associating environmentalism instead with "affects and sensibilities such as irreverence, ambivalence, camp, frivolity, indecorum, awkwardness, sardonicism, perversity, playfulness, and glee" (4). Timothy Morton's *Dark Ecology: For a Logic of Future Coexistence* (2016), with its emphasis on the negativity, melancholia, and strangeness of life in the Anthropocene, demands a similar rethinking of what it means to be "green." *Being Ecological*, as he calls it, means engaging with "feelings of unreality or of distorted or altered reality, feelings of the uncanny: feeling *weird*" (2).

Approached in this way, investigating modernism and its environments means asking questions like the curious one posed by art critic and Bloomsbury Group member Clive Bell in his essay introducing the art of "The English Group" at the Second Post-Impressionist Exhibition in 1912: "How, then, does the Post-Impressionist regard a coal-scuttle?" For Bell, the question is one of modernist formalism: the artist, he writes, "regards it as an end in itself, as a significant form related on terms of equality with other significant forms" (Kolocotroni et al. 193). The twenty-first-century reader might reasonably ask, "What's a coal scuttle?" having no image of one in their minds, impressionist or otherwise. For the English artists of the Second Post-Impressionist Exhibition, analyzing a coal scuttle might entail attention to its volume, shape, and form; for the environmental humanist it means reactivating the infrastructure and everyday habits of residential coal use, reminding readers that a coal scuttle is the specialized small bucket used to carry small quantities of coal from a home's central storage bin to the fireplace in which it will be burned, thus connecting the post-impressionists to the energy systems of industrial Europe, topics to which we will return in Chapters 1 and 2.

This book, then, is part of a growing movement to refashion both the objects and the methods of the first wave of ecocriticism, a movement rooted in American nature writing, into a more expansive vision, one that sees slums and concentration camps, skyscrapers and factories, landfills and strip mines as just as much the province of the environmental humanities as untrammeled nature. By doing so, we might reinterpret and reevaluate modernist artifacts that were previously ignored by a version of ecocriticism that was looking for environmentalism, and as a result failed to see what Buell calls environmentality.

Techno-Optimism and Ecomodernism

Consider, for example, a difficult case like that of Frank Lloyd Wright's utopian plan for Broadacre City, which was essentially an early vision of the garden suburb. Wright envisioned the future as a pastoral idyll in which every citizen would be granted an acre of land in a so-called garden city that would solve the environmental and social problems caused by industrial modernity: "Imagine spacious landscaped highways, grade crossings eliminated, 'by-passing' living areas, devoid of the already archaic telegraph and telephone poles and wires . . . joined at intervals with fields from which the safe, noiseless transport planes take off and land" (44). Wright sketched a world made up of "diversified units" into which different life functions would be sorted: dwelling here, work there, leisure yet another place, all "within a radius of a hundred and fifty miles of his home and now easily and speedily available by means of his car or his plane. This integral whole composes the great city that is seen embracing all of this country—the Broadacre City of tomorrow" (44). In the guise of an ecological utopia, Wright wrote a recipe for low-density settlement, long commutes, and stratospheric energy demands: what we now know, because we've since built many versions of this suburban dream, to be an ecological nightmare.

Those who saw themselves as modern in the early twentieth century, especially before the First World War, saw their cultural moment not unjustifiably as marking an important transition between the obviously pollution-causing fossil fuel energy systems inherited from their Victorian forbearers and a utopian future powered by electrified technologies, whose environmental impacts (because distanced from the point of use) were far more difficult to see or understand, and which might be eliminated entirely as a result of some new form of power generation just over the horizon. "Men urged by their necessities and desires have laboured for many thousands of years at the task of subjugating the forces of Nature," observes William Morris (most famous for his utopian novel *News from Nowhere*) in his 1884 lecture on "Useful Work versus Useless Toil." But now, he argues, "the struggle with Nature seems nearly over, and the victory of the human race over her nearly complete. And . . . we note that the progress of that victory has been far swifter and more startling within the last two hundred years than ever before" (Kolocotroni et al. 29).

Such prognostications are common in the technophilic writing of the years before the outbreak of the First World War, when scientists, social historians, artists, and the popular media increasingly understood their era as being on the winning end of a struggle to harness the forces of nature. Henry Adams, dazzled by the inventions on display at the 1900 World's Fair, calculated that "at the rate of progress since 1800, every American who lived into the year 2000 would know how to control unlimited power" (460). The new century was just three years old when, having only recently got the wheels turning on their cars, inventors would take to the skies in controlled, powered flight. In 1904, motoring enthusiast A. B. Filson Young, whose fame was such that James Joyce would subsequently seek his support in the promotion of *Dubliners*, had already predicted the displacement of internal combustion automobiles with electric cars, writing in *The Complete Motorist* that "on the day when a cheap, light, and compact means of storing a great power of electricity is discovered we shall see the last of the motor-car as we know it at present" (34). E. M. Forster's 1909 science fiction fable "The Machine Stops" depicts a civilization that has secured free and unlimited energy—How? No one knows; we are told merely that humanity has "harnessed Leviathan" (6).

Modernism's visions of its futures share a marked tendency to overestimate the pace of progress and to underestimate the unintended consequences and negative externalities of new technologies. Those modernist tendencies are still dominant today, despite the great swell of environmentalist discourse and activism since the mid-twentieth century. In one instance the popularity of environmentalist discourses has combined with modernist technophilia to produce a movement called "Ecomodernism," an environmentalist group that advocates pursuing technological solutions to today's challenges, embracing innovation, entrepreneurship, and geoengineering in contrast to more pastoral or conservation-based approaches to our ongoing environmental crisis. As they write in their founding manifesto of 2015, ecomodernists "affirm one long-standing environmental ideal, that humanity must shrink its impacts on the environment to make more room for nature, while we reject another, that human societies must harmonize with nature to avoid economic and ecological collapse" (Asafu-Adjaye et al. 6). The so-called ecomodernists have borrowed one of modernism's most emblematic literary forms, the manifesto, and they have also tapped into one of its favorite expressive modes and prominent cultural legacies: techno-optimism, a belief that the problems caused by modern technology can be solved by more and newer technology. Scientists and engineers have proposed a panoply of strategies to solve the problem of climate change, including carbon sequestration, cloud farming, fertilizing the oceans with iron powder (to promote carbon absorption by plankton), pumping sulfate particles into the stratosphere, and even installing space-based mirrors to deflect solar radiation. While any of these strategies might work, a knowledge of modernism and its environments might make us think twice about rushing to implement them, especially before trying other simpler and less risky solutions.

Chapter Summaries

Over the last century or so the meaning of modernism has multiplied, and the meaning of the environment has consolidated into a singularity. The crisscrossed trajectory of modernism's fragmentation and the environment's unification may have been less than causal, but it was much more than coincidental. The present volume describes the space opened by this chiasmus. We inherit the environmental crisis identified in the 1970s from the modernizers and the modernists of the early twentieth century, regardless of the fact that they imagined their environment in terms we no longer share. Reading them in order to understand their environmental imaginary, we might come to a better understanding of the historicity—and the inevitable blindnesses—of our own.

A book like this is made as much from what the finished product excludes as from what it includes. We were forced to make some hard choices. A chapter on waste was, unfortunately, thrown away, or at least shelved for gleaning or reuse. Ocean and arctic ecosystems remain largely unvisited; crucial supply chains and industries remain relatively underexamined. We decided to focus historically on the period between 1880 and 1940, with a few outliers to either side—an era that corresponds (from the perspective of literary studies) recognizably to that of high modernism, and that also indexes (from an energy systems perspective) a crucial series of energy regime transitions. This decision also helps us hold true to our grounding assumption: that the present ecological emergency renders modernism newly legible to ecocriticism. Wherever we can, we leave signposts for future research, gesturing to a broad range of material and questions that have yet to be explored by modernist ecocritics, though they are often only that: gestures or scattered seeds.

Chapter 1, "Modernism's Energy Environments," explores the high-modernist period as part of a historical process Paul Valéry called the "general energizing" of the world, in which technological developments like electrification, artificial fertilizer, and automobility caused humanity to get bigger and go faster by orders of magnitude. These changes caused a corollary change in modern subjectivity in which energy became the dominant metaphor for human being, doing, and dwelling in the modern world. We introduce readers to an exciting new development in environmental studies called the energy humanities, which redefines historical periods based on their energy regimes, and as a result draws new insights from their cultural artifacts. Modernism, read through the lens of the energy humanities, becomes a cultural production of coal, steam, electricity, and petrol.

Chapter 2, "Modernism's Urban Environments," takes up the urban origins of modernism as a counterintuitive occasion for ecocritical critique. Exploring representations of the city in texts by Charles Baudelaire, Virginia Woolf, Alfred Döblin, Robert Musil, T. S. Eliot, Richard Wright, Henry Roth, Franz Kafka, and others, we analyze the artificial environments modernity built in its own image, along with the supply chains and transportation systems on which they depended, and the pollution they produced. Our research includes utopian and dystopian visions of the modern metropolis, examining the city of the planners and the city of the *flâneurs*—the city of the skyscraper and of the crowd.

Chapter 3, "Modernism's Animals," addresses the animals populating modernist culture as modernity's intimate other, ambivalently a part of and apart from the moderns' self-conception. We examine representations of a wide range of species—dogs, cats, rats, and insects commensal with urban ecosystems; imaginary animals; animals hunted as "big game"; animals raised on factory farms; and animals driven to extinction—and introduce the new ways of understanding animal being emergent in the work of Darwin, Freud, and others. Examining the work of visual artists including Umberto Boccioni, Constantin Brancusi, and Pablo Picasso, and authors such as Willa Cather, Zora Neale Hurston, Jean Toomer, William Faulkner, A. A. Milne, and Marianne Moore, this chapter offers one of the first extensive surveys of modernism from the perspective of animal studies.

Chapter 4, "Modernism in the Wilderness," follows a trail that leads to the literary genealogies and legal frameworks that sustain the contemporary idea of the wilderness. It is an excursion through the work of writers like Samuel Clemens, Arthur Conan Doyle, Joseph Conrad, Virginia Woolf, Ernest Hemingway, Marianne Moore, and Wallace Stevens. We argue that textually and materially, modernity is characterized by radically divergent attitudes toward the wilderness, which is represented at times as a hostile adversary and at others as a place of refuge and renewal. Not only does telling this story expand our sense of modernism's geography and archive, it also provides a thicker history of why we have come to think and feel as we do about the wilderness in the present day.

Finally, in Chapter 5, "The Climate of Modernism," we shift away from our dominant focus on high modernism, and take up in earnest the expansive definition of modernism laid out by the pioneering critics of the new modernist studies. We trace a cultural history of modernist thought about weather and climate from Samuel Johnson to Olafur Eliasson, and a literary history of weather and climate from Virginia Woolf and Robert Musil to Zadie Smith and Kate Tempest. We examine the modernist forms inscribed in the land art movement of the 1970s, at the dawn of the environmentalist movement in the United States. We introduce the concept of the Anthropocene as a way to understand the relationships between modernism and its contested legacies at the dawn of the twenty-first century. And finally, building on Jesse Oak Taylor's concept of "atmospheric reading," we demonstrate that atmospheric conditions could be unruly and conspicuous in modernist fictions, even when they were supposed to stay in the background. Likewise, modernism itself refused to stay put between the dates that traditionally bound it: the land artists took "its faith and vaulting promise," as Geoff Dyer writes, "into the wilderness" (Loc 832). And contemporary writers continue to use modernist forms and styles to represent the environmental crises that define the twenty-first century.

1

Modernism's Energy Environments

Gasoline is divine
—F. T. MARINETTI

Power
Power! Power like a paw, titanic power ripped through the earth and slammed against his body and shackled him where he stood. Power! Incredible, barbaric power! A blast, a siren of light within him, rending, quaking, fusing his brain and blood to a fountain of flame, vast rockets in a searing spray! Power!
—HENRY ROTH

"Nothing is easier, than to point out in history books the omission of remarkable phenomena that have occurred so slowly as to be imperceptible." So wrote the French poet Paul Valéry in 1931. "An event that takes place over a century does not figure in any document or any collection of memoirs." That could describe the geological pace of climate change, but climate change was not what Valéry had in mind. He was thinking, he writes, of "the discovery of electricity and the conquest of the earth by its different uses." This brings him to a bold and startling claim: "This general energizing of the world is more pregnant with consequences, more capable of transforming life in the immediate future than all the 'political' events from the time of Ampère to the present day" (1962: 10). By putting the word "political" in scare quotes, Valéry signals that the distinction between political history and "general energizing" is exactly what he means to cast into doubt.

The "Ampère" to whom he refers is Andre-Marie Ampère, an early experimenter with electromagnetism after whom the ampere—the standard measuring unit of electric current—was named. Ampère's life straddled the French Revolution; born into a monarchy, he lived his adult life in the French Republic, whose utopian energy became closely associated with the promise of electricity. By name-dropping Ampère in this passage, Valéry reveals that the "political" events he mentions might in fact serve as a way to obscure the importance of one political event in particular: the republican revolution, and perhaps the enlightenment more generally, as the crucial origin of the political order of liberal democracy under which we currently still live in the West, at least by most accounts. Valéry's claim appears both bold, insofar as it foregrounds energy as a political force, and sheepish, insofar as it stops just short of positing a causal relationship between the general energizing and the republican revolution, a relationship that remains suggested rather than stated outright.

It is only relatively recently that historians have begun to attend to the omissions of which Valéry accused them. And more and more, they are agreeing with him. According to J. R. McNeill and Kenneth Pomeranz, editors of the seventh volume of the *Cambridge World History* (2015), "Human energy use has multiplied somewhere between fifty- and one hundred-fold since 1750, with the largest increases coming in the twentieth century," though they warn that even that figure "greatly understates the increase in effective human energy use, as the efficiency with which our technologies convert combustion into the motion, heat, or light we desire has increased anywhere from 35 times (today's best diesel engine versus a 1750 steam engine) to 1,600 times (today's halide light versus a tallow candle)" (10). Since humans started burning fossil fuels, according to McNeill in another essay in the same volume, "Our species probably used more energy . . . than in all of prior human history," making "our time wildly different from anything in the human past"

(55). McNeill therefore considers this general energizing to be "the most revolutionary process in human history since domestication" (55). In this radical acceleration, modernism emerged.

By and large, the modernists would probably have been flattered by Pomeranz's characterization of their era's wild difference from the one that preceded it. They would have professed a devout faith in the ability of technology to deliver them from one victory to the next. Discussing the new developments in theoretical physics for a generalist audience, Frederick Soddy, who was awarded the Nobel Prize in chemistry in 1922 for his work on radioactive isotopes, recognized in 1912 that "discoveries in connection with the recently explored field of radioactivity have put an entirely different complexion on the question as to how long the energy resources of the world may be expected to last" (16). Long before nuclear power was industrially viable, Soddy and others understood that the mass-energy equivalence portended "sufficient potential energy to supply the uttermost ambitions of the race for cosmical epochs of time" (17). Lewis Strauss, then the chair of the United States Atomic Energy Commission, speculated in 1954 that it would not be "too much to expect . . . that our children will enjoy in their homes electrical energy too cheap to meter" (9). In 1923 Leon Trotsky claimed from the USSR that "Man has already made changes in the map of nature that are not few nor insignificant. But they are mere pupils' practice in comparison with what is coming," and he looked forward to a world in which "Man" will "earnestly and repeatedly make improvements in nature. In the end, he will have rebuilt the earth, if not in his own image, at least according to his own taste" (Kolocotroni et al. 230). When Trotsky penned this utopian vision, global carbon dioxide levels were around 300 parts per million, according to the most recent NASA data; now, with carbon dioxide levels over 411 parts per million, we have realized, perhaps belatedly, that the world of our creation is one not of fantasy but of nightmare. Our children are unlikely to enjoy energy too cheap to meter, but our children's children's children on down for 20,000 years will inherit a world bearing the signature of the radioactive isotopes released in pursuit of that dream.

Like Trotsky, Valéry was exuberantly optimistic when imagining the political revolution of the enlightenment as a function of the technological revolution of electricity. Almost eighty years later, Dipesh Chakrabarty, in an essay addressing itself to the Anthropocene, would suggest a very similar relationship between energy and politics, but with much less optimism: "The mansion of modern freedoms stands on an ever-expanding base of fossil-fuel use. Most of our freedoms so far have been energy-intensive" (208). This is a realization as terrifying as Valéry's was once, to the moderns, inspiring. It is weakly mitigated by the qualification "so far," which nevertheless strongly suggests the need to imagine new freedoms that might not depend so heavily on the energy intensity that produced the old ones.

Fredrick Buell describes the fossil fuel era, including the nuclear age, as an "'age of exuberance'—an age which is also, given the dwindling finitude of the resources it increasingly makes social life dependent on, haunted by catastrophe" (276). When viewed from the retrospect of the Anthropocene, the first electrical age appears as an age of relative innocence regarding the environmental costs of energy production. Jean-Francois Mouhot argues that "we have arrived at the present situation (mostly) in good faith, with the conviction that modernity would bring the masses freedom from toil, and without any chance of knowing the climatic consequences of our burning of fossil fuels" (qtd. in Johnson xii). "The average consumer [in the United States]," writes Bob Johnson in *Mineral Rites: An Archaeology of the Fossil Economy*, "has until recently participated in carbon's jubilee with an unmetered innocence" (xii).

This past age—characterized by the combination of a general energizing enabled by the burning of fossil fuels with a general innocence about their environmental and climatic consequences—is also the age of the emergence and dominance of modernism as a set of aesthetic forms and recurrent themes. That age of innocence and exuberance is now over. And because it is over, we feel more intensely the paradoxes and contradictions of modernist art, particularly where they come to bear on the environment. Some of the stranger, more uncomfortable aspects of modernism, like the strident manifestos of the Futurists, as well as some of its lesser-known works—like Valéry's "Outlook for Intelligence"—take on a new centrality for understanding modernism from the present historical vantage of the Anthropocene. And many of modernism's most revered texts can and ought to be productively reread and understood anew. It might even be true to a certain extent to say that now—in the time of catastrophic mass extinctions and accelerating climate change—is the first time we've been able to see them properly at all.

Electricity

In May of 1936, five years after Valéry wrote about general energizing, the French painter Raoul Dufy was commissioned by the electrical authority of Paris—*La Compagnie Parisienne de Distribution d' Électricité*—to paint a large fresco as part of the 1937 International Exhibition of Art and Technology in Modern Life. The result, titled *La Fée Électricité* (*The Electricity Fairy*), was a huge 600-square-meter mural pulsing with vibrant color that covered one of the concave walls of the *Pavillon de la Lumière et de l'Électricité*. It was a grand narrative, done on a grand scale, one in a long tradition of modernist monuments to technological progress, including Thomas Hart Benton's panorama *America Today* of 1931, composed of ten room-sized canvas panels, and Diego Rivera's 1931 portable mural *Electric Power*, a fresco of plaster supported by steel and concrete, depicting New York power plant workers surrounded by the industrial sublimity of generators and turbines.

Dufy's mural—still on display in what is now the Paris Museum of Modern Art—narrates the history of the discovery and domestication of electricity from the eighteenth century to the modernist moment and represents 110 key figures significant to that history, including Ampère. In the center section of the mural is a deep blue depiction of the Ivry-sur-Seine power station with the generators at the bottom, a ball of lightening in the center, and a few Greek gods perched on the top, looking as if they might be stone sculpture sentries—a pantheon in honor of the power station's Promethean modernity. Dufy's enchanted vision was a pitch-perfect representation of the dominant modern attitude toward electricity: a tremendous secular pride in the accomplishments of science and technology combined with a rapturous wonder produced by electricity's illuminated spectacle.

In 1915, on a smaller, more reproducible scale, the American art journal *291* published Francis Picabia's "mechanomorphic," a series of relief prints titled after people but depicting, in the style of mechanical drawing, technological artifacts. The most famous and most often reproduced among these mechanomorphic portraits is *Portrait of a Young American Girl in the State of Nudity* (Figure 1), which depicted, underneath its title printed in all caps, a mechanical drawing of a spark plug from a typical car engine. Much like the

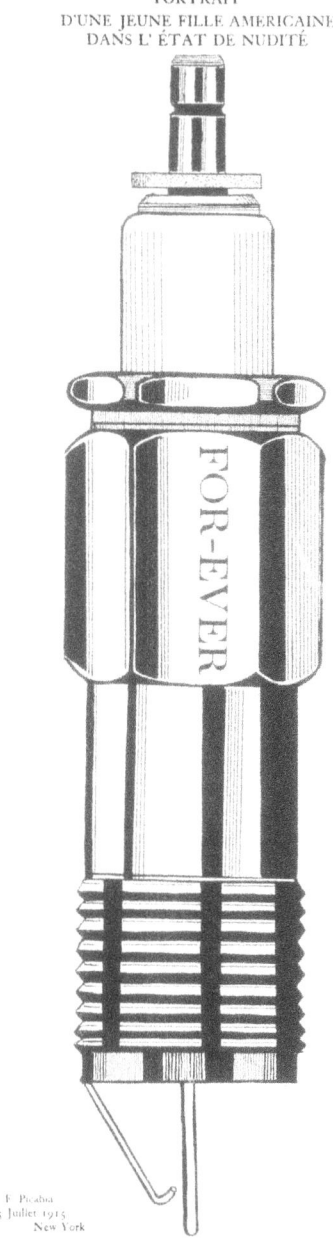

FIGURE 1 Portrait of a Young American Girl in the State of Nudity, *Francis Picabia*.

"ready-mades" of Marcel Duchamp, the effect of *Portrait of a Young American Girl in the State of Nudity* relies on wrenching the mechanical drawing from its utilitarian context, resituating it in the world of art, and captioning it to create a wholly new, often wryly humorous, meaning.

There are a number of ways to read Picabia's intent, but one of them is to see in the juxtaposition of the title and the represented object an attempt to connect the presumed beauty of the young girl's nude body to the supposed sexiness of the automobile; to equate the spark of attraction with the spark of ignition; to mix the exhilarations of sex and speed. Picabia's young American girl and Dufy's fairy both gendered electricity as feminine, suggesting an attractive, wild, and dangerous force of nature whose power could be harnessed, if at great risk, by the heroic efforts of rational men of science and politics. At the Hoover Dam, which in 1937 began feeding water and electricity to parts of Arizona and Southern California, a commemorative sculpture and plaque makes the danger of the undertaking explicit. "They died," the plaque says of the ninety-six men who perished in accidents during the five-year construction of the dam, "to make the desert bloom."

Of all the ways that the moderns imagined and figured "general energizing," electricity was perhaps the most prominent as well as the most exuberantly optimistic. For a lot of artists, cultural commentators, and politicians in the first part of the twentieth century, electrification stood as a synecdoche for the astonishingly rapid and intense general energizing that characterized the period. Valéry makes this move in the passage from *The Outlook for Intelligence* when he substitutes electrification for "general energizing" in successive sentences. Dufy's fresco does something similar by making electricity the centerpiece of a painted narrative of modern progress. Picabia's mechanomorphic spark plug was yet another approach.

The modernists were by no means the first to understand the symbolic potential of electricity and fossil fuels. Inspired by a variety of theories about the energetic basis of human life from vitalism to the second law of thermodynamics, nineteenth-century writers embraced the idea of the electric text, drawn especially to the possible analogies between electrical energy and the figurative power of art, understood in terms of its capacity to "move" its audience, as Bruce Clarke and Linda Henderson in *From Energy to Information: Representation in Science and Technology, Art, and Literature* (2002), Paul Gilmore in *Aesthetic Materialism: Electricity and American Romanticism* (2009), and others argue. Following a different trajectory of technological imagery and influenced by Freud's use of thermodynamics to explain psychic energy, Peter Brooks suggests that in novels by Zola, Verne, Balzac, and others, "plot is, most aptly, a steam engine" (44). More importantly, Brooks argues that machines in nineteenth-century texts "are a *mise-en-abyme* of the novel's narrative motor, an explicit statement of the inclusion within the novel of the principle of its movement" (45). Electrification is everywhere: it inflects Emerson's theories of literary inspiration in "The Poet," where he describes the poet as a "conductor of the whole river of electricity; it becomes an "immense reservoir of electrical energy" for Baudelaire; and it wells up in Whitman's poetry of "the body electric" with its "instant conductors" in *Leaves of Grass*.

In 1920 Vladimir Lenin hit a similar note with the full force of his exuberant faith in the Russian revolution when he defined communism as "Soviet power plus electrification" (419). The idea took popular hold in the USSR to such an extent that, as Susan Buck-Morss recounts, "the kilowatt hour was proposed as 'an index of cultural progress'" (140). Fast-forward to April 1986 when a nuclear reactor exploded at the Chernobyl nuclear power plant in the Ukraine, then a part of the USSR. The human and ecological catastrophe that ensued was among the largest in human history; it killed thousands, displaced hundreds of thousands, and created an uninhabitable exclusion zone for a thousand-mile radius around the plant. And it produced "a major political and social shock that contributed to shattering confidence in the communist system and the myths that helped to hold it together" (Yergin 380).

The USSR's worship of the kilowatt ended, four years after the Chernobyl accident, with the end of the USSR. The West's worship of general energizing is still ongoing. What is striking about reading Valéry's assertion together with Lenin's is that electrification becomes the leitmotif for both capitalist and socialist development; two warring modes of production, and two warring narratives of human progress, united under the sign of electrification. In the early 1970s, when the United States, along with much of the rest of the world, found itself in the grip of another energy crisis, the architectural historian Rayner Banham echoed Valéry and Lenin from about five decades away when he called electrification "the greatest environmental revolution in history since the domestication of fire" (qtd. in Kern 29). What all these examples have in common is a sense of wonder and utopian hope that vested electricity with the power to transform politics, culture, and society. What distinguishes Banham's remark is that, instead of political revolution—implied in Valéry, explicit in Lenin—he lights on something they both passed over: environmental revolution.

There can be no doubt that electrification transformed society and that it did so in time with the rise and reign of high modernism. A simple analogy, with all its obvious and serious limits, might help carry the point: what the railroad was to the nineteenth century and to the Victorian period, electrification was to the twentieth century and high modernism. In his 1934 *Technics and Civilization*, Lewis Mumford argued that electrification marked an epochal transition out of what he called the paleotechnic age, whose spirit lived, as it was formed, in the coal mine: "From the mine came the steam pump and presently the steam engine: ultimately the steam locomotive and so, by derivation, the steamboat. From the mine came the escalator, the elevator . . . the subway for urban transportation. The railroad likewise came directly from the mine" (158). Mumford called the age of electricity the neotechnic age, which implied an escape from the mine, although that turned out to be only so much wishful thinking: electrification created unprecedented demands for the energy of fossil fuels. Nevertheless, electrification marked a major transformation.

There were some powerful voices of skepticism about electrification in the period of the first construction of the big grids, a subject to which we return in Chapter 2, but their sound was faint amid the victorious din of technological progress, at least until they were rediscovered by the environmentalist movement in the 1960s and 1970s. One of the most poignant critiques made at the time was less about the environmental consequences of electrification than it was about the way it fundamentally changed lived experience. In his 1928 memoir of a year spent in his beach house in Cape Cod without electricity, *The Outermost House*, Henry Beston wrote that electrification was making people lose touch with the natural rhythm of night and day, a rhythm with which and by which humans had lived for the entire life span of the species up until the electrical revolution: "We now have a dislike of night itself. Are modern folk, perhaps, afraid of night? Do they fear that vast serenity, the mystery of infinite space, the austerity of stars? . . . Today's civilization is full of people who have not the slightest notion of the character or the poetry of night, who have never even seen night" (qtd. in Nye 10).

Beston is often considered an early model for environmentalist writing, falling in a lineage including Henry Thoreau and Aldo Leopold. His emphasis on the way that electrification completely disrupted the diurnal rhythms of human life by attenuating the difference between night and day, however, might also remind us that some of the most important modernist novels, like James Joyce's *Ulysses* (1922) and Virginia Woolf's *Mrs. Dalloway* (1925), returned to the solar day as their fundamental narrative unit—the measure of time appropriate to tell the story of a character or even a whole city—a "day in the life." Not everything that happens in *Ulysses* or *Mrs. Dalloway* happens on the day on which the novels are set; but everything that doesn't happen on that day is remembered on that day by a character living in that day. Even as the characters in the novels restlessly cast their thoughts forward in anticipation and backward in reminiscence, the day as the limit of the present holds those characters together in both a formal and a lived unity. But as Beston's lament makes clear, Joyce and Woolf only seized on the day as a narrative, fictional, novelistic unit at the moment of its phenomenological weakening under electrification—just as it could no longer be considered a natural and normalized unit of lived urban experience. To see Joyce's and Woolf's choice in this way is to see in their work a reaction to modernization, and thus as more reactionary—or perhaps conservationist—than we are accustomed.

Case Study: Joyce and Electricity

Let us take an extended look at the way electrification can be apprehended in the works of one high-modernist writer in particular: James Joyce, whose fictions are peppered with references to electrification that index his ambivalence on the subject—a combination of obsession and aversion, fetish and phobia. In *A Portrait of the Artist as a Young Man* (1916), college boy Stephen Dedalus pointedly yawns through his professor's lecture on electricity. The narrator conveys this in an irony-drenched language freighted with the vocabulary and principles of electrical engineering: "The droning voice of the professor continued to wind itself slowly round and round the coils it spoke of, doubling, trebling, quadrupling its somnolent energy as the coil multiplied its ohms of resistance" (210). The sentence complicates its most obvious and immediate meaning, which is simply that Stephen is bored and uninterested in the lecture, by employing the language of electricity to describe Stephen's indifference to the language of electricity.

Stephen's indifferent stance would, a few years later in *Ulysses*, turn into an anxious one. On the afternoon of June 16, 1904, he walks past the Fleet Street power station in Dublin, and feels a bolt of fear pass through him as he hears "the whirr of flapping leathern bands and hum of dynamos from the powerhouse." "Beingless beings," he thinks, "Stop! Throb always without you and the throb always within. Your heart you sing of" (199). The electrical grid appears to Stephen as a living thing and also as a kind of rival, with its own song, its own being, and its own heart. In fact, the novel as a whole is driven by (largely unseen) electrical forces, as Hugh Kenner has influentially argued: "The day . . . that *Ulysses* reflects would have been impossible a generation earlier, before electric trams were moving people quickly about a large city. Dublin's tram system, in 1904 the world's most extensive, gets Stephen Dedalus from Dalkey to Sandymount, and Leopold Bloom from the baths to Sandymount, both by 11 a.m." (11). It is noteworthy, however, that Stephen and Joyce are more concerned with the symbolic potential of electrical energy than with the pragmatics of its generation, leaping to the anthropomorphic "heart" of the machine rather than to the coal, steam, and steel at its material base; it remains for the ecocritic today to reconstruct this history from its textual traces.

The brief encounter between Stephen and the electrical grid in *Ulysses* has a counterpart in "The Dead," the (very long) short story that closes Joyce's 1914 collection *Dubliners*. "The Dead" stages its climactic scene in the luxurious rooms of the Gresham Hotel in central Dublin. After returning to their room late at night, Gretta Conroy tells her husband Gabriel the story of Michael Furey, a boy who worked in the Galway gasworks and who loved Gretta so much that he stood outside her window serenading her in a cold night of lashing rain, became ill, and died. "I think he died for me" (220), she says to Gabriel, driving him momentarily mad both with jealousy for Gretta's lingering feeling for Furey and with envy of Furey's youthful ardor for Gretta. Gabriel realizes his greatest love rival is a dead boy, a ghost. Although it is possible that Furey died for love of Gretta, as she supposes and as Gabriel seems to accept, it is more likely that he died of the kind of respiratory ailment so common among gasworks workers at the time, pneumoconiosis, which often went under the name consumption—aggravated, perhaps, by his night serenading Gretta, but certainly not caused by it alone. "Who was he?" Gabriel asks Gretta. "He was in the gasworks" (219), she replies in an Anglo-Irish vernacular, meaning idiomatically simply that he worked in the gasworks, but also carrying in its literal sense the idea that he was somehow in them and of them.

The Gresham Hotel advertised itself at this time as one of the first in the city to boast of electrical lighting. This was made possible in 1903 when the Pigeon House generating plant in Ringsend went online, enabling a substantially expanded array of electrical lighting and electrical tram service in the city. But on the night that Gabriel and Gretta are staying at the Gresham, the electricity isn't working—outages were fairly common in the early days of electrification. The porter offers them a candle, but Gabriel refuses it. "We don't want any light," he says, "we have light enough from the street" (216). When the porter leaves, the room remains dimly illuminated by "a ghostly light from the street lamp" that "lay in a long shaft from one window to the door" (216). That street lamp, as Luke Gibbons points out, was one of the last gas lamps in Dublin; in 1904 the city was in the process of "upgrading" its street lamps from gaslight to electric light. And the ghost of Michael Furey, a boy "in the gasworks," streams into the room from that "ghostly light." The transition from gas lighting to electrical lighting, a technological shift of momentous proportions that, at the same time, didn't feel, or may not have felt, particularly momentous in terms of everyday experience, is allegorized in "The Dead." Lurking just below the surface of Joyce's story of sexual jealously is a very different story about technological change and energy transition, a story linked to Stephen's ruminations on electricity in *A Portrait of the Artist as a Young Man* and *Ulysses*. Joyce's writing was shot through by electrification; his plots were partly structured by it; his Dublin cityscapes were indelibly marked by it; and his characters' sensibilities were significantly shaped by it.

The Energy Humanities

Electrification was only part of the story of the general energizing, even though it so often stood for the modernists as a synecdoche for the whole. This brings us to a tricky point when it comes to thinking seriously about energy regimes and their relationship to culture. To the extent that electricity often served the moderns as a synecdoche for energy, that operation grossly oversimplified the reality of the situation. Modernist energy regimes were profoundly mixed, comprised of biomass fuels like wood and whale oil; hydropower; wind power; fossil fuels like coal and oil and the many other products, like coal gas in the case of coal or gasoline and kerosene in the case of oil, derived from them; and, later, nuclear fission. Unlike these primary energy sources, "Electricity is always a secondary energy source, produced by some primary energy source" (Kander, Malanima, and Warde 258). Electricity is a way of transporting the energy created by falling water or burning coal or splitting atoms from the site of generation to the site of consumption.

What made electricity magical, beyond its glorious spectacle, was that it sequestered many of the dirty consequences of energy production far away from the site of energy's consumption. Among other things, this meant that the local pollution associated with producing energy—like the smog that came with burning coal—was no longer a necessary part of the experience of consuming energy. Like the airplane and the automobile in this respect, electricity is a charismatic converter of energy that occludes one's view of energy's origins and mode of production. High modernism, as Hal Foster has persuasively argued, was particularly prone to "aestheticist occlusion[s] of the socioeconomic bases of technology" because "they made a fetish of technology. They treated it apart from mode of production and turned it into an object of art" (7). Growing epistemological barriers and lengthening supply chains made it easy for users of technology in the twentieth century to disconnect their patterns of consumption from their social and ecological effects. This disappearing act was as much a part of the wonder that surrounded electrification as were the wondrous special effects that could be achieved with it. Unmasking this trick has become a central task of the growing field of the energy humanities.

Doing so requires an understanding of what Debeir, Deléage, and Hémery call "energy systems" and "converter chains," the organizations, technologies, and infrastructure by which energy is converted to work: "An energy system is the original combination of diverse converter chains which draw on determined sources of energy and depend on each other, initiated or controlled by classes or social groups which develop and consolidate on the basis of this control" (108). An ecocritical take on the "general energizing" shifts focus away from the technological things of modernism—the charismatic converters, like automobiles, airplanes, and electrical lights—and refocuses on the supply chains and waste streams that vastly exceed them in space and time and which link them intimately and ultimately to the natural environment.

But how—getting past the converters—can we theorize the relationship between energy and culture? As late as 1958, Raymond Williams, the eminent British literary critic, the founder of cultural studies as we know it today, and author of one of the canonical texts of ecocriticism, *The Country and the City*, made the case in favor of general energizing even while fully acknowledging the consequent environmental damage. His argument was based in part on his own Welsh working-class background:

> At home we were glad of the Industrial Revolution, and of its consequent social and political changes. True, we lived in a very beautiful farming valley, and the valleys beyond the limestone we could all see were ugly. But there was one gift that was overriding, one gift which at any price we would take, the gift of power that is everything to men who have worked with their hands. It was slow in coming to us, in all its effects, but steam power, the petrol engine, electricity, these and their host of products in commodities and services, we took as quickly as we could get them, and were glad. . . . Any account of our culture which explicitly or implicitly denies the value of an industrial society is really irrelevant: not in a million years would you make us give up this power. (9)

It is an extraordinary passage that reads painfully today, but that perfectly exemplifies a common conceptual impasse, the short circuit between energy and environment. "Not in a million years would you make us give up this power," he writes, defiantly admitting that no argument, no matter how persuasive or scientifically verifiable, could ever make him see things differently. There is a deep irony in the use of the figure of speech "not in a million years," since of course in an absolutely literal sense it takes millions of years of organic life cycles to produce the fossil fuels whose burning powers the mode of human life Williams here defends. The use of fossil fuels represents, in Jennifer Wenzel's words, "the burning or harvesting" of "compressed time" (Szeman et al. 8). Matthew Huber refers to fossil fuels in his book *Lifeblood: Oil, Freedom, and the Forces of Capital* (2013) as the "biotic concentration of time—the product of millions of years of concentrated solar energy, or what Jeffrey Dukes refers to as 'buried sunshine,'" which "allows for the temporal *acceleration* of the pace and productivity of production" (7; original italics). As the physicist Frederick Soddy wrote in a popular scientific text of the early twentieth century, "The power [of a technology] is neither in the machine nor in the mining; its origin is more ancient . . . the energy of the sunshine in the carboniferous era, millions of years before there was such a thing as a man" (102). In Williams's refusal to give up the power of fossil fuels for another million years, all that compressed time and buried sunshine is projected from the past into the future. At the current rate of consumption, however, humanity will burn through its carbon reserves long before then.

Williams, for his part, acknowledges that the "new power brought ugliness: the coal brought dirt, the factory brought overcrowding, communications brought a mess of wires" (10). But he professes faith that such problems will very soon be solved by technological advances: "New sources of power, new methods of production, improved systems of transport and communication can, quite practically, make England clean and pleasant again, and with much more power, not less. Any new ugliness is the product of stupidity, indifference, or simply incoordination" (Williams 10). That was 1958. A generation earlier Soddy had written something eerily similar in its techno-optimism: "It is possible to look forward to a time, which may await the world, when this grimy age of fuel will seem as truly a beginning of the mastery of energy as the rude stone age of Paleolithic man now appears as the beginning of the mastery of matter" (16). After touring the Niagara Falls hydropower turbines in 1906, H. G. Wells saw a similar utopian future, describing the dynamos as "clean, noiseless, and starkly powerful. All the clatter and tumult of the early age of machinery is past and gone here; there is no smoke, no coal grit, no dirt at all . . . [just] softly humming turbines" (1019). In more recent years, many ecocritics have lost faith in future technological fixes to the polluting excesses of industrial society—even hydropower, a low-carbon source of electrical energy, causes significant impact through dam construction—while the self-styled ecomodernists, as we saw in our Introduction, have held on to it.

All this is to say that even a critic like Williams—a Marxist, a progressivist, and a pioneer in the realm of thinking about the relationship between culture and politics—cannot, in the late 1950s in Britain with a working-class background that seemingly bound him to equate energizing with liberation and empowerment, think clearly at all about energy or energy regimes. He does *see* clearly, however, just how much of a difference the modern energy regime has made to his own way of life, and just how polluting that regime is. But knowing that doesn't result for him in a theoretical paradigm for culture and society that includes it, let alone makes it central. In Williams's once definitive and still influential cultural studies handbook of 1976, *Keywords*, the notion of power or general energizing he discusses here simply does not appear at all—neither does "energy," "climate," "environment," "environmentalism," or "nature." At the time, such things did not seem to pertain to cultural studies; indeed, they may have seemed its very antithesis. Now, cultural critics think very differently, even if we are as trapped and enabled by fossil-fueled modernity as Williams was.

As we saw in the writings of figures like Valéry, Lenin, Soddy, Beston, and others, a general theory of culture's relationship to energy began to develop in the late nineteenth and early twentieth centuries. But a theory of culture's relationship to its specific energy regime—that is to say, a theory about culture's relationship to *how* the general energizing occurred, which in this case was through the increasing use of fossil fuels—did not develop until much later. Williams's position in "Culture is Ordinary" marks a moment in cultural criticism before energy and energy regimes became objects of inquiry in themselves. One of the opening moves of a real debate about the relationship between energy regimes and culture was taken in 1994 by Vaclav Smil, an eminent environmental scientist and theorist of energy. In *Energy in World History*, he issued a statement that, were it to be accepted as true, would end all speculation about the relationship between culture and energy: "Timeless literature, painting, sculpture, architecture, and music show no correlation with advances in energy consumption" (qtd. in F. Buell 274). Of course, Smil is not an expert on literary culture, and his assertion, far from deterring interested critics, instead provoked them to discover previously overlooked connections between culture and energy. Frederick Buell engages Smil by refusing his foreclosure and remaking it as a speculative project: "Perhaps the gap between energy and culture can be credibly bridged and made available to the traffic of a new field of study" (275).

There is a whole new critical industry living and growing in Buell's "perhaps" that calls itself the energy humanities. This new critical idiom drew a positive charge from two negatives at its origin. Smil's categorical denial in 1994 of the relevance of energy to art was one. The other was a review article published by Amitav Ghosh in 1992 that he titled "Petrofiction," by which he meant to designate a subgenre of fictions about oil encounters. His argument was that such petrofictions, like the one he was reviewing in the article, Abdelrahman Munif's quintet of novels *Cities of Salt*, were exceptionally and—given the modern world's dependence on oil—surprisingly rare. Why, Ghosh asks, "when there is so much to write about, has this encounter proved so imaginatively sterile?" (30). Ghosh ventures three answers. The first proposes a generalized cultural repression of any awareness of the oil energy regime: "To the principle protagonists in the Oil Encounter (which means, in effect, America and Americans on the one hand and the peoples of the Arabian Peninsula and the Persian Gulf on the other), the history of oil is a matter of embarrassment verging on the unspeakable, the pornographic" (29). The second faults the institutional professionalization of a whole class of literary elites in the university system, particularly in the United States and Europe, whose "fictional gaze has turned inward," making the prospect of an "American writer taking on the Oil Encounter . . . literally inconceivable" (30). Finally, novelistic form itself may be too limited to properly represent the oil encounter: "We do not yet possess the form that can give the Oil Encounter a literary expression" (31).

By pointing to the rarity of petrofictions even while discussing one of the exceptions to his own speculative rule, Ghosh was making a point superficially similar to Smil's—that most works of art turn away from considering the sources of the general energizing from within which they were produced. But it is one thing to say, like Ghosh, that novelists have largely ignored the oil encounter, and entirely another thing to argue, like Smil, that works of art are unaffected by the dominant energy regime in which they are made and consumed. Just about ten years after Ghosh published "Petrofiction," critics like Imre Szeman and Peter Hitchcock (2010) began to turn Smil's and Ghosh's arguments on their heads. In a special issue of *American Book Review* in 2012, Imre Szeman and Graeme MacDonald remade Ghosh's title "petrofiction"— originally conceived to denote novels that were explicitly about the oil encounter—into a term that might apply instead to any cultural artifact produced within an energy regime dominated by fossil fuels. Whether such artifacts explicitly treated fossil fuels or not, they were, for Szeman and MacDonald, "petrofictions" by virtue of being produced and published in the hydrocarbon age. Perhaps, they speculate, every fiction written in the era of petromodernity ought to be considered as a petrofiction, including the works of authors we might otherwise never associate with an interest in the energy industry. In the opening vignette of E. M. Forster's *Howards End* (1911), for example, the narrator assures us that "pouring in petrol" is one of many "actions with which the[ir] story has no concern" (14). An ecocritic concerned with the story of energy—its modes of extraction, consumption, and its ecological impacts—might read this against the grain, seeing in Forster's dismissal of the significance of gassing up a mode of paralepsis: a rhetorical strategy meant to emphasize a point it pretends merely to be passing over.

By 2017, for Imre Szeman and Dominic Boyer, the editors of *Energy Humanities: An Anthology*, the relationship between modernity and energy had become axiomatic: "To be modern is to depend on the capacities and abilities generated by energy." To realize this, according to them, "necessitates a fundamental reconsideration of our understanding of the forces that have given shape to modernity" (1). Such a reconsideration, according to Johnson, requires us to acknowledge that "fossil fuels are more than what our language permits us to see" and then to articulate "a proper *energy heuristic* to tease out the hidden material functions they perform behind the scenes to birth us into a second nature" (2–3; original italics). One such heuristic proposed by Patricia Yaeger takes its name and its method from the work of Fredric Jameson by modifying his formulation "the political unconscious" to reflect the concerns of the energy humanities: the energy unconscious. Yaeger's energy unconscious is a useful tool to help us discover energy regimes in modernist cultural texts that may not show any direct or explicit concern with them (Yaeger et al. 306, 309–10).

As thinkers of the Anthropocene, Szeman and Boyer shift focus from a passive sense of energizing—as if this massive liberation of energy for human use over the last 130 or so years had no particular cause, like a gift from Nature or God, or by force of a kind of collective will—to a focus on energy *dependence* or *addiction*. This reframing marks a transition away from the utopian, progressive thrust of Lenin, Valéry, and Banham to something much more fatalistic, or nihilistic—from the story of energy told as comedy to a new, environmentally aware version told as tragedy. Unlike their precursors, Szeman and Boyer are explicitly interested in the process of converting energy into work; in the fuels that catalyze these processes, like oil and coal; and in the by-products of such processes, like the carbon dioxide released into the atmosphere.

To really acknowledge the points made by Szeman, Boyer, and Ghosh, we thus need to reconceive modernity and modernism around the "general energizing" that made them possible. How will such a reconceptualization affect how we think about modernism? Asking how energy regimes affect cultural production is a much more difficult question than asking how they affect modern life more broadly. It is a question that has given cultural critics a great deal of trouble, mainly because so many investigations come away with disappointing results. "Why has it been so difficult," asks Szeman, "to locate a literary archive for what now appears to be so important a social and historical force?" (228).

Using another strategy to reconceptualize energy use, we might redraw some boundaries around modernism using the history of energy regimes. According to Frederick Buell, 1870 marks the time when "more energy is extracted from fossil fuels than from photosynthesis"; 1890 when "more than half of global energy comes from fossil fuels." And finally, "One might consider postmodernism in relation to the 1973 OPEC crisis, a moment in which narratives of petromodern futures and US hegemony were deeply unnerved, and so, too, the self-certainties of Oil-electric-coal capitalism" (280). Having established that fossil fuels are and have been "an energy source that organizes life practice in a more fundamental way than we've ever allowed ourselves to believe" (Szeman 230), and having reconceived the periodization of modernism around the history of a succession of energy regimes dominated by coal and oil (for Szeman, "oil has to be seen as hegemonic," even in the nuclear age, simply because it produces so much more of the world's energy [230]), we must still grapple with a fundamental difficulty, which "comes as a revelatory surprise to almost everyone who engages in critical explorations of energy today"—namely, that "the importance of fossil fuels in defining modernity has stood in inverse relationship to their presence in our cultural and social imaginaries" (Szeman 227).

There were and are, of course, exceptions to Szeman's rule. Coal was particularly visible in the UK, where nearly half a million people were working in the mines by 1880; the number of miners peaked in the decade of high modernism's high-water mark, growing to over a million people between 1913 and 1922 before falling rapidly after the Second World War according to the British government's Department for Business, Energy, and Industrial Strategy. Many works of modernist art protested the mining and burning of coal, which was by a wide margin the dominant form of energy use in the modern era. Emile Zola's 1885 novel *Germinal* depicts the hellish conditions of the coal mines in rural northern France, while in England the novels of D. H. Lawrence offer an extensive inquiry into the social, personal, and ecological costs of coal dependency. In *Lady Chatterley's Lover* (1928), Lawrence gives voice to one of his most full-throated critiques of industrial capitalism. The novel depicts the ecologically and socially devastated colliery district of Tevershall, with its "industrial population" laboring away "in the pits" and killing their souls for wages and their bodies with pollution; and then it contrasts that vision with a fantasy of small-scale agriculture, a world where, in a famous image, men "were educated to *live* instead of earn . . . to be naked and handsome and to sing in a mass and dance the old group dances, and carve the stools they sit on . . . that's the only way to solve the industrial problem" (266).

In 1937 George Orwell set out to see the coal mines in Northern England on a supposition not that far off from Szeman's: that "our civilization, *pace* Chesterton, is founded on coal, more completely than one realizes until one stops to think about it" (21). What follows is what critic Justin Neuman calls an energy recognition scene, "a moment, often surprising or unexpected, when writers and artists imagine their way across the vivid and tangible materiality of locomotives, lightbulbs, automobiles, and other technologies to the energy systems on which they depend" (152). After a grueling tour of the labyrinthine underground tunnels in which miners put in eleven-and-a-half-hour days shifting, on average, two tons of rock and coal every hour, Orwell concluded that "the miner can stand as the type of the manual worker, not only because his work is so exaggeratedly awful, but also because it is so vitally necessary and yet so remote from our experience, so invisible, as it were, that we are capable of forgetting it as we forget the blood in our veins" (34). Orwell's metaphor about forgetting the blood in our veins lends a fleshy, tactile reality to Szeman's "inverse relationship" between oil dependence and oil's presence in the cultural texts of oil-dependent societies. If workers liberated from manual labor—intellectuals and artists included—routinely failed to think about coal, it wasn't only because coal was mined far away from city centers. It was also because there was something "humiliating" in watching "coal-miners working. It raises in you a momentary doubt about your own status as an 'intellectual' and a superior person generally. For it is brought home to you at least while you are watching, that it is only because miners sweat their guts out that superior persons can remain superior" (34).

Another exception to the "inverse relationship" rule was Upton Sinclair's 1927 novel *Oil!*, which, like his earlier *King Coal* (1917), concerned itself directly with the fossil fuel energy regime on roughly the same theory—that modernity's fossil fuel dependence was, and is, practically invisible to the modern cultural imaginary. But again, like Orwell, Sinclair was more "committed to international socialism" than he was to thinking through what fossil fuel dependence might mean in itself to the modern condition, as Stephanie LeMenager argues (69). In *Living Oil: Petroleum Culture in the American Century* (2013), LeMenager theorizes the affective impasse of living in petromodernity in part through her reading of *Oil!*. She points out that the novel's opening chapter narrates in great detail the pleasures and thrills of driving an automobile on California's roads. The novel, she concludes, both critiques the horrors of oil extraction and capitalist modernity while, at the same time, it "generates a series of aesthetic images and environmental emotions that valorize driving and even the process of oil extraction, showing both of these industrial-era activities as modes of facilitating the body's capacity for self-extension toward other life" (69). The result of the novel's combination of a naturalist critique of the fossil economy with a descriptive narration of the oil economy's pleasures is, predictably perhaps, impasse: "Even for one of the most ideologically driven American novelists," LeMenager concludes, "the aesthetic pleasures of petroleum undermine political solutions" (70). This is a damning assessment considering that *Oil!* is, like *The Road to Wigan Pier* (1937), one of the rare modernist works that attends to oil—or to other fossil fuels like coal or natural gas—as a central element of plot.

Ironically, though critical of coal mining, Lawrence, for his part, was just as prone to romanticize the new form of power produced by burning coal as the most technophilic of moderns. In *Women in*

Love (1920), for example, Ursula Brangwen's sexuality is described in terms of electrical energy: "A dark flood of electric passion she released from him, drew into herself. She had established a rich new circuit, a new current of passionate electric energy, between the two of them, released from the darkest poles of the body and established in perfect circuit" (313). E. M. Forster depicts the automobile as an unambiguously malevolent force in *Howards End*, a case he makes by following automotive supply chains back to the rubber plantations of colonial West Africa and projecting the automobile's impacts forward to the smog and suburban sprawl they presage. And yet not even Forster can avoid the erotic pull of internal combustion, as he demonstrates in his posthumously published novel *Maurice* (1971). There Forster uses a motorcycle to propel the "passion" between Maurice and Durham that flowers when the two skip school on the latter's motorcycle, speeding away under a teacher's gaze:

> The machine was powerful, he reckless naturally. It leapt forward into the fens and the receding dome of the sky. They became a cloud of dust, a stench, and a roar to the world, but the air they breathed was pure, and all the noise they heard was the long drawn cheer of the wind. They cared for no one, they were outside humanity, and death, had it come, would only have continued their pursuit of a retreating horizon. (60)

Modernist writers like Zola, Lawrence, Forster, and Orwell did turn their gaze to coal, and appear therefore to disprove Szeman's theory of the inverse relationship between the prevalence of fossil fuels and their representation in culture. But those modernists did not generate thereby a theory of the general energizing of modernity. Orwell's focus was instead on the coal miner—as the ideal type of the worker—who exemplified his commitment to the working class as the central protagonist of socialist revolt. He was reading for the political unconscious, whereas we, as ecocritics or petrocritics, are reading for the energy unconscious. While the preceding examples demonstrate that modernist energy regimes did make dramatic appearances in modernist texts, it remains to be seen how we might read modernist texts as petrofictions in the expanded critical sense, in particular when energy makes no immediately obvious appearance in the text. We still need, *pace* Johnson, an "energy heuristic" for reading texts for energy when energy is not explicitly thematized; and we still need, *pace* Szeman, to "locate a literary archive."

Missing Modernist Energy Epics: Three Case Studies

Marcel Duchamp's gnomically titled sculpture *The Bride Stripped Bare by her Bachelors, Even (The Large Glass)* constitutes one of the major works of his eclectic and provocative career; it is a modernist monument (over nine-feet tall and six-feet wide) on par with *Ulysses* or *À la recherche du temps perdu*. Duchamp began work on it in 1915 and declared it "definitively unfinished" in 1923. He composed it of varnish, oil, wire, dust, and metal on two rectangular panels of glass. It is difficult to describe, and it has proven even more difficult to interpret—a tribute to high-modernist recalcitrance. Marjorie Perloff cautions viewers against literalism, arguing that "Duchamp's enigmatic *Large Glass* . . . exerts a special fascination for the viewer who keeps trying to extract meanings that the artwork blocks at every turn. Art becomes play, endlessly frustrating our longings for certainty . . . mocking the solemnity of the explicator who is determined to find the key" (34). But while granting that *The Large Glass* is not a roman à clef waiting to be unlocked by an ecocritical key, reading the work as a manifestation of general energizing reveals a compelling narrative, clarifying many of the work's central elements and helping viewers to understand what is at stake in Duchamp's erotic-mechanical assemblages.

The theme of automobility helps explain the medium of the "glass" itself—two panes divided by a horizontal hinge—which becomes legible as a surreal version of a car windshield, specifically as a magnified version of the hinged windscreen of the iconic Model T Ford. If, as Enda Duffy proposes in *The Speed Handbook: Velocity, Pleasure, Modernism* (2009), "the car was modernist mobile architecture," then *The Large Glass* was the car remade as modernist sculpture (6). Duchamp produced a narrative companion piece in the form of *The Green Box* (1934), a hand-produced collection of 320 notes, sketches, and other items. In one of the notes, he recounts a road trip he took with the artists Guillaume

Apollinaire, Gabrièle Buffet, and Francis Picabia in 1912, a trip that inspired *The Large Glass*. Through the narrative materials of *The Green Box*, it becomes clear that Duchamp thought of his work as a meditation on the erotic life of the human machine. As Linda Dalrymple Henderson argues, "The theme of *The Bride* . . . is sexual interaction" among "biomechanical or purely mechanical creatures" (91). Duchamp describes the Bride as "basically a motor"—a motor that, like many of the mechanical figures in the work, is imagined as running on a peculiar kind of gasoline. "The Bride," he continues, "being a motor which transmits her timid-power.—she is this very timid-power—This timid-power is a sort of automobiline [sic], love gasoline, that, distributed to the quite feeble cylinders, within reach of the *sparks of her constant life*, is used for the blossoming of this virgin who has reached the goal of her desire" (42; original italics). Reading *The Large Glass* from an energy systems perspective underscores Duchamp's sense of the specifically violent and sexualized characteristics of petroleum energy systems, epitomized by the up-and-down thrusting of pistons in a two-stroke motor. The affective qualities conjured by petroleum come into tighter focus when contrasted with the smooth circular motion of the water-wheel and hand-driven chocolate grinder in the lower frame of *The Large Glass*, machines whose motions suggest onanism and autoeroticism.

Seeing the whole of *The Large Glass* framed in the windscreen of a Ford Model T clarifies the experiences and impressions that gave it form. But what of literary texts that seem formally and thematically indifferent to petromodernity? What if we try to read a modernist classic like *A la recherché du temps perdu* as a petrofiction? What could we learn about Proust, or about Proust's historical and cultural milieu, or about ourselves? The name Marcel Proust inevitably summons to mind an image of cookies dipped in tea; but only the most devoted aficionado will be aware that in preliminary drafts of *In Search of Lost Time* it was the smell of gasoline, not the taste of a *petite madeleine*, that served as a trigger for the sudden shifts in consciousness Proust calls *mémoire involuntaire*. Proust, it turns out, was infatuated with the smell of gasoline. He muses ecstatically in *Contre Sainte-Beuve*—a posthumously published mélange of literary criticism, autobiographical prose, and social commentary begun in 1907 and abandoned in the fall of 1908—about the "smell of petrol," in a way that differentiates his relationship with petroleum from the way he thought, spoke, and felt about the coal, electric, biomass, and muscular energy systems also caught in the representational web of his writing (48).

Proust writes rapturously in *Contre Sainte-Beuve* of the "sky-coloured, sun-coloured petrol" he sees spilled on the street (19, 27, 48). Even as the waste product of incomplete combustion or in its spilled state, gasoline is for the novelist an object of sensory enjoyment, creating rainbows on the ground. Though suffering from chronic asthma no doubt worsened by environmental pollutants, he writes that "the smell of petrol came into [his] room quite simply as the most intoxicating of all the summer smells of the country, the smell that summed up both its beauty and the joy of speeding over it" (48). In these passages, seeing spilled fuel on the ground or inhaling the fumes from a passing car brings back a memory from the previous summer when a lover awaited him at the end of a motoring adventure: "She had stayed behind, thirty miles off . . . [a distance which he] would cover so quickly in the car when the time came to go back" (48–49). For Proust, the smell of gasoline brings back involuntary memories: "All these the smell of the passing automobile had restored to me, whilst inviting me towards pleasures to come—for it [gasoline] is a smell of summer, of power, of freedom, and nature, and love" (50). Saturated with sexual significance and evoking an almost magical form of mobility, petroleum powers a fantasy of heterosexual conquest, and it also fuels the motor of involuntary memory, the unconscious processes whereby our brains connect perceptual stimuli (a phrase of music, a taste, a sound, a smell) with unrelated emotional states, opening wormholes to lost pasts. Figuratively and literally, petroleum moves him. We might say that the smell of petrol is a better vehicle for the metaphor of involuntary memory than the more familiar madeleine; but that leaves us to reckon with why Proust thought that the smell of petrol had to be sublimated, in the transition from his occasional writings to his fictions, into the madeleine—perhaps a future project for a dedicated petrocritic.

We are not suggesting that *In Search of Lost Time* is the great oil novel for which Ghosh, Nixon, and the energy humanists were searching. That honor belongs to one of the greatest unread novels of all time: Robert Musil's 2,000-page opus, *The Man Without Qualities* (1943). Readers only discover the central role petroleum has in shaping the plot and aesthetics of the novel after 119 chapters have passed. Like Proust, Musil's subject is the aristocracy on the brink of the Great War, in this case the Austro-Hungarians of Vienna, from within whose Imperial and Royal halls we observe Ulrich, the eponymous man without qualities, as he observes the doomed Hapsburg monarchy as it plans a peace celebration on what we know is the eve of war. Ulrich finally learns from the bank director Leo Fischel what so much international squabbling and palace intriguing has been about: "Galician oil fields, that's what!" (672).

The Galician oil fields, which were indeed integral to German war plans, made Austria-Hungary one of the top oil-producing regions in the world in the years before the Great War. When Ulrich discovers the oil plot, his friend Arnheim tries to buy his silence, offering to take him in as a partner in his "great industrial enterprise" (695). The Austrian military turns out to be involved as well, hoping to trade Galician oil contracts for German artillery and munitions. Though never acknowledged openly, everything comes back to oil: "If Arnheim has the Galician oil fields and a contract to supply the Army, we naturally have to protect our frontier. We also have to install oil bases for the Navy on the Adriatic, which will upset the Italians . . . our neighbors will arm too" (1092). In Great Britain, the buildup to war saw Winston Churchill order the British Navy to convert its fleet from coal to oil power, doubling down on the country's commitment to a resource not present within its borders. In short, *The Man Without Qualities* presciently understood the lead-up to the Great War, from inside the great game of the power struggle in Europe, as both an oil war (the kind with which we are all too familiar today) and as the first large-scale energy transition from coal to oil—a perspective one might not expect to find in the pages of literary high modernism.

Innervations and Enervations

Valéry's "general energizing" was ultimately about a great deal more than powering machines. It affected every aspect of human life on every scale. At the highest level, the population explosion of the twentieth century required a massive increase in humanity's ability to harvest caloric energy through agriculture. As Soddy noted in 1926, a million calories represents the energy needs of one person for one year (118). The Haber-Bosch process for chemically fixing nitrogen from the atmosphere in order to manufacture fertilizer—invented in 1909, industrialized in 1913—enabled increases in agricultural yields that were orders of magnitude greater than any other innovation in agriculture before or since. Nitrogen was a scarce resource before Haber-Bosch, which meant that fertilizer, often in the form of ammonia, was a limited and expensive agricultural input. Scientists already knew that nitrogen was superabundant in the air, but Fritz Haber was the first to figure out how to make it accessible to chemical engineering. Once he did, and once he partnered with Carl Bosch at the German firm BASF to create an industrially scalable process for doing so, the planetary nitrogen cycle was fundamentally altered. Previously accepted limits to agricultural growth were shattered, and with them, understood limits, like those theorized by Thomas Malthus in the nineteenth century, to population growth. The Haber-Bosch process increased the amount of nitrogen available for human use, which in turn increased the availability of energy in the form of food calories, enabling a massive human population boom. This increase in caloric energy must be considered, alongside electrification and fossil fuels, a crucial aspect of the "general energizing" that characterizes the modernist era, even if Valéry himself wasn't thinking about calories when he coined the term.

There are not many explorations of the way that Haber-Bosch might have affected modernist aesthetics, but it is possible to find a few footprints. Aaron Rosenberg's paper from the 2016 Modernist Studies Association Conference, "Nitrogen Fixations: From Waste to World War," reveals some of the fascinating ways the nitrogen cycle does appear in modernist literature, though they have heretofore rarely been remarked upon. Rosenberg informs us that before Haber-Bosch, "The richest natural source of nitrogen ever discovered" was still guano, a combination of seabird and bat droppings, the biggest deposits of which were mostly found on remote Pacific islands. "It is no exaggeration to suggest," writes Rosenberg, "that the business of empire in the late nineteenth century ran on guano." This was true in two distinct ways: because guano was used to fertilize "the crops that fed expanding populations" and because guano supplied "the active ingredient in gunpowder and high explosives." Guano increased farm yields at the same time that it intensified the destructive capacities of empire—and the British Empire had the best access to it of any of the European powers at the time, giving them tremendous competitive advantages over their European rivals. Rosenberg offers what is, as far as we are aware, the first exploration of the appearance of the nitrogen cycle—either as guano or as chemically fixed from the air—in modernist literature, opening up new ecocritical perspectives on novels like Joseph Conrad's *Lord Jim* (1899–1900) and H. G. Wells's *In the Days of the Comet* (1906).

Ecocritics have tried to come to terms with absences, like that of the nitrogen cycle, through theories of genre. High modernism, they might claim, didn't produce genres that could easily accommodate something, like the Haber-Bosch process and the human alteration of the nitrogen cycle, whose scalar import was planetary. Science fiction, which tends toward the scale of the planetary, is suited to incorporating something like Haber-Bosch into its purview, which returns us to Ghosh's assertion that the realist novel is a poor form for representing the oil encounter. It seems logical for our purposes tentatively to extend his argument even further: that the realist novel might be an inadequate form for narrating the general energizing of the twentieth century as well. Consider William T. Vollman's two-volume *Carbon Ideologies* (2017), which in most respects is an encyclopedic act of investigative journalism into the culture and industry of energy in the United States, but which operates on the fictional conceit of a narrating voice addressing itself to unborn generations dealing with the aftermath of our present energy-intensive economy. Neither a novel nor entirely a straightforward work of nonfiction, Vollman's genre-bending work is an attempt to discover a narrative mode suited to representing the fossil fuel and nuclear energy regimes of the present.

Unlike at the macro level, we do find in high modernism a lot of attention paid to the general energizing at the micro level. On this score it is worth remembering that Valéry's "general energizing" appeared in its original French as "*cette innervation générale.*" "Energizing" is probably the right translation of "innervation" in the context of Valéry's remarks about electricity, but "innervation" translates literally and directly as "innervation," whose primary definition springs from the biological sciences and means "the supply of nerve fibres to, or disposition of nerve fibres within, an organ or part" (OED). In more colloquial terms, to be innervated is to be excited or energized, a physiological and psychological state that came to characterize for many contemporaries the defining affect of the modern age. Just as often, however, the general energizing could lead to enervation—a weakened state of nervousness or overexcitement. As early as 1881 Thomas Beard published a best-selling book called *American Nervousness: Its Causes and Consequences*. His theories about physiological nervousness were not unrelated to electricity as both a cause and a cure; he also coauthored a standard textbook on electroshock therapy (Duffy 2016: 89).

The general energizing thus refers not only to an increase in the ability of humans to marshal natural energy resources for their use but to a series of new concepts for understanding human life itself as essentially defined by the body's energy inputs and outputs. Energy in this context is the thing that animates human beings, and it was the subject of intensive study and elaboration in modernist texts. For the moderns, "to be energized," as Duffy puts it in "High-Energy Modernism," "is to be excited: the physical body, the nervous system, the capacity for alertness, what is called the will, collude." "To be alive" in the modernist period, he continues, "is to be full of energy" (87). Duffy suggests a number of thought-provoking formulations to describe the conceptual break that would mark the transition into modernism as the move from an "age of materialism" to an "era of energetics" (96). In the twentieth century, energy became "the prime attribute by which we know and name nothing less than life" (87).

Unlike the macro level of the nitrogen cycle, this micro level of the general energizing—on which the epistemology and the phenomenology of everyday life was radically altered—had very clear and profound effects. "Modernist art," writes Duffy, "shows people trying to recreate themselves as energetic, and to imagine the material world energized, at the moment of the birth of the new economy of energy" (95). In 1905, Albert Einstein established the theoretical equivalence between mass and energy, which helped popularize the equivalence between life and energy. The general theory of relativity primed the public to expect a practically unlimited access to new and greater forms of energy, since theoretically it could be liberated from any and all matter. Everything, the moderns were coming to believe, was energy, including, and especially, sex. Jean Toomer's 1923 lyric poem "Her Lips Are Copper Wire," from his experimental novel *Cane*, combined electrical current and sexual energy in keeping with the new thinking: "Telephone the powerhouse," the speaker commands, "then with your tongue remove the tape / and press your lips to mine / till they are incandescent" (101). In this image the consummation of the kiss closes the circuit and lights up the lover's lips, linking the circulation of electricity in the city with the circulation of erotic desire between the speaker and their addressee. Others saw this analogy between sex and energy as a cause for anxiety. D. H. Lawrence, for example, saw the general energizing as a drain on sexual potency. As Lawrence has his protagonist Mellors lament of the British people in *Lady Chatterley's Lover*, "Their spunk is gone dead. Motor-cars and cinemas and aeroplanes suck that last bit out of them" (238). On the level of the human subject, one could be innervated as in Toomer or enervated as in Lawrence, but what these opposing cases exemplified together was the epistemological takeover staged by a new modernist metaphorics of energy.

Oil as Hyperobject

We may no longer be living in an age of modernist energy exuberance, but we are ever more enmeshed in an age of petromodernity; and in that fact we can see clearly our profound continuity with the moderns, even if our acute and general awareness of it differentiates us from them in another way. When Elizabeth Bishop published her poem "Filling Station" in 1965, the first oil shocks of the 1970s were still a decade away. The poem is clearly a petrofiction—both in Ghosh's sense of the term as a fiction about oil and in Szeman's sense of the term as a fiction composed in the time of petromodernity—that has yet to be identified as such in the extant criticism, despite the hiding-in-plain-sight obviousness of its title. It reveals the extent of our enmeshment in oil as if it were a revelation to the speaker, resulting in a rush of revulsion that, in the end, settles back into a strange lyricism.

"Oh, but it is dirty!" the speaker exclaims of the titular rural gas station where she is refueling her car while observing her immediate environment, "oil-soaked, oil-permeated / to a disturbing, over-all / black translucency" (127). The exclamatory apostrophe of the opening line leaves the reader waiting to find out what, specifically, is dirty until the second line, "—this little filling station," just long enough to suggest something much bigger as the allegorical subject of the poem: petromodernity itself. To that end, the filling station appears to be occupied by a whole nuclear family: mother, father, two sons, and a dog, all of them covered in oil. "Do they live in the station?" the speaker asks incredulously (127). "We all do," a petrocritic might answer. She begins to notice many of the accoutrements of domesticity: a porch with a "grease-impregnated" wicker sofa on it, some comic books lying on top of a "big dim doily" draped over a matching wicker table. She takes offense, seemingly arbitrarily, from the doily in particular, apostrophizing again, "Why, oh why, the doily?" But this question answers itself, since the word "doily" is made, literally, of the word "oil." The poem ends with an image of oil cans carefully arranged in rows softly saying their name, "Esso—so—so" to "high-strung automobiles." For Ross Barrett and Daniel Worden, oil is usually "contained—in our cars' gas tanks, in pipelines, in shale, in tar sands, in distant extraction sites" (qtd. in Hensley and Steer 66). But as a unified image of petromodernity, "Filling Station" asks readers to see the viscosity and hegemonic agency of oil, and to see as illusory the boundary between this speaker, whose life is powered frictionlessly and cleanly by oil, and the family whose lives are covered in it: a whole reality that, like Bishop's very language, is "oil-soaked, oil-permeated." "Filling Station" thus parodies and undoes our everyday containment strategies for living in petromodernity.

2

Modernism's Urban Environments

Cities were more attractive and densely populated year by year; the Berlin of 1905 was not like the city I had known in 1901 . . . which in turn paled beside the Berlin of 1910. Vienna, Milan, Paris, London, Amsterdam—whenever you came back to them you were surprised and delighted. The streets were broader and finer, the public buildings more imposing, the shops more elegant.

—STEFAN ZWEIG

No first visitor to the newer industrial centres but is aware of a certain shriveling up of man's importance before the aggregate of material construction. The sense of proportion is dwarfed by the mere divergence in size and stability, as the weak, unprotected human body is contrasted with vast levers and furnaces, which at any moment could crack him like an eggshell, or shrivel him up like sawdust.

—C. F. G. MASTERMAN

Metropolis and Modernity

The silent film *Metropolis* (1927), a sprawling work of expressionist science fiction with a script by Thea von Harbou and directed by her husband, Fritz Lang, opens with a long shot of the city of the future, its gleaming skyscrapers overlaid by the film's title in gothic lettering, to the triumphant strains of a score by Gottfried Huppertz (Figure 2). At first, the problems of the urban environment—its pollution, congestion, disease, danger, and noise—seem to have been solved by modern technology. New transportation systems, building materials, and energy sources have produced a long-dreamed-of utopia. Techno-optimism of this kind is, as we note in our Introduction, one of the most significant themes and enduring legacies of modernist art. Nowhere is it more prominent than in depictions of and visions for the city, conceived as an artificial environment that could be built to express human nature and satisfy human desires, while totally replacing and dominating the natural world from which it rises.

In Lang's film, however, the utopian view of the metropolis is short-lived. The skyline of the city's towers fades into darkness as

FIGURE 2 *The city of the future, frame shot from* Metropolis.

the viewer is plunged underground through a montage of tight-focus shots emphasizing violence and chaos: pumping pistons, churning gears, ticking clocks, and venting steam form the base of the city's soaring architectural superstructure. Aurally, frantic rhythms and atonal phrases supplant major chords. As a clock strikes noon or midnight, thousands of identical workers in black coveralls, heads uniformly shaven, shuffle in Brechtian misery in and out of a factory gate, like so many links in the chain of industry. Lang's film symbolizes the economic asymmetries produced by urbanization through the vertical separation between the technocratic executive who controls the city from high atop his "New Tower of Babel," while, as intertitles proclaim, workers are confined to levels of the city "deep below the earth's surface." In this dark, subterranean space, the many toil and die, while high above, the few play Greco-Roman sports and frolic on sunlit rooftops. Physically, the groups appear almost as different as the Morlocks and the Eloi of H. G. Wells's *The Time Machine* (1895), two species evolved, after thousands of generations of class segregation, from one parent species. In other words, the dream city is also a nightmare, a space of toxicity, mechanization, and death; its soaring skyscrapers hide the misery of teeming masses, who include not only the laborers described earlier but also the women of *Metropolis*, for whom the city is a space of patriarchal control. These dystopian themes tap an equally deep vein of the modernist urban imagination, which perceives urban land as wasteland, or land laid waste.

In these and countless other ways, *Metropolis* dramatizes modernity's conflicted attitudes toward its urban environment, which is at once the central subject of modernist art and the necessary condition of its emergence. The metropolis is, we might say, modernism's native habitat. Modernism's coteries are named for neighborhoods or cities at large: the Vienna Secession, the Harlem Renaissance, the Bloomsbury Group, the Left Bank, and the Chicago school, to name a few. Meanwhile, its writers became synonymous with specific cities: Charles Baudelaire and Marcel Proust with Paris, Alfred Döblin with Berlin, Robert Musil with Vienna, Langston Hughes with New York, Virginia Woolf with London. "Trieste-Zurich-Paris," writes James Joyce, after the final "yes" of Molly Bloom's monologue in *Ulysses*, in homage to the cities that gave him refuge while he was writing the great novel of his native city, Dublin, which he referred to as the "Hibernian metropolis." "Jerusalem Athens Alexandria / Vienna London," writes T. S. Eliot, sketching the metropolitan cultural geography of *The Waste Land*.

But while the metropolis is the site of modernism's fondest fantasies, it is also the source of its deepest fears. For every modern who loves the city—"What a lark! What a plunge!" thinks Virginia Woolf's Clarissa Dalloway, as she steps out into a busy London street (3)—there are those who love to hate it; "So many," muses a speaker in T. S. Eliot's *The Waste Land* contemplating a similar crowd, but coming to a very different conclusion: "I had not thought death had undone so many" (ln. 63). The modern metropolis promised economic opportunity and social mobility, and its swelling throngs likewise found increased opportunities for recreation, socialization, and the consumption of material and social goods. But life in industrial cities also brought increased stress, regimentation, and surveillance, longer working hours, more pollution, and greater divisions between rich and poor. Both of these extremes drew the attention of the artists we have come to know as modernist.

Whether the burgeoning city of the late nineteenth and early twentieth centuries is celebrated as a wonderland or derided as a wasteland, those living there share a sense that the conditions and pace of life in a realm built of coal and steel represent something new in the nature of human experience, which demands new representational modes and new administrative strategies. Many critics make cases for the city's centrality to modernism, including Desmond Harding in *Writing and the City* (2002) and Andrew Thacker in *Modernism, Space, and the City* (2015). Malcolm Bradbury observes in "The Cities of Modernism" that "the literature of experimental Modernism which emerged in the last years of the nineteenth century . . . was an art of cities, especially of the polyglot cities which, for various historical reasons, had acquired high activity and great reputation as centers of intellectual and cultural exchange" (96). Or, as David Harvey puts it in *The Condition of Postmodernity* (1989), "Modernism, after 1848, was very much an urban phenomenon, that . . . existed in a restless but intricate relationship with the experience of explosive urban growth" (25–26).

Texts about the city become testing grounds for what Raymond Williams, in *The Politics of Modernism* (1989), calls "metropolitan perception," which according to Jed Esty is "the single term that best captures the multiple contextual dimensions needed to historicize modernist practice" (3). In another influential study, *The Country and the City* (1973), Williams describes modernity's Janus-faced relationship with urbanization this way: "On the city has gathered the idea of an achieved center: of learning, communication, light. Powerful hostile associations have also developed: on the city as a place of noise, worldliness and ambition" (1). Modernism's love-hate relationship with the city is a rare point of agreement in an otherwise fractious field. In *All That Is Solid Melts into Air* (1982), Marshall Berman gives voice to the consensus view when he describes the city as a "dynamic new landscape in which modern experience takes place, . . . a landscape of steam engines, automatic factories, railroads, [and] vast new industrial zones . . . that have grown over night, often with dreadful human consequences" (18).

Urbanization produced dire environmental consequences as well—problems like the pollution of air, water, and soil—which receive prominent treatment in modernist art as subjects worthy of aesthetic attention for the first time. As Walter Benjamin observes, "With Baudelaire, Paris for the first time became the subject of lyrical poetry" (170), while in T. S. Eliot's words, modernism would take "the scream of the motor horn, the rattle of machinery, the grind of wheels, the beating of iron and steel, the roar of the underground railway, and the other barbaric cries of modern life; and . . . transform these despairing noises into music" (qtd. in Crawford 139). Given our current environmental crisis, however, it is not enough to hear the music of modernity in the sounds of the urban technoscape, as many modernist critics have done. We must learn to listen ecocritically as well; to search within and beyond urban texts for evidence of and responses to the environmental impact of modernization, a legacy in light of which modernism— from Eliot's poetry to Lang's films—acquires a new legibility.

The Built Environment

Our task in this chapter is to uncover the ecological and environmental implications of modernist urban theory and practice. We examine why and how the city became the dwelling place of the modern subject and the favored subject of modernist art, paying specific attention to the way urban texts address the environmental consequences of industrial modernity, which were vividly and pressingly apparent to the modern urbanite. The urban epic is one of modernism's most ubiquitous forms, and the city constitutes the largest entity regularly imagined by modernist literature, enabling texts to capture (and readers then and now to visualize) the ecological impact and social transformation of the species at its new industrial scale. Beginning with Lang's *Metropolis*, we take an artistic and literary tour of modernist cities real and imagined, surveying their transportation networks, waste treatment systems, and other aspects of the built environment. By emphasizing large-scale processes and by thinking of the city as an ecosystem, we are inspired by the urban theorist and activist Jane Jacobs, who writes in her foreword to the 1993 edition of *The Death and Life of Great American Cities* (1961) that "to investigate either natural or city ecosystems demands the same kind of thinking. It does not focus on 'things' and expect them to explain much in themselves. Processes are always of the essence; things have significances as participants in processes, for better or worse" (xxvii).

We will observe two such large-scale processes in modernist urbanism. The first leads toward greater urban density, a trend that is already well established when we pick up our story with the proto-modernisms spawning in Paris and London in the 1850s. During this phase, urbanization is powered by coal and shaped by fixed-path, fixed-time transportation systems like ships and trains; its architecture is likewise expressed in fixed-site infrastructure such as factories, bridges, and skyscrapers. Within and through these infrastructures, the moderns were alternately awed or alienated by the rising city, and they were habituated to new modes of being regimented by the timetables and terminals of public transportation. From an ecological perspective, rapid urban growth in the period between 1850 and 1950 represents one of the most significant transitions in human history, matched only by the shift from hunter-gatherer to settled agricultural societies in the late Neolithic period. Growing cities were the focal point of new architectural forms such as the factory, the skyscraper, and the department store, and they were enabled by new infrastructural forms such as railroad networks, electrical power grids, highways, and sanitation systems. Cities transformed the lifeworlds of millions of human beings and, in turn, these new urban agglomerations radically transformed their surrounding environments. The steam engine—and later the diesel engines and gas turbines that Vaclav Smil calls the "prime movers of globalization"—would transform the very idea of surrounding environments. By the second half of the twentieth century, with the advent of air travel and telecommunications, space itself was transformed, so that the world's centers of industry and finance became what Saskia Sassen (1991) calls "global cities," nodes in transnational supply chains. In the nineteenth-century metropolis, however, coal was king; as David Nye argues, "Not only did steam railroads and steamboats supply the produce, fuel, and raw material that the city demanded, not only did they carry off the products of the dense factory districts; stationary steam engines were the throbbing heart of the new industrial city, turning the wheels of commerce" (82).

Coal-fired steam engines may have been the heart of the nineteenth-century metropolis, to borrow Nye's metaphor, but if so, they were a diseased heart. Steam engines consolidated urban development and drove the first industrial revolution, but the coal combustion that powered them befouled urban environments, devastated human health, and degraded natural ecosystems. "The city is made of man; that is the last word to say of it," American novelist Robert Herrick crows in his novel *The Gospel of Freedom* (1898); it is "brazen, unequal, like all man's works, it stands a stupendous piece of blasphemy against nature. Once within its circle, one must forget that the earth is beautiful" (103). In *The Culture of Cities* of 1938, the American historian and urban theorist Lewis Mumford makes the case in greater detail, arguing that "urban agglomeration produces ... depletion in the natural environment," citing various negative externalities accruing from the city: "The blare of light in the evening sky blots out half the stars overhead," he begins, citing a benign-seeming light pollution before moving on to call attention to "the rush of sewage into the surrounding waters [which] converts rivers into open sewers," making typhoid "endemic" in big cities (252). For most of those who experienced the explosive, haphazard urbanization of the late nineteenth and early twentieth centuries first hand (and, we might add, for those who experience a similar phenomenon in the cities of the Global South today), it seemed self-evident that urbanization came at the cost of the natural environment.

If the city produces a host of environmental problems, it also fosters innovations designed to solve these problems, solutions that come with their own unintended consequences. We focus on three of these "solutions": the skyscraper, electrification, and the automobile. These technologies define the second phase of modern urbanism, alleviating many of the problems associated with nineteenth-century urbanism (air pollution and overcrowding in particular) but leading to skyrocketing energy intensity and a demographic dispersion away from high-density city centers into low-density suburbs and exurban corridors. These stages follow sequentially in the Global North while much of the Global South, by contrast, has witnessed industrialization and centralization concurrently with the adoption of automotive and electronic technologies. Automobility was a particularly potent force of decentralization. Electrification, on the other hand, was an unambiguous environmental good, one that put in place the possibility of ending the domestic combustion of coal, but it too became a force of decentralization as the growing electrical grid allowed for a redistribution of population and production. This changing technoscape had profound impacts on the way urbanites imagined and experienced their environments, particularly for women, people of color, and the urban poor, many of whom could not afford or were forbidden access to new technologies. The second half of this chapter considers landscapes of urban dispossession and questions of environmental justice in texts by Edith Wharton, Virginia Woolf, and Elizabeth Bowen as well as Ralph Ellison, Theodore Dreiser, and Richard Wright.

The City Rises

In 1850, depending on how one defines the boundaries of urban areas, there was at least one city—and possibly three—with a population of over a million people, in a world with a total human population of around 1.25 billion. The largest of these by far (and the only one for which we have reliable data) was London, whose population had surpassed a million people by the time of the 1801 decennial census; in 1851, the year of the Great Exhibition, that number had reached 2,630,782, according to the Office of National Statistics. The next largest city in the 1850s was likely Beijing, then the capital of the Qing dynasty under the new Xianfeng emperor. Edo (modern-day Tokyo) and Paris followed close behind, each hovering around the million mark. New York City, four times larger than any other city in the Americas in 1850, boasted only half a million people, and then only by combining the populations of its independent borough cities. By 1950, with the post–Second World War population boom only just beginning, the total human population had doubled to 2.5 billion and the number of urban areas exceeding a million residents had grown to over fifty. While this doubling of total population was unprecedented in the history of the species (and it would double again in the next half-century), the rate of urbanization during the same period is even more striking. In 1850, only an estimated 3 percent of the population lived in cities containing more than a hundred thousand people, while over the next hundred years that number grew logarithmically. By 1950, at least 30 percent of the global population consisted of urban dwellers; and sometime around 2008, as Mike Davis estimates, "for the first time the urban population of the earth will outnumber the rural . . . a watershed in human history comparable to the Neolithic or Industrial revolutions" (1).

London was not the first urban area with a population in excess of a million people. Anthropologists estimate that ancient Rome at its height contained between half a million and a million people, while Baghdad was likely the first urban area to exceed one million, as it did between the seventh and the ninth centuries CE, followed by Constantinople at the height of the Ottoman Empire. As these examples demonstrate, preindustrial cities—particularly those serving as administrative centers for vast empires—could achieve massive size, but these were the exception rather than the rule. Industrialization, which was already well underway in the England of 1850, would both enable and require such concentrations of human and natural resources on an ever-enlarging scale. Indeed, it could be said that during the century between 1850 and 1950, the city itself became an object of mass production.

The 1851 Great Exhibition in Hyde Park burnished Britain's reputation as the self-professed "workshop of the world" in its aggregation of resources, products, people, and technology from around the globe. Its iconic architectural work, The Crystal Palace—a building composed of cast iron and plate glass erected in Hyde Park—served as a symbol of transparency, light, and the benefits of a newly ascendant commodity culture. For tourists in London who took special trains to the exhibition, however, the city they left behind was increasingly choked by sulfurous smog. Industrial and human waste had transformed the "sweet Thames" of Edmund Spenser's "Prothalamion" (1596) into a stream of contagion, pollution, and death. Life expectancies for the immiserated population, as Beverley Cook and Alex Werner of the Museum of London observe, was a mere thirty-seven years.

London in the 1850s was at once a magnet and a midden, as Charles Dickens avers at the beginning of *Bleak House* (1852–53), where its 2.5 million residents encounter

> as much mud in the streets as if the waters had but newly retired from the face of the earth, and it would not be wonderful to meet a Megalosaurus, forty feet long or so, waddling like an elephantine lizard up Holborn Hill. Smoke lowering down from chimney-pots, making a soft black drizzle, with flakes of soot in it as big as full-grown snowflakes—gone into mourning, one might imagine, for the death of the sun. (3)

In this passage readers discover, already emergent in the Victorian period, an ironic narrator, a geological time frame, and a vivid sense of environmental catastrophe. There is air pollution bad enough to blot out the sun; soot falls like snow from the sky; the teeming masses of industrial laborers, already pouring into the city in vast numbers on steamships and trains, overwhelm the local transportation, housing, and sanitation infrastructure. Gone is the city Wordsworth described in "Composed Upon Westminster Bridge, September 3, 1802," with its "Ships, towers, domes, theaters and temples ... bright and glittering in the smokeless air." This world has been swallowed up, in Dickens's time, by "Fog everywhere. Fog up the river, where it flows among green aits and meadows; fog down the river, where it rolls defiled among the tiers of shipping and the waterside pollutions of a great (and dirty) city" (3).

Air pollution is a subject of frequent concern across a wide range of modernist texts. Eliot's "Portrait of a Lady," the second poem in *Prufrock and Other Observations*, begins "Among the smoke and fog of a December afternoon" and concludes with the speaker imagining the lady's death, which would leave the speaker "sitting pen in hand / With the smoke coming down above the housetops" (8, 12). Eliot's "The Love Song of J. Alfred Prufrock" animalizes the London fog, imagining it as a catlike creature that "rubs its back" and "its muzzle on the window panes," "lingers," and falls "asleep" outside the buildings of the city (3). Eliot's images of a polluted city reveal a direct line from Dickens's Victorian melodrama, through literary naturalism, to the depiction of a toxic urban milieu in a high-modernist aesthetic conception. In *The Waste Land*, Eliot imagines London "under the brown fog of a winter noon" where the Thames "sweats / Oil and tar" (208; 267–68). In *The Mechanic Muse*, Hugh Kenner argues that "if Eliot is much else, he is undeniably his time's chief poet of the alarm clock, the furnished flat, the ubiquitous telephone, commuting crowds, the electric underground railway" (25). From an ecocritical perspective, it is equally true that Eliot is modernism's principal poet of urban pollution. The large-scale coal gasification plants, or "gasworks" as they were called, which were used in urban areas and many small towns from the middle of the nineteenth century to generate fuel for municipal lighting and heating, inundated whole districts with foul smells and toxic pollutants.

Between 1899 and 1901, Claude Monet made three trips to London to paint the cityscape, in pursuit of the visual effects created by the interaction between sunlight and the infamous London Fogs, and by 1904, he had produced over a hundred of the paintings. On some of the canvases, such as *Houses of Parliament in the Fog* from 1903 (Figure 3), the Palace of Westminster is almost completely obscured by smog. Years later, in 1918, he would remark to his friend René Gimpel that what he loved "more than anything in London is the fog . . . without the fog London wouldn't be a beautiful city" (qtd. in Corton 184). Monet was interested in the fog as an aesthetic effect, as indeed impressionism writ large favored perception over the accurate representation of nature. The fog acted like an Instagram filter, which was all the more powerful because it was real. Art critics tend to think of Monet's impressionism as an innovative modernist style, a way of "making it new" in painting. In *The Decay of Lying* (1891), long before Monet had started painting the London Fogs, Oscar Wilde quips, "Where, if not from the Impressionists, do we get those wonderful brown fogs that come creeping down our streets, blurring the gas-lamps and changing the houses into monstrous shadows?" (47). Reading modernism under the banner of environmentalism entails understanding this style not only as a style of perception but as a mode of realist mimesis: an attempt to paint the city the only way it could authentically be seen at that time, through the dense haze created by airborne particles

FIGURE 3 Houses of Parliament in the Fog, *Claude Monet*.

of sulfur dioxide. Six years before Eliot described "yellow smoke" and "yellow fog," in "The Love Song of J. Alfred Prufrock," Dr. H. A. des Voeux delivered a paper to the Coal Smoke Abatement Society proposing "smog" as a new term denoting "fog intensified by smoke" (OED). "Smog" filled a new lexical need with a rather satisfyingly onomatopoeic note of snarling menace—Tolkien names his dragon in *The Hobbit* (1937) "Smaug"—in a word that seemed, and still seems, a perfect union of signifier and signified, word and thing. By definition, only London could suffer London fog; but soon enough Los Angeles, Beijing, Mexico City, and a host of other metropolitan centers would be blanketed in what had come to be understood as smog.

Air pollution was not the only form of waste generated by the modern metropolis; the furious cycles of production and consumption that made the modernist city also made colossal amounts of trash, waste, and by-product materials that must be considered as much a part of the city as its skyscrapers and train stations. In the first great wave of urbanization between 1890 and 1930, "the overproduction and disposal of refuse," writes Michelle

Ty in "Trash and the Ends of Infrastructure," "became legible as a biopolitical problem" (607). In these years, "the treatment of urban waste underwent a comprehensive transformation" in which informal waste workers—people who in rural environments were called "gleaners" and in urban ones were called ragpickers, or chiffoniers in French—turned into formal wage workers in a new and growing regime of waste management. In the United States in the 1880s, a quarter of cities had organized trash collection; by 1914, 50 percent had it; and by the end of the 1930s, "all American cities with a population in excess of 100,000 had some form" of waste collection (616–17). The expansion of dumps and midden heaps, along with their expulsion further and further outside the city's official boundaries, contributed to a blurring of the conceptual line between city and country.

Indoor plumbing was still only just reaching the rich inhabitants of cities like London and Paris. In 1904, Leopold Bloom's house at 7 Eccles Street in Dublin has only an outhouse and a chamber pot, both of which get explicit use in *Ulysses*, in scenes that played a significant part in the scandal the novel caused upon publication. In London, Virginia Woolf used the royalties she earned from *Mrs. Dalloway* to install two lavatories and a bathroom in her Sussex vacation home, Monk's House (Rosner 7). The first line of her final novel *Between the Acts* (1941) produces a shock of incongruity: "It was a summer's night and they were talking, in the big room with the windows open to the garden, about the cesspool" (3). As first lines go, this one is a zinger. The unsuspecting reader is lured in through a series of grammatical and descriptive delays only to find, at the end, shit.

To discuss a cesspool at a garden party may be the height of bad manners in 1940s British society, but to us the greater scandal is that today over 2.3 billion people currently live without access to basic sanitation according to the World Health Organization, a number equal to the total number of people on the planet when Woolf was writing her final novel. By this metric—an index of the as-yet-undelivered promises of modernization—it seems depressingly true that, in Bruno Latour's phrase, "We have never been modern." The conversations about the cesspool in *Between the Acts* and Bloom's urban outhouse in *Ulysses* are important reminders of the unevenness of socioeconomic development. The Indian writer Mulk Raj Anand was inspired by his reading of James Joyce's *A Portrait of the Artist as a Young Man* (1916) to write a novel about spiritual and political liberation called *Untouchable* (1935). The novel's protagonist, an outcaste sweeper named Bakha, is forced to choose between two opposed (or seemingly opposed) sources of liberation: on the one hand, traditionalist nationalism like Gandhi's Swadeshi movement; and on the other, a sort of modernizing nationalism— here metonymized in the form of a mechanical toilet that would obviate the need for the untouchable sweeper class to which Bakha resentfully belongs. In the end, Bakha refuses to choose between the two, and thus in his own way, according to Jessica Berman, "resolves, at least for the moment, the paradox of Indian modernity" (115). His dilemma highlights the role that modern technologies like sanitation played not only in the history of (under)development but in the history of modernism, as Anand adapts Joyce's *Kunstlerroman* to a very different cultural idiom.

In many modernist fictions, the sewer indexed the moral corruption of the city and emblematized its gritty, dirty truth. In *Les Misérables* (1862) Victor Hugo called the sewer "the intestine of leviathan" and claimed that "the sewer is the conscience of the city" (1261)—in French, "conscience" means both conscience as a sense of moral responsibility and consciousness as self-awareness. Joyce took up Hugo's claims in *Ulysses* by using the sewer in a chapter called "Wandering Rocks" to map and to voice the synoptic perspective of the episode's omniscient narrator. The episode ends with "a tongue of liquid sewage" hanging out in ironic "fealty" to the British Vice Regal Cavalcade as it marches past the point where Dublin's Liffey River meets the Poddle River—a smaller tributary that was bricked over to serve the city as a sewer emptying into the Liffey (207). That confluence was, as Joyce would have known, the site of the first Viking settlement in the area, a marsh they called "Black Pool," which was eventually translated into "Dubh Linn" in Irish and then transliterated into "Dublin" in English. Joyce thus imagined Dublin's sewer in *Ulysses* not only as the conscience of the city but also as its nomos: the wellspring of its ancient identity and the index of its current depravity and ecological degradation (see Rubenstein 2014). In Carol Reed's film version of Graham Greene's *The Third Man* (1949), the villain Harry Lime traverses Vienna's postwar divisions frictionlessly and invisibly by traveling in the sewer system, until he is found out by our hero Holly Martins and hunted down by the police in a spectacular underground chase scene. Across literary genres then, from high modernism to the noir thriller, the city sewer often functioned, when it appeared in art, as a dark stage for morality plays about urban monstrosity and corruption. Sewers were also, on the other hand, one of the greatest achievements of modernization. The tension between the sewer as a monument of modernization and as its shameful, disgusting secret attracted a great deal of modernist attention.

"High" Modernism

When we watch Fritz Lang's film *Metropolis* today, vistas of the city's soaring architecture provide one of the film's primary visual pleasures. This was apparently also the case for its original audience, many of whom complained about the film's clumsy plot and long running time. The architecturally rendered towers, elevated roadways, and zooming sky trains of *Metropolis*—features we also encounter in the fiction of writers like Verne, Wells, and even Musil, as well as in sketches and renderings by Le Corbusier and Wright—pioneer what would become the dominant visual idiom of futurity in science fiction cinema. This urbanscape would characterize the Los Angeles of 2019 in *Bladerunner* (1982), the fully urbanized city-planet of Coruscant in *Return of the Jedi* (1983), and the Neo-Seoul spectacularly rendered in the film version of *Cloud Atlas* (2012), to name a few examples. Meanwhile, the cityscape of *Metropolis* also expresses the obsession with height that was enabled by the new technology contemporary to its era. On Ferris wheels and on the Eiffel Tower, in balloons, zeppelins, and airplanes, the "high" moderns surged skyward. This trend was epitomized by the skyscraper, which leaped out of the imaginations of planners and architects, into city skylines, and onto the canvases of cubist paintings as well as the screens of the newest mass media form, the cinema.

One unrealized paean to the skyscraper is Tatlin's Tower, a proposed Soviet "Monument to the Third International" designed in 1920. The 400-meter-tall steel tower, imagined as spanning the Neva River in Petrograd (contemporary St. Petersburg), would serve as a mass media projector casting images onto clouds over the city, and would house a giant lecture hall at the base of its symbolic double helix design. Skyscrapers also infiltrated nonarchitectural media, as we can see in *Parade*, a 1917 ballet featuring dancers from the famous Ballets Russes dressed in cardboard skyscraper costumes fashioned by Pablo Picasso. For this truly collaborative mixed-media modernist enterprise, Apollinaire wrote the program notes, Jean Cocteau scripted the scenario, and Erik Satie composed the music, whose score was punctuated by urban noises—typewriters, trains, dynamos, airplanes—to convey the soundscape of everyday urban life. Meanwhile, on January 23, 1931, in New York City, dozens of architects appeared at the Beaux Arts Ball dressed in costumes resembling the buildings of their own creation, including William Lamb as the Empire State Building and William Van Alen as the Chrysler Building.

In the real world, iron rail and the power of coal brought millions of people to cities, and once they arrived they had nowhere to go but up. Traditional construction techniques employing load-bearing walls and pedestrian stairways had once made vertical development above four or five stories unfeasible. Higher structures were enabled by improvements in the safety elevator (demonstrated by Elisha Otis at the 1854 New York World's Fair) and the advent of steel-frame construction techniques. Thus the steel rails of transport, turned vertically into the girders of skyscrapers, would transform the spatial imagination of the metropolis by decoupling population density from physical congestion. As Walter Benjamin writes, exaggerating slightly to make his point, "With iron, an artificial building material appeared for the first time in the history of architecture . . . the rail was the first iron unit of construction, the forerunner of the girder" (158). For Benjamin, skyscrapers embodied movement, translating the forward movement of the train into the upward thrust of the building.

The first office building to feature these construction technologies and building techniques was the Equitable Life Assurance Building in Manhattan, completed in 1870 at seven stories tall, followed by the Home Insurance Building in Chicago, a ten-story structure completed in 1885. Another important proof of concept was the Eiffel Tower, completed for the Paris exhibition in 1889. At over a thousand feet tall (108 stories) and at the time of its construction the tallest structure in the world, the Eiffel Tower bestowed upon its visitors a planner's eye view of the city that had previously only been available through maps, photographs, and models. And as a spectacle itself, it celebrated its innovative building materials, showing off the steel girders that in other skyscrapers would become a skeleton hidden by exterior skins of stone or glass. The Empire State building, completed in 1931, would rise to a height of 1,250 feet on 102 floors, enclosing over two million feet of office space, enough for over 15,000 workers, on a site in midtown Manhattan less than two acres in size. In comparison, the Crystal Palace had enclosed less than half this space while sprawling over a twenty-three-acre site.

All around the world, historians, urban planners, and progressive activists observed similar trends of dense development and debilitating pollution arising in the new cities of steam and steel. Chicago, for instance, hub of North America's railroads, grew from a town of fewer than 30,000 in 1850 to a metropolis of more than 3.5 million in 1900, an increase of over 10,000 percent. As the site of the World's Columbian Exhibition in 1893, Chicago became famous as the "White City": "Never had there been so much light in one place," writes historian Jane Brox, "and it was all electric: 200,000 incandescent bulbs traced the edges of the edifices, and countless more lit the interiors of the massive exhibition halls; 6,000 arc lights on twelve-foot-high posts lined the paths and walkways" (129). Meanwhile, the environmental impact of Chicago's rapid industrialization induced horror in many, including Pulitzer Prize winning author Hamlin Garland: "I shall never forget . . . the feeling of dismay with which . . . I perceived from the car window a huge smoke-cloud which embraced the whole eastern horizon, for this, I was told, was the soaring banner of the great and gloomy inland metropolis [networked by] tangled, thickening webs of steel" (qtd. in Cronon 10).

Carl Sandburg's most famous poem, "Chicago," celebrates the city's status as "Hog Butcher for the World, / Tool Maker, Stacker of Wheat, / Player with Railroads and the Nation's Freight Handler; / Stormy, husky, brawling, / City of the Big Shoulders" (3). Sandburg sees Chicago as a nexus of labor power and machine power that makes it a giant on the national stage. He praises Chicago's industrial might in the first person, taunting, "Come and show me another city with lifted head singing so proud to be alive and coarse and strong and cunning" (3). But this braggadocio is not merely athletic: Sandburg sees the city as "pitted against the wilderness" (3). In the work of modernization, Chicago is described as "Bareheaded, / Shoveling, / Wrecking, / Planning, / Building, breaking, rebuilding, /

Under the smoke, dust all over his mouth, laughing with white teeth / Under the terrible burden of destiny" (3). It is clear that Sandburg expects readers to celebrate the ecological and political relations he describes, if not to participate themselves in the shoveling and wrecking.

The sense of the helplessness and insignificance of individuals in relation to the size and scale of the city and industrial capital is one of the major themes of Alfred Döblin's vivid and depressing anti-bildungsroman *Berlin Alexanderplatz* (1929). Like Joyce in *Ulysses*, Döblin makes extensive use of montage to represent the metropolis by exploiting the gaps and fragments of metropolitan perception. Martino Stierli considers montage "the mode of perception specific to the mechanized metropolis" that "became defining for Western visual culture in the twentieth century," and he points to Döblin specifically as one of the technique's foremost literary practitioners (1). The protagonist of *Berlin Alexanderplatz* is a laborer in the construction industry, also a rapist and a murderer:

> The subject of this book is the life of the former cement worker and haulier Franz Biberkopf in Berlin. As our story begins he has just been released from prison . . . to see and hear this will be worthwhile for many readers who, like Franz Biberkopf, fill out a human skin, but, again like Franz Biberkopf, happen to want more from life than a piece of bread. (1)

Franz's story is interspersed, in the manner of filmic montage, with scenes of urban sensory overload, caused largely by the relentless and continual cycle of construction and demolition: "On the Alexanderplatz they're tearing up the road for the underground railway. People are made to walk on duckboards" (113). "Boom boom goes the steam pile-driver outside Aschinger's on the Alex. It's as big as a house, and it drives the piles into the ground like nobody's business. . . . Boom boom goes the steam pile-driver on the Alexanderplatz. Lots of people take the time to watch the pile-driver at work. A man at the top keeps pulling on a chain, and bam! The pile gets one on the lid" (155). There is a deep irony at play here: while the people gather to observe the sonic and visual spectacle of the construction site, Döblin's novel implies that these same individuals are, both figuratively and literally, being beaten down and hammered into place by industrial modernity. "I smash therefore I am," Döblin writes (159). In his version of Descartes's seventeenth-century adage updated for the machine age, the ultimate reality is force.

Alienation and the Crowd

Another main by-product of industrial urbanization—one exacerbated by the rise of tall buildings and the efficiency of rail and ship transport—was the urban crowd. In his poems and essays Baudelaire describes the emergence of a new form of "passionate spectator," the *flâneur*, who draws his energy from the unprecedented density of the urban crowd. He writes, "Multitude, solitude: equal and convertible terms for the active and productive poet . . . who walks alone with his thoughts"; this figure enjoys a "universal communion" or "ineffable orgy" in the city (1970: 20). "The painter of modern life," he writes, is he who "set[s] up house in the heart of the multitude . . . [who] enters into the crowd as though it were an immense reservoir of electrical energy" (1964: 9). As we discussed in Chapter 1, Baudelaire finds himself energized by city life, along with the young Marcel Proust, James Baldwin, James Joyce, and Virginia Woolf. In fact, according to the architect Rem Koolhaas in *Delirious New York* (1978), the pleasure to be found in urban crowds is the reason why, in the period of high modernism, the urban resort Coney Island "on summer Sundays . . . becomes the most densely occupied place in the world." As "the total opposite of Nature," New York "has no choice but to counteract the artificiality of the new metropolis with its own Super-Natural" (33).

Caroline Meeber, the protagonist of Theodore Dreiser's *Sister Carrie* (1900), escapes from her farmland home in rural Wisconsin in search of the particular energy that suffuses the urban crowd. When she arrives in Chicago, "the life of the streets continued for a long time to interest Carrie. She never wearied of wondering where the people in the cars were going or what their enjoyments were. Her imagination trod a very narrow round, always winding up at points which concerned money, looks, clothes, or enjoyment" (39). In New York, she seeks out the epicenter of the urban experience, hoping to find "that hour, when Broadway is wont to assume its most interesting aspect . . . [when] theaters were just beginning to receive their patrons," a time when Carrie can absorb "the curious enthusiasm of a great city bent upon finding joy in a thousand different ways" (342). Virginia

Woolf regarded the urban crowd in a similar way, writing in her essay "Street Haunting: A London Adventure" of how walking the city streets enables us to "shed the self our friends know us by and become part of that vast republican army of anonymous trampers, whose society is so agreeable after the solitude of one's own room" (155).

Other thinkers of the period viewed the crowd with much more skepticism. The German sociologist Georg Simmel found it enervating and alarming. In his landmark investigation, "The Metropolis and Mental Life" (1903), he argued that urban industrial systems, through "the swift and continuous shift of external and internal stimuli" quite unlike the "slower, more habitual, more smoothly flowing rhythm" of country life, inflicted profound psychic stress on their inhabitants (325). "Metropolitan individuality," Simmel writes, is a mode of being that favors industrial traits such as "punctuality, calculability, and exactness" and produces an affective reserve or "blasé outlook" (328). The modern urbanite, in Simmel's account, "becomes a single cog as over against the vast overwhelming organization of things and forces which gradually take out of his hands everything connected with progress, spirituality and value" (337).

Simmel's dystopian conclusions about the negative effects of the urban environment may seem, to the modern ear, more a reflection on the hyperbolic representation of urbanism in Lang's *Metropolis* rather than a response to any existing city of the early twentieth century, but Simmel was not alone in feeling oppressed by the machinery of modernity. Such sentiments can be found at both the top and the bottom of the socioeconomic ladder, from the drawing rooms in the novels of Edith Wharton to the mean streets in those of Dreiser and Henry Roth. Lily Bart, the downwardly mobile protagonist of Wharton's *The House of Mirth*, speaks of her urban alienation just before she dies of a drug overdose: "I have tried very hard but life is difficult, and I am a very useless person. I can hardly have been said to have an independent existence. I was just a screw or a cog in the great machine I called life" (433). In addition to seeing herself as a cog in a machine, Lily also understands herself as a commodity on the marriage market. "Isn't marriage your vocation?" an admirer asks during one of their flirtations early in the novel. "She sighed. 'I suppose so. What else is there?'" (26). Lily is, as she herself says, "horribly poor—and very expensive"—much like the city itself (26).

The representation of urban environments through machine and market metaphors—or through the corporeal metaphors examined earlier in the chapter—implies a false sense of design or control. As Ulrich, the protagonist of Robert Musil's *The Man Without Qualities*, observes, the systems have simply grown too vast and complicated. To understand modernity, Ulrich declares, "I should need to have all the qualities, and do all the things, I cannot possibly have and do. You must be enough of a mathematician to see that it would take a lifetime to plan a single carom shot in that fashion; it boggles the mind!" (622). For Ulrich, the problem is "solved" by breaking the rules of the game and rejecting the illusion that the complexities of urban environments and modern economies can be understood at all. "I step up to the table," he says, referring to the vector-analysis of his billiards metaphor, "and the problem is solved. . . . All the crucial processes of life take place beyond the scope of the conscious rational mind. Man's greatness is rooted in the irrational" (622).

As Musil was writing in Vienna in the first decades of the twentieth century, sociologists at the University of Chicago began to take the city itself as an object of scientific analysis and to search for patterns in its apparent chaos, for a rationality behind the seemingly irrational. Neither the image of city as machine nor the metaphor of the market seemed adequate to describe the phenomena in which they were interested, including physical infrastructure, social life, and landscape as an integrated system. Instead, with an ambition to document rather than to dictate and with a largely more positive sense of urbanization's effects on society, Chicago school sociologists borrowed from ecosystem approaches to the biological sciences as they investigated the city. R. D. McKenzie and his colleagues defined ecology as "that phase of biology that considers plants and animals as they exist in nature, and studies their interdependence, and the relations of each kind and individual to its environment" (288). Then, they extrapolated: "In the absence of any precedent let us tentatively define human ecology as a study of the spatial and temporal relations of human beings as affected by the selective, distributive, and accommodative forces of the environment" (288). Adding the dimension of culture to human ecology, sociologist Robert E. Park calls the city,

> More than a congeries of individual men and of social conveniences—streets, buildings, electric lights, tramways, and

telephones, etc. . . . The city is, rather, a state of mind, a body of customs and traditions, and of the organized attitudes and sentiments that inhere in these customs and are transmitted with this tradition. . . . It is a product of nature, and particularly of human nature. (1)

This lyrical description, especially noteworthy in a sociology text of the 1920s, foreshadows Jane Jacobs's ecological approach and the neighborhood focus that would define the New Urbanism movement that emerged in the 1980s. Describing the ideal neighborhood environment, Jacobs would put it this way: "The bedrock attribute of a successful city district is that a person must feel personally safe and secure on the street among all these strangers. He must not feel automatically menaced by them" (38). Woolf, Baudelaire, Joyce, and anyone else who loved the city likely felt the same way; Le Corbusier, Ford, and others, meanwhile, wanted no people on the streets at all, regarding walking as inefficient and the street as a domain of automobiles.

Motor City

In *The Man Without Qualities* Musil offers a wry caricature of modernist urban planning:

An obsessive daydream has been a kind of super-American city where everyone rushes about, or stands still, with a stopwatch in hand. Air and earth form an anthill traversed, level upon level, by roads live with traffic. Air trains, ground trains, underground trains, people mailed through tubes special-delivery, and chains of cars race along horizontally, while express elevators pump masses of people vertically from one traffic level to the next, instantly sucked in and snatched away by the rhythm of it. . . . Questions and answers synchronize like meshing gears; everyone has only certain fixed tasks to do; professions are located in special areas and organized by group; meals are taken on the run. Other parts of the city are centers of entertainment, while still others contain the towers where one finds wife, family, phonograph, and soul. (26–27)

We could dwell at great length on these few sentences, in which Musil deploys a relentless and disturbingly prescient parody of what we have called modernism's hallmark techno-optimism. Between the comic moments—"people mailed through tubes special-delivery," a special tower to house one's "soul"—Musil diagnoses several crucial features of modernity at large (time-consciousness, specialization, fast food), and of the modernist urban planning movement in particular, which worked hard to reconfigure the mixed-use metropolis of the nineteenth century into cities regulated by areas of single-use zoning. The separation of residential and industrial areas offered one potential solution to urban environmental and health concerns. One of the earliest and most influential theorists of the suburb was Ebenezer Howard, who advocated for the creation of "garden cities" (Figure 4) of 30,000 people in his influential *Garden Cities of To-morrow* (1898). "Town and country *must be married*," Howard wrote, predicting that "out of this joyous union will spring a new hope, a new life, a new civilization" (18–19). Instead, we got the suburb.

"Two economic events—the advent of the AC electric grid and of automotive transport," writes historian Douglas Rae, "ended the urbanism-friendly age of centered development. Together these events created the deep technological basis for almost limitless mass mobility—people moving and living where they please, across virtually every region of a continental nation" (21). From a purely practical perspective, in William Cronon's similar account, it was "the rise of the diesel truck [that] eventually undermined the technological tendency toward centralization that the railroads had promoted" (259). The theory behind suburbanization, as Marshall Berman describes it, was to create "a modernized version of pastoral: a spatially and socially segmented world—people here, traffic there; work here, homes there; rich here, poor there; barriers of grass and concrete in between, where haloes could begin to grow around people's heads once again" (168). The environmental cost of traversing such distances through the burning of fossil fuels continues to be paid. In New York City, questions of zoning, highway construction, and urban renewal reached their zenith in the conflict between Robert Moses and Jane Jacobs over the Lower Manhattan Expressway, which Moses planned to plow through Washington Square Park along with much of SoHo and Little Italy. While Jacobs

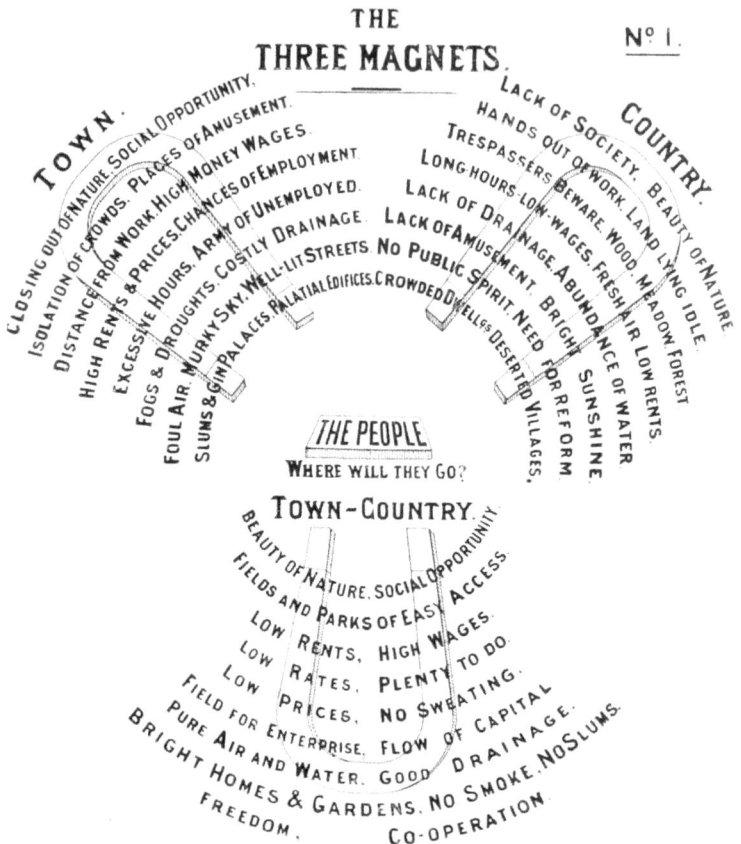

FIGURE 4 *"The Three Magnets," from Ebenezer Howard's* Garden Cities of Tomorrow.

succeeded at blocking this project, Moses's legacy survives in the Brooklyn-Queens Expressway, the Cross Bronx Expressway, the Staten Island Expressway, and many of the bridges that speed car transit between Manhattan and surrounding boroughs.

Environmental concerns inspired Frank Lloyd Wright and Le Corbusier, the two most famous architects of their era, in their competing visions for the ideal city. Their plans and proposals addressed the same set of problems—pollution, over-population, traffic, congestion, and noise—but come to startlingly different conclusions, both representative of important modernist trends. In texts like *The Disappearing City* (1932), Wright argued that "the value of this earth, as man's heritage, is pretty far gone from him now in the cities centralization has built. And centralization has over-built them all" (3). In a seemingly "green" move, he argued that the city's "perpetual to and fro excites and robs the urban individual of the meditation, imaginative reflection and projection once his as he lived and walked under clean sky among the growing greenery to which he was born companion" (3). Worse still, the effects of the city, in Wright's estimation, will be passed on to urban children: "Out of machines he can create nothing but machinery," Wright laments, and "children grow up, herded by thousands in schools built like factories, systematically turning out morons as machinery turns out shoes" (3). In its propagation of itself, the city is "like some tumor grown malignant . . . like some cancerous growth" (21). As a solution to the problem of the city, Wright offered small, planned, suburban communities such as Broadacre City, discussed in our Introduction, which emphasized the family-tended plot of land in an attempt to get back to nature. When mass-produced suburbs metastasized across the landscape after the Second World War, such thinking tied our culture to energy-intensive lifestyles, long commutes, and low population densities while accelerating ecosystem disruption and increasing the rate of anthropogenic climate change.

In Europe, the architect and urban planner Le Corbusier was likewise strident in his criticism of the paleotechnic city: "The advent of the machinist era has provoked immense disturbances in the conduct of men, in the patterns of their distribution over the earth's surface and in their undertakings," he writes in his modernist architectural manifesto *The Athens Charter* (1923). This shift represents "an unchecked trend, propelled by mechanized speeds, toward concentration in the cities, a precipitate and worldwide evolution without precedent in history. Chaos has entered the cities" (48–49). For Le Corbusier, it was self-evident that "the more the city expands, the less the 'conditions of nature' are respected within it. By 'conditions of nature' we mean the presence, in sufficient proportions, of certain elements that are indispensable to living beings: sun, space, and verdure. . . . The individual who loses contact with nature is diminished as a result" (55). In his solution, Le Corbusier imagined dense but isolated skyscrapers surrounded by green space. As in Wright's Broadacre City, residents of these communities were intended to make extensive use of transportation technologies like airplanes and cars, but no thought was given to how these technologies might be fueled or the pollution they might cause. Skyscrapers and highways have come to dominate cities around the world, which would have delighted Le Corbusier, but our transportation systems remain powered by the paleotechnic energy produced by burning fossil fuels, which he and the other moderns would have found deeply distressing. In fact, modernism's utopian visions for the metropolis foundered on its ignorance of the energy systems on which the realization of its dreams would depend—an issue we took up in depth in Chapter 1.

Until the introduction of the affordable, mass-market automobiles first sold by Henry Ford in 1908, suburbanization remained a dream; the new, cleaner, healthier life in the suburbs was only available to a very few, while the urban poor continued to be plagued by the city's public health hazards. The mass-market automobile, however, was a truly game-changing technology, one that did more than any other to disrupt the dense urban centers characteristic of the period of high modernism. For Ford, disrupting the city was a deliberate ambition: "The modern city," he wrote, was "A Pestiferous Growth," the "suppression of all that is sweet in its natural environment" (154). As Ford saw it, "The 'problem of the city'" was intractable; "The ultimate solution will be the abolition of the City, its abandonment as a blunder" (156–57). "We shall solve the City Problem," he wrote, "by leaving the City" (157).

Several critics have devoted entire volumes to the study of modernism's relation to the automobile, including Ray Batchelor (1994), Sara Danius (2002), John DeWitt (2002), Deborah Clarke (2007), Enda Duffy (2009), David Gartman (2009), and Dan Albert (2019). The transportation sector—which includes cars and trucks as well as petroleum-burning airplanes and ships—at present constitutes 28 percent of US emissions on an annual basis, according to the US Environmental Protection Agency; globally, transportation accounts for almost 15 percent of CO_2 emissions, a major cause of climate change. The supply chains, manufacturing processes, and waste streams associated with automobiles consume resources on a vast scale. Burning petroleum for fuel generates other forms of pollution as well, including the sulfurs and nitrogen oxides that contribute to smog and acid rain; further ecological harm is associated with extracting, refining, and transporting petroleum and other fossil fuels. Leaded gasoline, introduced in 1922 to solve the problem of engine knocking and used extensively until the 1970s, generated massive amounts of airborne lead pollution, with catastrophic consequences for human health, particularly among children. When we think about the challenges facing environmentalism today, the enduring appeal and enormous ecological impact of automobility is a prime concern.

In the period of late modernism, Elizabeth Bowen reflects on the exodus of the middle class from the urban core to a suburban world of new construction and semi-detached homes that could be Broadacre City in her chilling story "Attractive Modern Homes" (1941). It begins: "No sooner were the Watsons settled into their new home than Mrs Watson was overcome by melancholy" (88). The fantasy of fulfillment through suburban home ownership and a desire for the new is shown to be a sham: "The semi-detached house was box-like, with thin walls. . . . The rooms still smelled of plaster, the bath of putty. The stairs shook when the wardrobe was carried up: the whole structure seemed to be very frail" (88). In the new suburb, all the residents are "pioneers" surrounded by the sound of unfinished construction, the "persistent hammering from unfinished houses" that serves as the soundtrack of suburbia (981). As the melancholic housewife of the story's opening line succumbs to severe isolation and depression, she asks her husband, "Why aren't the two of us having a better time?" (98). It is the question we are all asking of life in the Anthropocene.

Environmental Justice in the Modernist Metropolis

In this final section, we turn to some questions of environmental justice in the modernist metropolis. Even in the modern urban wasteland, costs and benefits are unequally distributed. As Paul Outka argues in *Race and Nature* (2008),

> Although both people of color and whites are deeply engaged in environmental struggles, the nature each group is concerned with remains markedly different. One environment is inhabited, toxic; the other is uninhabited, wild, pure, untouched except by

the gaze of the privileged visitor. American wilderness in all its empt(ied) glory remains a largely white preserve, while urban, polluted landscapes have long been identified with people of color. (1)

In London, poverty and pollution aggregated downriver and downwind, toward the poorer districts of the East End. "The East End had the highest density of factory chimneys," writes Christine L. Corton, "as well as houses packed tightly next to each other, all with their own domestic chimney pots puffing out smoke" (20). In the United States, immigrants arriving in New York by ship from Europe register the dislocations of arriving in the city in their narratives, as we see at the beginning of Henry Roth's *Call It Sleep* (1934). Roth's novel is set in "May of the year 1907, the year that was destined to bring the greatest number of immigrants to the shores of the United States" (9). David, the novel's young Yiddish-speaking protagonist, clings to his mother's skirts as they pass through Ellis Island: "Before her the grimy cupolas and towering square walls of the city loomed up . . . she tried to smile" (16). In the tenements of the Lower East Side, "There were four rooms in the flat they lived in. There were eight windows. Some faced 9th street, some faced avenue D, and one looked out upon the dizzying pit of an airshaft" (144).

Similarly, the gleam of the "White City" was specifically beyond the reach yet constantly within the desiring gaze of its black residents, who supported it with their labor and capital, as we see clearly in Richard Wright's *Native Son* (1940), a novel set in the Chicago of the 1930s. In an essay on the invention of his antihero, "How 'Bigger' Was Born" (1940), which is often published as a preface to the novel, Wright argues that

> the urban environment of Chicago, affording a more stimulating life, made the Negro Bigger Thomases react more violently than even in the South. More than ever I began to see and understand the environmental factors which made for this extreme conduct. . . . Chicago's physical aspect—noisy, crowded, filled with the sense of power and fulfillment—did so much more to dazzle the mind with a taunting sense of possible achievement that the segregation it did impose brought forth from Bigger a reaction more obstreperous than in the South. (xv)

Early in the novel, Bigger and his friends are walking the streets of Chicago's South Side, penniless, when their eyes are pulled skyward by the iconic technology of modernity: the airplane. In a scene of skywriting that will remind many readers of a similar scene in Woolf's *Mrs. Dalloway* (discussed in Chapter 6), Wright describes how Bigger and his friends "laughed again, still looking upward. The plane sailed and dipped and spread another word against the sky: GASOLINE . . . 'Use Speed Gasoline' Bigger mused, rolling the words slowly from his lips. 'God, I'd like to fly up there in that sky'" (20).

In this moment, Wright brings together affective desires for power and freedom with the fossil fuel era's most charismatic converter of energy—the airplane, seen here advertising its own fuel. However, Bigger's Futurist fantasy is, as Wright's novel insists, stillborn on the wrong side of the color line: "Every time I think about it I feel like somebody's poking a red-hot iron down my throat," Bigger explains, "Goddammit, look! They got things and we ain't. They do things and we can't. It's just like living in jail" (23). A black man in the White City looking up at the plane in which he will never fly, Bigger feels an inevitable sense of alienation that leads to violence. In Ralph Ellison's *Invisible Man*, a similar sense of dispossession leads a rioting group of tenement dwellers to burn down their own building, an act cast by the novel as a desperate but necessary form of liberation from the structural racism of the urban built environment. "I couldn't believe it," the unnamed narrator thinks, "couldn't believe they had the nerve." But "where will you live?" he asks Scofield, the leader of the campaign. "You call this living?" Scofield fires back (544). After systematically and carefully evacuating the residents of the building—pausing along the way for Scofield to visit his own apartment and soak his mattress in kerosene, saying, "Ain't the bedbugs going to get a surprise!"—Scofield gives the final command: "Okay, mens. We got everybody out. Now starting with the top floor, I want you to start striking matches" (548).

African Americans who undertook the Great Migration to the industrial North from the agrarian South often felt even more alienated in the urban environment. One of the best examples of the feelings of stress and dislocation produced by the modern city can be found in Rudolph Fisher's "The City of Refuge," a short story first published in *The Atlantic Monthly* and anthologized in Alain Locke's *The New Negro* (1925), one of the seminal texts of the Harlem Renaissance. In this story, the protagonist, King Solomon Gillis, arrives in New York "dazed and blinking" and is shunted into a "long, white-walled corridor, the impassible slot-machine, the terrifying subway train—he felt as if he had been caught up in the jaws of a steam-shovel, jammed together with other helpless lumps of dirt, swept blindly along for a time, and at last abruptly dumped. . . . 'New York! Penn Terminal—all change!'" (57). Gillis "had shot a white man [in his home state of North Carolina] and, with the aid of prayer and an automobile, probably escaped a lynching" (58). Gillis had imagined Harlem as a utopia, a place where "you had rights that could not be denied you; you had privileges, protected by law. And you had money. Everybody in Harlem had money. It was a land of plenty" (58). In the city, however, he finds himself "meditating in a room half the size of his hencoop back home, with a single window opening into an airshaft" through which "waste noises" emanate: "Waste odors of a score of families, seeking issue through a common channel; pollution from bottom to top—a sewer of sounds and smells" (61). Exploited by con men and unwittingly used to fence illegal drugs, Gillis finds nothing but exploitation in the "city of refuge," and the fact that his eventual arrest is conducted by a black police officer provides his only consolation. As these diverse texts suggest, from the tenements of Harlem to those of the Lower East Side and from the slums of London to those of Berlin, the view of an airshaft looks more or less the same.

Under extreme forms of urban alienation, the exhilarating view of the city from above, promised by the airplane, skyscraper, or camera lens, remains tantalizingly inaccessible. Without that access, the city becomes nothing more than an airless trap. How can one envision an escape from the city's hovels to its soaring vistas? Roth and Ellison devise imaginary methods that allow their protagonists to commune with the pulsing energy that drives the modern city (See Rubenstein 2010: 191–92). David in *Call It Sleep* (1934) thrusts a metal dipper into the third rail of a Lower East Side elevated train track, nearly killing himself and causing a power outage, but nevertheless touching for a moment the forces that power the city. Similarly, the eponymous protagonist of Ellison's Invisible Man siphons electricity from Monopolated Light and Power into his basement squat, illuminates it with a thousand light bulbs, and fills it with the sound of multiple gramophones. "I love light," he says. "That is why I fight my battle with Monopolated Light and Power. The deeper reason, I mean; it allows me to feel my vital aliveness" (6–7). Those who experience the worst of the city find ways, however dangerous or illegal, to demand it make good on its promises.

3

Modernism's Animals

> *Rocking itself and rising up a trifle from the floor, it stretched forth a tortoise's serpentine head; then, suddenly taking fright, retreated into its shell. This tortoise was the consequence of a whim of Des Esseintes's, which antedated his departure from Paris. One day, while gazing at a shimmering Oriental carpet . . . he had thought: it would be a good idea to place upon this carpet something that moves, and is dark enough in hue to set off the brilliance of these tones.*
>
> —J. K. HUYSMANS

Modernism's "Snorting Beasts"

In the preceding chapters we explored the energy ecosystems and urban environments of modernist art and literature. We called attention to the overwhelmingly destructive implications of industrial modernity's desire to "make it new," to borrow Ezra Pound's phrase, and detailed the negative externalities generated in pursuit of the "beauty of speed" glorified by F. T. Marinetti and others. Given this account of the field, our readers might expect that modernism's intellectual and physical environments—the former infamously difficult, prone to abstraction and introspection, the latter urban and marked by a preference for built spaces—would be hostile to most forms of animal life. Moreover, many of the suggestive tracks and signs that point toward modernism's animals lead us instead to machines. The "snorting beasts" (49), "beautiful shark" (50), and "serpent with explosive breath" (51) of Marinetti's "Founding and Manifesto of Futurism," for instance, all turn out to be automobiles, while the mysterious sea monster spotted in Jules Verne's *20,000 Leagues Under the Sea: A Tour of the Underwater World* (1870) is in fact Captain Nemo's nuclear-electric submarine, the *Nautilus*. Once the search has begun, however, the sheer biodiversity in modernist art and literature, not to mention the crucial thematic, formal, aesthetic, and ethical roles that animals play, will likely surprise new students and seasoned scholars alike. This chapter surveys that biodiversity, engaging the work of writers such as Franz Kafka, Joseph Conrad, Virginia Woolf, Zora Neale Hurston, and Jean Toomer; artists like Umberto Boccioni, Constantin Brancusi, and Georgia O'Keeffe; and thinkers including Charles Darwin and Sigmund Freud, whose work reframes the way the moderns act toward and feel about their animal environment.

The Modernist Menagerie

Consider Umberto Boccioni's *Unique Forms of Continuity in Space* (Figure 5), a sculpture that exemplifies some of the most distinctive motifs and frequent themes of modernist art. Its form is at once classical in gesture—its armless torso echoes the *Winged Victory of Samothrace*, a work cited by Marinetti in his "Founding and Manifesto of Futurism"—and transgressive in execution. Violence is not only a theme of the work but a part of its production history. Boccioni, having completed a wax mold and plaster cast of *Unique Forms* in 1913, died in 1916, after being trampled by horses during a cavalry exercise as a soldier in the Great War. The bronze we see today was cast posthumously in 1931. The striding figure before us is powerful, almost threatening, despite its relatively small stature. It might be a nightmare from our distant past or a prophecy of evolution yet to come. Not fixed upon a single plinth or in a single form but crossing the void between two, the sculpture is dynamic in both the kinesthetic and ontological senses of the term. Its anthropomorphic features blend with what seem to be machine components and the body parts of nonhuman animals, fused through mutation to evoke a new, hyper-accelerated mechanical

FIGURE 5 Unique Forms of Continuity in Space, *Umberto Boccioni*.

mythology. From one angle, the head looks human; from another, it appears to be a hammer or tool. Boccioni's work is a modern minotaur, a hybrid that evokes the human-animal-machine as a nexus or in a state of flux, emphasizing the machine-like qualities of animals and the animalistic qualities of machines.

Zoologists have only been able to identify and describe about 1.5 million species in our biosphere, a fraction of the estimated 7 million species alive today. In this chapter we follow several branches of the phylogenetic tree of modernist life, surveying dozens of wild and domesticated animals across a variety of literary and literal landscapes—a small fraction of modernism's biodiversity. Limited though it may be, our account implies a significant revision of the standard view in which, as Steve Baker writes, "the animal is the very first thing to be ruled out of modernism's bounds" (20). On the contrary, we think it is fair to say that modernism is a veritable *Animal Farm* (George Orwell, 1945). As they do in Orwell's allegory, the animals of modernism have escaped the enclosure of children's literature in which they had been caged since the medieval period. Freed from these conventions of genre and form, they range from the high modernism of Virginia Woolf, James Joyce, and T. S. Eliot to the more popular modes pioneered by writers like Rudyard Kipling and Jack London.

The most famous animal of modernist literature is undoubtedly Franz Kafka's Gregor Samsa, who, in the opening line of *The Metamorphosis* (1915), wakes after a night of unsettling dreams to find his body transformed into that of an *ungeziefer*—a "monstrous vermin" in the Stanley Corngold translation (3). The idea that Samsa is a "cockroach" entered the story in the process of translation, while the German word is significantly more general in denotation though negative in connotation. After making a detailed study of Kafka's descriptions of Gregor's animal form, novelist Vladimir Nabokov, himself a lepidoperist, concludes that Gregor "belongs to the branch of 'jointed leggers' (Arthopoda), to which insects, and spiders, and centipedes, and crustaceans belong" (473). Nabokov notes with some regret that he cannot be more specific, because Kafka fails to report how many legs Gregor's new body has, saying only that they are "numerous." It should be no surprise, however, that Kafka's experimental prose would thwart pseudoscientific attempts to find a stable place for a being like Gregor on a phylogenetic tree of life. Instead, Kafka's work explores environments where the human animal is perpetually in a process of becoming other animals and—as in the case of the ape Red Peter, the protagonist of his short story "A Letter to an Academy" (1917)—vice versa. In Kafka's works, even inanimate objects are constantly taking on attributes of language, cognition, and memory in ways traditionally understood to be distinctly if not uniquely human in nature.

Whatever his species, Kafka's Gregor Samsa has become a creature commensal, in biological terms, with the Anthropocene. The word "commensalism," from the Latin for "eating at the same table," is used by ethologists (scientists who study animal behavior) to describe relations between two species in which one benefits from the other, for instance, in the way that cockroaches benefit from communities of larger host humans. Gregor believes that his physical transformation into an insect is related to the stress of his job as a traveling salesman, and more generally, to the accelerating pace of modern life: "What a grueling job I've picked! Day in, day out—on the road . . . the torture of traveling, worrying about changing trains, eating miserable food at all hours, constantly seeing new faces" (4). It is easy to connect Kafka's creature with the other "vermin" commensal with urbanized humans. The protagonist of Eliot's "The Love Song of J. Alfred Prufrock" (1915) imagines himself in several insect forms, including a crustacean with "ragged claws / Scuttling across the floors of silent seas" (lns 74–75), or wriggling under the gaze of others like an insect on a pin.

One finds rats "popping up irrepressibly in modernist texts," as Maud Ellmann puts it (14). There is the rat "dragging its slimy belly" (ln. 188) across the pages of Eliot's *The Waste Land* (1922) and feeding with cosmopolitan indifference on the corpses of English and German soldiers alike in Isaac Rosenberg's "Break of Day in the Trenches" (1916). The "piercing death-cries" of poisoned rats dominate the emotional landscape of Hugo von Hofmannsthal's "Chandos Letter" (1902), one of the pivotal works of early German modernism, whose protagonist experiences a crisis of subjectivity and language upon imagining "the knotted impotent convulsions" of a poisoned rat colony (92). It would not be long before the Great Powers of Europe would use such poisons on human animals in the battlefields of the First World War, treating soldiers as vermin deserving extermination. The common or black rat, *Rattus rattus*, is the ultimate human-commensal species, widely regarded as one of the most damaging of all the invasives that have accidentally accompanied global trade. In a rather ironic twist, in the early twentieth century the rat rapidly became the favored animal or model organism for modern scientific research.

Close on the heels of modernism's rats, so to speak, are its cats. Eliot himself became a "cat person" late in his career, giving us the *Old Possum's Book of Practical Cats* (1939), adapted by Andrew Lloyd Webber in the famous musical, *Cats*, which premiered in London in 1981. Joyce was a cat person too, recording three distinct orthographic variations of the cat's "Mkgnao" in *Ulysses*, a novel notable for its attention to the creatural dynamics of biological and social reproduction. Joyce also composed a children's book, *The*

Cats of Copenhagen, for his grandson, Stephen James Joyce, which was posthumously published with illustrations by Casey Sorrow in 2012. While children never had the opportunity to encounter Joyce's cat story in the twentieth century, English speakers likely encountered Wanda Gág's illustrated children's story *Millions of Cats*, which has been in print continuously since it was first published in 1928. Japanese writer Natsume Sōseki satirizes Japanese society in the process of modernization from a feline perspective in *I am a Cat*, which was published in ten serial installments during 1905 and 1906. Jacques Derrida describes Baudelaire, Rilke, and Lewis Carroll as cat lovers in *The Animal That Therefore I Am*, a book that begins with an account of the feeling of being beheld naked by one's pet. Glenn Willmott adds Oscar Wilde, Wilde, W. B. Yeats, Ezra Pound, and the graphic artist George Herriman to the list of modernism's "cat people," arguing that "in their rendering of cat-life" modernist writers "variously rebelled against what they perceived to be sentimental anthropomorphism in nineteenth-century ideology," using "animal primitivism to promote new structures of feeling about the animal in human life" (848).

Modernism's dog people include Djuna Barnes, who structures the famously shocking final scene of her novel *Nightwood* (1936) around an interspecies encounter of an ambiguously if undeniably erotic nature, with protagonist Robin Vote down "on all fours" joining a dog in sexual play (139). Kafka's Joseph K. dies "like a dog" at the conclusion of *The Trial* (1925) in the Willa and Edwin Muir translation, "as if the shame of it must outlive him" (1968: 229), while to live "like a dog" in J. M. Coetzee's novel *Disgrace* (1999), where David Lurie becomes "the dog-man" in an act of self-imposed penance, means a life "with nothing. . . . No cards, no weapons, no property, no rights, no dignity" (2000: 146, 205). American writer Jack London (1876–1916) sniffed through the world from a canine perspective in novels like *The Call of the Wild* (1903) and *White Fang* (1906), and Woolf writes *Flush* (1933), a best-selling imagined biography from the perspective of Elizabeth Barrett Browning's cocker spaniel. A rabid dog bites Tea Cake, Janie's lover, in a climactic scene of Zora Neale Hurston's *Their Eyes Were Watching God* (1937). In Hurston's depiction of the 1928 Okeechobee hurricane, which left a trail of devastation from Puerto Rico across Florida and deep into the Carolinas, the novel's protagonist, Janie, nearly drowns amid a riot of animal and human bodies before Tea Cake risks his life to save hers: "The dog stood up and growled like a lion, stiff-standing hackles, stiff muscles, teeth uncovered as he lashed up his fury for the charge. Tea Cake split the water like an otter, opening his knife as he dived. . . . They fought and somehow he managed to bite Tea Cake high up on his cheek-bone once" (198). Animal encounters can be lethal, the novel suggests, but animal drives animate our human being.

Willa Cather, Zora Neale Hurston, and William Faulkner remind their readers of the encounters between humans and the cows, pigs, horses, and other agricultural animals that make up the daily life of rural modernism. In Cather's *O Pioneers!* (1913) and *My Antonia* (1918), humans share their most intimate feelings more easily with cows than with people. The cows in Faulkner's *The Sound and the Fury* talk more than some members of the Compson family, and when the pageant falters in Woolf's *Between the Acts*, "the cows took up the burden. . . . One had lost her calf. In the very nick of time she lifted her great moon-eyed head and bellowed. . . . The cows annihilated the gap; bridged the distance; filled the emptiness and continued the emotion" (2008: 96). Stories of intimate interspecies relations are preserved in Hurston's pioneering works of ethnobiography, including *Mules and Men* (1935) and *Tell My Horse* (1938); the destruction of these modes of life by industrial modernity is mourned in the work of D. H. Lawrence. Lawrence writes in *The Rainbow* (1913) that at one time people "knew the intercourse between heaven and earth. They took the udder of the cows, the cows yielded milk and pulsed against the hands of the men, the pulse of the blood of the teats of the cows beat into the pulse of the hands of the men" (10). Modern farming, by contrast, "has become a great industrial enterprise," a fact celebrated by President Coolidge in his 1925 "Address Before the Annual Convention of the American Farm Bureau" (n.p.). Modernization meant that Fordist and Taylorist approaches to labor and supply-chain management had begun to be applied to agriculture in earnest, so that animals were disassembled and repackaged as products on an industrial scale. Modernism contends with this aspect of animal existence as well. Upton Sinclair's *The Jungle* (1906) is the most famous text in this regard, offering an account of Chicago's industrial abattoirs gruesome enough to trigger the passage of federal legislation including the Meat Inspection Act and the Pure Food and Drug

Act of 1906. More experimental and equally shocking is Alfred Döblin's *Berlin Alexanderplatz* (1929), in which pigs are given a sightseeing tour of Berlin's slaughterhouse: "You are entering a new model. . . . I'll be going the other way, dear little piggies, because I'm a human. I'll be going through this door here, but we'll see each other soon enough" (127).

Beyond these commensal species and domesticated animals range modernism's "wild" life. To name a few: Old Ben, the elusive bear of Faulkner's *Go Down, Moses* (1942), a novel that ends with the unsettling image of a tree "alive with frantic squirrels" (314). "My mother is a fish," muses Faulkner's Vardman, cryptically, in *As I Lay Dying* (1930) (84). For Lawrence, meanwhile, animals represent a primitive nature, a savage potentiality controlled, disavowed, and repressed by social norms. The poetry of Marianne Moore—filled with pangolins, flightless birds, octopi, and other creatures—presents a veritable menagerie. For Rebecca West, in "Indissoluble Matrimony," a story first published in Wyndham Lewis's *Blast* of 1915, the animalized biracial protagonist Evandine becomes a seal to escape her husband's attempts to murder her. Finally, we come back around to modernism's strange hybrids and archaea: creatures like Lewis Carroll's Jabberwocky and Snark, Kafka's Odradek, Boccioni's *Unique Forms* and Picasso's minotaurs, and the compendium of imaginary creatures that wander the Hundred Acre Wood of A. A. Milne's Winnie-the-Pooh stories. The latter, to which we return at the end of this chapter, is particularly noteworthy for the way it negotiates the nexus of animals, sentimentality, childhood, and experiment as it operates across audiences young and old.

When we survey the visual art of the *fin de siècle*, the First World War, and the interwar period—and investigate movements such as impressionism and post-impressionism, pointillism and fauvism, surrealism and cubism—we are likewise struck by the prevalence of modernism's animals. They are everywhere: *Les fauves*—the group of Parisian artists including André Derain and Henri Matisse known for their bold use of color—translates literally as "wild beasts." In the Metropolitan Museum's collection, animals populate dreamscapes such as Marsden Hartley's *Berlin Series, No. 2* (1914) and Franz Marc's *Fighting Cows* (1911), and they fight on the battlefields of Roger de la Fresnaye's prophetic *Artillery* (1911). Henri Rousseau, who never left his native France, took his inspiration from the botanical gardens of Paris and created surreal, implausible paintings of animal encounters, such as with the tiger in *Surprised!* (1891), a beast of prey illuminated by a lightning bolt. The horsepower driving the torrent of construction in Boccioni's *The City Rises* (1910) is literally *horse* power. Modernism's animals range from ominous (the exotic beasts that populate the canvases of Henri Rousseau and Salvador Dali) to humorous (Henri Matisse's goldfish and Alberto Giacometti's cats). They emerge in all of modernism's visual idioms, from Giacomo Balla's futurist dachshund in *Dynamism of a Dog on a Leash* (1912) to the minimalism of Constantin Brancusi's *Bird in Space* (1923).

If modernism had a spirit animal, it would be Brancusi's *Bird in Space*. The sculpture seems to defy physics, offering us a meditation on flight and speed stripped to its most abstract and minimalist gesture, bound by no gravity save that of the human mind. Having pursued the figure and idea of birds in flight over many decades, here "Brancusi sought to convey the essential nature of a bird, elegantly soaring upward in flight, without the need for traditional representational forms" (Cleary n.p.). There is something of a paradox here: the symbol of flight has evolved beyond the need for wings. An anecdote from the work's circulation history adds another, distinctly modernist twist: Brancusi produced nine bronzes and seven marbles in this particular series, and when one of the birds was being shipped from Paris to New York for a 1926 exhibition, US Customs officials refused to allow the object entry, categorizing the shipment not as art but as "Kitchen Utensils and Hospital Supplies," subject to an import tax of 40 percent of the declared value. Ironically, the exhibition's curator, Marcel Duchamp, achieved fame for his revolutionary "ready-mades," which operated precisely through the seizure of mass-produced, utilitarian objects (a bicycle wheel, a urinal, a shovel) and their exhibition as art.

Darwin and Freud: Theorizing the Animal

Two axial transformations revolutionized the way animals were understood between the mid-nineteenth and the mid-twentieth centuries, setting the stage for the production and reception of the works listed earlier. These stories are widely known, but their familiarity does nothing to diminish their importance to the history of modernism. Charles Robert Darwin (1809–82) was no modernist, but it would be hard to exaggerate the way his insights have shaped modernity. His career as a naturalist began somewhat quixotically. He studied science only as a hobby alongside the serious business of theology, until an opportunity arose to serve aboard the HMS *Beagle* as the ship's naturalist on a survey trip around the world. The planned two-year voyage lasted for five, and when Darwin finally returned, he had amassed a trove of material that would feed a lifetime of literary and scientific production. Early essays established his reputation as a geologist, and his narrative account, *Voyage of the Beagle* (1839), was a surprise bestseller. It took him twenty years to puzzle through the apparent paradoxes of species distribution and adaptation he had encountered in remote areas such as the Galapagos Islands and to hone his thinking about the effects of natural selection. He published *On the Origin of Species* in 1859 to popular acclaim, and the theory of evolution gained widespread circulation within a decade. At the most fundamental level, *On the Origin of Species* reminds us that people are animals too, providing a revolutionary account of the human species that connects us with the web of life, destroying divine accounts of the privileged origins and exalted destiny of "Man." In subsequent work, Darwin researched questions of human evolution and sexual selection, and then turned to seemingly more humble concerns, with his final book examining the behavior of earthworms and their effects on ecology and geology.

Among other things, Darwin's research on natural selection and the so-called survival of the fittest shattered the idea that nature was static and unchanging (whether as a product of divine creation or, according to broad scientific consensus, as an achievement of equilibrium over time) and unsettled long-standing hierarchies that had separated and elevated the human from the rest of animal nature. Benjamin Bateman argues in *The Modernist Art of Queer Survival* (2017) that Darwin's conception of "survival as competition, violent assertion, [and] self-preservation" is little more than the "loose legacy of evolutionary thinking as it has been and continues to be hijacked by ideologies of capitalism, heteronormativity, and rugged individualism" (1). For Gillian Beer, meanwhile, "The key concepts for natural theologians seeking to display God's workings in the material world were *design* and *creation*. Darwin, on the contrary, was trying to precipitate a theory based on *production* and *mutation*" (xviii). Some, like Beer and Bateman, see Darwin's fingerprints everywhere; for others, like Philip Armstrong, "The impact of Darwinian evolutionary theory on the cultural terrain of modernity proved to be erratic, partial and sometimes contradictory. Its potentially revolutionary undermining of beliefs about human supremacy were mostly inhibited (or ignored) due to the widespread interpretation of evolutionism as another of modernity's narratives about progress towards an ever-more advanced human state" (142).

Of equal importance in changing the way generations of modernists felt and thought about animals is the work of Sigmund Freud and his drive/instinct theory of the psyche. As with Darwin, it is impossible to offer a concise summary of Freud's various impacts on modernism: in W. H. Auden's elegiac terms from "In Memory of Sigmund Freud" (1939), "he is no more a person, but a whole climate of opinion" (275). The relationship between Darwin's zoology and Freud's psychoanalysis can be seen to frame modernism's understanding of animals at large, as Carrie Rohman argues: "The discourse of species in modernism is specifically framed by this dialectic between Darwinism and Freudianism, which further explains the centrality of the human/animal dichotomy in literature of the period" (22). With respect to the role of animals in his work, two main trends emerge. In his case studies (accounts of his analysis of and conversations with individual clients) Freud encourages readers and patients to interpret animals not in zoological terms but as symbols pointing back to elements of human drives and experience. In his *Analysis of a Phobia in a Five-year-old Boy* (1909), Little Hans's fear of horses turns out to be, in Freud's analysis, symbolic of the child's fear of his father; the Rat Man's morbid terror of the creature for which he is named represents, as Freud argues in *Notes Upon a Case of Obsessional Neurosis* (1909), a displaced fear of punishment. Most famously, the Wolf Man's childhood nightmares—he dreams about a pack of wolves that stare at him while perched in a tree outside his window—in Freud's analysis have nothing to do with actual, or even fairytale, wolves. Instead, for Freud they represent the deferred impact of a traumatic childhood experience, specifically, the boy's having witnessed the "primal scene" of his parents' sexual activity.

Frequently in Freud's work, animals are invoked to symbolize that which is antagonistic to culture—to symbolize humanity's other. In *Civilization and Its Discontents* (1930), Freud writes that as animals, human beings are "creatures among whose instinctual endowments is to be reckoned a powerful share of aggressiveness" (58). What Freud describes pejoratively as "the original animal part of our nature" is associated with libidinal drives and the id: prerational parts of the unconscious mind operating purely according to the pleasure principle and never with our positive attributes or altruistic behaviors (58). The human capacity for violence, in Freud's analysis, "reveals man as a savage beast," a conclusion clear to "anyone who calls to mind ... the horrors of the recent World War" (58). This savagery he summarizes in the formula "*Homo homini lupus*": a man is a wolf to man. It seems to us, however, that here Freud is guilty of a classic case of psychological projection: feared, hunted, and hated, wolves have been the victim of human savagery for centuries. In North America, government-sponsored extermination programs devastated populations, while the Eurasian wolf (*Canis lupus lupus*), once widespread across Europe and Asia, was deliberately hunted to extinction in most of northern and western Europe by 1800. Even in the years when Freud was writing, thousands of wolves were deliberately being killed in the forests of Eastern Europe every year.

As the example of Freud's wolves makes clear, if we seek beyond the walls of museums and the pages of texts and examine the treatment of actual animals and their environments during this period, we face some hard truths. A responsible ecocritical approach to modernism must wrestle with the fact that the human treatment of animals (human and nonhuman) in the late nineteenth and early twentieth centuries veered between chilling instrumentality, unintentional disaster, and deliberate ecocide. In other words, while modernism's ideal in the animal realm might be Brancusi's *Bird in Space*, its reality is closer to Martha, the last surviving passenger pigeon, who died at over twenty-eight years of age in a Cincinnati Zoo on September 1, 1914. At their height, the population of passenger pigeons (*Ectopistes migratorius*, the wandering migrant) in North America exceeded three billion, making it the most populous bird species on the planet in the mid-nineteenth century. Within fifty years, however, it had been hunted to extinction, the last wild bird of the species shot in 1901. Today the most populous bird on the planet is the domesticated chicken: there are at least twenty-two billion of them, according to the United Nations Food and Agriculture Organization. Thus, to think seriously about modernist animals demands an unflinching investigation of the cultural and ecological practices that helped to perpetuate the (ongoing) Holocene Extinction, the sixth major extinction event in the history of life on earth and the first to be caused by human activity.

John Muir, who lived to see the passenger pigeons' extinction, writes of witnessing their annual migration: "It was a great memorable day when the first flock of passenger pigeons came to our farm," as he recollects in "A Paradise of Birds" (78). Riffing on the species' Latin name, he goes on to describe how "the beautiful wanderers flew like the winds in flocks of millions . . . so large that they were flowing over from horizon to horizon in an almost continuous stream all day long . . . like a mighty river in the sky" (78). Muir sharply contrasts this exalted descriptive mode with the response of his peers, such as one "practical old sinner," who subscribes to the view that "they were made to be killed, and sent for us to eat . . . and I must confess that meat was never put up in neater, handsomer-painted packages" (79). In this anecdote we see the tragedy of modernity's conception of the natural world as simultaneously infinite and instrumentalized, views habituated by even those most receptive to the views of Darwin or Freud.

Economics and Ethics

Animals are often seen by humans not only across a chasm of ontological privilege but also (figuratively and literally) down the barrel of a gun. In the late nineteenth century alone, species reduced to, or near to, extinction include elephants hunted for ivory and whales for oil, along with many species of herons, terns, hummingbirds, egrets, ibises, owls, and other birds hunted for sport or for the plumage to decorate hats. To satisfy this latter market alone, by the 1880s "more than five million birds were being massacred yearly," writes Douglas Brinkley, in what he describes as a "genocide" (11). As Burkhard Bilger elaborates, "In London, the feather market went through nearly a third of a million egrets in 1910 alone. . . . Some ladies had taken to wearing whole birds on their heads by then—an economical choice, given that feathers were more costly, by weight, than anything but diamonds" (70). Figure 6 shows Deborah Kerr as Edith Hunter in Michael Powell and Emeric Pressburger's 1943 film *The Life and Death of*

FIGURE 6 *Deborah Kerr's bird hat, frame shot from* The Life and Death of Colonel Blimp.

Colonel Blimp. Kerr's costume was accurate to the period of the film's setting, 1902; the whole-bird hat, astonishing all on its own, is just part of what appears to be a nearly all-animal outfit. At the same time, spectacularly misguided experiments were undertaken to spread exotic species around the globe. One attempt in the 1890s, well known in the birding community, to bring every bird mentioned in Shakespeare's plays to New York's Central Park, resulted in the introduction of invasive pest species such as European sparrows and starlings to North America.

Another invasive species that impacted American ecosystems was the boll weevil, a beetle that feeds on the buds and flowers of the cotton plant and was responsible for more economic damage than any agricultural pest in US history, according to the US Department of Agriculture. The poet Jean Toomer, a self-professed amalgam of "French, Dutch, Welsh, Negro, German, Jewish, and Indian" ancestry, records the ecological and economic catastrophe of the boll weevil plague that devastated the cotton economy of the rural South in his poem, "November Cotton Flower":

Boll-weevil's coming, and the winter's cold,
Made cotton-stalks look rusty, seasons old,
And cotton scarce as any southern snow,
Was vanishing; the branch, so pinched and slow . . .
Drouth fighting soil had caused the soil to take
All water from the streams. (7)

Plagues of insects are among the oldest of literary tropes, dating at least to the book of Exodus, but the infestation of *Anthonomus grandis* moved north across the Mexico/Texas border in 1892 and spread through the cotton-growing regions of the American south at the staggering rate of 150–200 miles per year, reaching all growing regions by 1920. Not only ecologically but also culturally invasive, the beetle sparked folk songs especially popular among the poor of cotton-growing regions, a group that "often suffered the most" from the economic dislocations caused by the blight (Hall n.p.). These dislocations were, in turn, major drivers of the Great Migration.

Many farms not destroyed by the blight were driven under by the Great Depression in the subsequent decade, or fell victim to the Dust Bowl droughts presaged by the dry streams and parched soils in Toomer's poem. Economic losses to American cotton producers from the original infestation through 2013, when a multi-decade boll weevil eradication program was declared complete, are estimated to have exceeded twenty-three billion dollars, according to data gathered by the US Department of Agriculture.

To prevent erosion on railroad sidings and abandoned farms, a government-funded project paid farmers to plant kudzu, a perennial vine native to Asia that was first displayed in the United States at the 1876 Centennial Exposition in Philadelphia. In our own time, kudzu is known as the plant that swallowed the South after having destroyed entire ecosystems. The economic and ecosystems costs of invasive kudzu are almost impossible to monetize. Mono-crop farming, desertification, drought, invasive species, and extinction events: all of these are aspects of modernism's environments.

Bird in Space and *Ectopistes migratorius*, elation and extinction, are two extremes in the vast archive of modernism. *Bird in Space* is not a commentary on species loss, and Kafka's beetle Gregor Samsa knows nothing of the beetle *Anthonomus grandis*, but to elucidate the shaping force and pervasive influence of animal encounters and species discourse in the art and literature of modernism, to bring Brancusi's bird into dialectical tension with *Ectopistes migratorius* and Kafka's beetles into dialogue with Toomer's, we turn to the methods and insights of animal studies.

The interdisciplinary field of animal studies aims to investigate the relations between human and nonhuman animals and to trace the ecological, social, and ethical implications of those relations across different times, cultures, and ecosystems. In his introduction to animal studies, Paul Waldau identifies one of the central missions of the field as the imperative to tell "the entire story about our past with other living beings" with the ultimate goal of "going beyond our own history . . . and developing perspectives on animals' realities" (2–3). There is something more than a little utopian in this formulation, not only in its quantitative boundlessness (recall our planet's estimated seven million species) but also and more fundamentally in terms of epistemology: it remains questionable how much can be known about animals' realities. But there is also something undeniably enticing about animal encounters, an urgency that is related not only to our present-day ecological emergency but also, in more modernist terms, to the promise of transcending the feelings of alienation that Marx and subsequent sociologists identified as one of the defining consequences of capitalist modernity.

Like the broader environmental movement, animal studies began to consolidate as a field during the 1970s, with philosophers often pointing to Peter Singer's 1975 *Animal Liberation: A New Ethics for our Treatment of Animals* as a foundational text. Singer, an ethicist and moral philosopher, introduced a profoundly normative dimension to the emergent field, aligning animal studies with political activism promoting issues such as vegetarianism, veganism, and animal rights. Vegetarianism, of course, wasn't invented by the hippies in the 1960s; Mohandas Gandhi was delighted to find a vegetarian restaurant in London while he was studying law there in 1888; and, in fact, the nineteenth century was a burgeoning period for vegetarian movements and animal rights advocacy more broadly. As Gandhi writes in his autobiography, he joined the Vegetarian Society in England, "subscribed to the weekly . . . and very shortly found myself on the Executive Committee" (50). It was through an interest in interspecies ethics that Gandhi formulates and rehearses his *intra*-species ideas of mutual aid: "I saw that the writers on vegetarianism . . . had arrived at the conclusion that man's supremacy over the lower animals meant not that the former should prey upon the latter, but that the higher should protect the lower, and that there should be mutual aid between the two as between man and man" (50).

Other prominent vegetarians and animal rights activists influential among the modernist coteries include Edwin Carpenter, the famous socialist and early gay rights activist; Annie Besant, a prominent Theosophist, who argued that one should abstain from eating not only meat but also, like many vegans today, any food the production of which might involve cruelty to animals; and Arnold Hills, who enjoyed widespread notoriety as the architect of the Vital Food movement, which promoted uncooked vegetarian food as the key to spiritual and physical health. In the United States, vegetarians gathered at the Chicago World's Fair of 1893 to attend the World's Vegetarian Congress, where "more than 200 vegetarian delegates met" in "the largest gathering of like-minded food reformers in history" (Shprintzen 156).

An immense trove of material on vegetarian modernism awaits scholarly exploration, beginning in *Ulysses* with Leopold Bloom's disgust at watching the patrons of the Burton restaurant: "Stink gripped his trembling breath: pungent meatjuice, slush of greens. See the animals feed" (138). "Am I like that?" Bloom asks himself, before fleeing to Davy Byrne's pub for a glass of burgundy and a gorgonzola cheese sandwich. As J. M. Coetzee reminds us in the voice of Elizabeth Costello, herself an expert on James Joyce, "Let me say it openly: we are surrounded by an enterprise of degradation, cruelty and killing which rivals anything that the Third Reich was capable of, indeed dwarfs it, in that ours is an enterprise without end, self-regenerating, bringing rabbits, rats, poultry, livestock ceaselessly into the world for the purpose of killing them" (63). Modernization brought with it both industrial agriculture and campaigns against cruelty to animals, including the formation of the first American Society for the Prevention of Cruelty to Animals (SPCA) in 1866; the passage in England of the Cruelty to Animals Act in 1867; and the American Anti-Vivisection Society in 1883, which campaigned against experimentation on live animal subjects.

Though attitudes and policies did not shift fast enough to save the passenger pigeon, popular movements—often grassroots campaigns led by women—developed in support of conservation. Wild birds could be saved from extinction, activists realized, only by shifting consumer choices at the retail level. Harriet Lawrence Hemenway and her cousin Minna Hall began a boycott of the millinery trade in Boston and founded a society to campaign for the protection of birds, leading to the establishment of America's Audubon societies and the passage of the Migratory Bird Treaty of 1918, the first international agreement of its kind.

Marianne Moore, the influential poet and editor, used her work to advocate for conservation. In "He 'Digesteth Harde Yron,'" a poem about species loss and flightless birds, Moore examines the way human beings have for millennia hunted these creatures to extinction for the thrill of sport, for the beauty of their feathers, and for other organs, likewise conspicuously consumed:

> Six hundred ostrich brains served
> at one banquet, the ostrich-plume-tipped tent
> and desert spear, jewel-
> gorgeous ugly egg-shell
> goblets, eight pairs of ostriches
> in harness, dramatize a meaning,
> always missed by the externalist. (100)

Wanton carnage has driven the "aepyornis / or roc that lived in Madagascar, and / the moa" to extinction and significantly reduced the geographic range of other species (99). Moore's poem calls for a "Heroism" to "contradict a greed that did not wisely spare / the harmless solitaire // or great auk in its grandeur." She calls humanity to account for an "unsolicitude" toward nature that has "swallowed up / all giant birds but . . . this one remaining rebel" (100). Seen through an ecocritical lens, Moore's poetry not only attempts to change practices of human consumption through poetic exposure but also calls for stronger protections for animal rights and habitats at the policy level.

While promoting animal rights remains important to animal studies, more recent work "has focused less on the treatment of animals and more on disrupting traditional philosophical distinctions between 'the human' and 'the animal,'" as Michael

Lundblad and Marianne DeKoven write in the introduction to their edited collection *Species Matters: Humane Advocacy and Cultural Theory* (3). This theoretical turn has focused critical attention on the idea of "speciesism," a term used to critique the assumption of human superiority, which leads to the exploitation of other animals and of the world more broadly. In *Animal Studies: An Introduction* Waldau puts the status quo this way, calling attention to religious and utilitarian justifications for speciesism: "Claims about humans' rightful place and privileges are sometimes anchored in religious beliefs that humans were invested with superiority by a divinity who prizes humans more than other living beings. Exceptionalist claims have also been based on the conclusion that humans simply have enough power to impose their domination on others, thereby making humans' privileged place just and moral" (8). Paola Cavalieri, meanwhile, in an essay from *Species Matters*, faults the tradition of Descartes and Plato: the "doctrine of human ontological and moral superiority," she argues, has been based "on the allegation that all and only humans are free insofar as they are antinatural and rational beings" (52). For Derrida, as one might predict, the deciding factor is language, as he writes in *The Animal That Therefore I Am*: "Men would be first and foremost those living creatures who have given themselves the word that enables them to speak of the animal with a single voice and to designate it as the single being that remains without a response, without a word with which to respond" (14). Instead of a boundary between Homo sapiens and other animals, Giorgio Agamben suggests in *The Open: Man and Animal* that we should think instead in terms of an "open wound" or "central emptiness" between humans and other animals (7, 92).

Modernism's critique of human exceptionalism is various and thorough, its probing of the open wound of the species boundary deliberate and often painful, and it thus offers the most exciting points of resonance for scholars of animal studies in the present day. There are numerous common threads between the current fascination with the ethics and politics of the species boundary and the formal concerns of early twentieth century avant-garde art. John Berger, in the title essay of his book *Why Look at Animals?* (2009), describes the context this way: "The 19th century, in western Europe and North America, saw the beginning of a process, today being completed by 20th century corporate capitalism, by which every tradition which had previously mediated between man and nature was broken" (12). Berger is referring to the folkways and practices of rural daily life, which came under threat in the era of migration to the city and were forgotten behind the walls of the factory farm. As Philip Armstrong argues, "During the first half of the twentieth century, the movement known as modernism brought about a . . . discrediting of sympathetic and sentimental engagement with animals in the aesthetic sphere. . . . The modernist break with the past entailed, and in many ways depended upon, a revaluation of human-animal relationships" (134). Conversely, affirming the value of animal life and the vitality of animal perspectives allowed some modernists to challenge exceptionalist claims about humanity's ontological privilege, replacing firm species boundaries and techniques of human mastery with a sense of common and interpenetrating modes of being.

Philosopher Thomas Nagel asked in 1974, "What is it like to be a bat?" While Nagel's famous argument is less about the lived experience of flight or the sensorium of echolocation than it is about the problem of other minds, his initial question was a live one for the modernists. Inhabiting the perspective of animal realities is precisely the goal of many modernist experiments. Franz Marc asked in an essay from 1911: "How does a horse see the world, how does an eagle, a deer or a dog? How poor and how soulless is our convention of placing animals in a landscape familiar to our own eyes rather than transporting ourselves into the soul of the animal in order to imagine his perception?" (178). In her short story "Kew Gardens," first published privately in 1919, Woolf asks a similar question, not only of four human couples, out for a walk on a hot July day, but also with regard to invertebrates:

> In the oval flower-bed the snail, whose shell had been stained red, blue and yellow for the space of two minutes or so, now appeared to be moving very slightly in its shell, and next began to labour over the crumbs of loose earth which broke away and rolled down as it passed over them. It appeared to have a definite goal in front of it. . . . Brown cliffs with deep green lakes in the hollows, flat, blade-like trees that waved from root to tip, round boulders of grey stone, vast crumpled surfaces of a thin crackling texture—all these objects lay across the snail's progress between one stalk and another to his goal. (1989: 91–92)

From beginning to end in this quotation, the perspective shifts from that of a human looking down (literally) upon a snail to that of the snail itself, from whose perspective pieces of soil seem like "brown cliffs" and stalks of grass are as tall as "blade-like trees." We return to human consciousness across the bridge of Woolf's em-dash, with an increased appreciation for the lifeworld of the snail as well as for our own.

Teddy Bears and Heffalumps: Imagining Extinction

In the twenty-first century we can assume that most of our readers, whether or not they identify as environmental*ists*, share our conception of *the* environment as a space of entanglement and feedback loops. We have grown up understanding that as organisms, our bodies are only nominally singular, and are in fact made up of countless microorganisms upon which life depends. As Donna Haraway puts it, "*Homo sapiens* have never been human, at least not in any luminous, singular, self-making sense"; instead an ecological sensibility teaches us that "we are 'a bundle of multispecies reciprocal inductions . . . in debt to and at risk to and with each other'" (18). But how was this conception different a hundred years ago?

An influential and indicative voice in this regard was Ernest Thompson Seton, one of the founders of the Scouting movement. For Seton, as he writes in *Wild Animals I Have Known* (1898), nature challenges the doctrine of human exceptionalism by the networks and commonalities connecting every living creature: "Man has nothing that the animals have not at least a vestige of, the animals have nothing that man does not in some degree share. Since, then, the animals are creatures with wants and feelings differing in degree only from our own, they surely have their rights" (12–13). Seton's wildly popular book, along with William Long's *School of the Woods* (1902), would spark the so-called "nature fakers controversy" with the president of the United States. The avid hunter Theodore Roosevelt wrote an article for *Everybody's Magazine* in 1907 in which he accused Seton and others of being "nature fakers" because they had falsely sentimentalized and anthropomorphized animals. Despite a conservation record that included the foundation of the National Parks and the protection of over 200 million acres of land, Roosevelt was keen for the public to see the president as "a slayer not a lover of animals," as one headline in the *Boston Globe* put it.

In President Roosevelt's "Nature Fakers" article, conservationist writers such as John Muir, whose relationship with Roosevelt we discuss in Chapter 4, were praised, but authors such as Jack London were denigrated for their supposed exaggeration of animal intelligence and compassion. We can only imagine what Roosevelt would have to say about Kenneth Grahame's explicitly anthropomorphic children's novel *The Wind in the Willows* (1908), or of the depiction of animals in the work of one of the twentieth century's most beloved and imaginative authors, A. A. Milne. Roosevelt's passion for big-game hunting recalls a famous scene from *Winnie-the-Pooh*. In the story, first published in 1926, Christopher Robin mentions casually one day that he has seen an animal he calls a heffalump. "I saw one once," Piglet claims, not wanting to be outdone, "at least, I think I did," he reconsiders, "only perhaps it wasn't" (56). Winnie-the-Pooh resolves immediately to catch one of these mysterious creatures, and sets out with a rather frightened Piglet to "dig a Very Deep Pit" in the hope that "then the Heffalump would come along and fall in" (56, 58).

What is a heffalump? A distinctly modernist hybrid that springs from Christopher Robin's unconscious, fused through parapraxis (mispronouncing "heffalump" for "elephant") from the memory fragments gleaned from a day at the zoo or the circus, two distinctly modern ecosystems. While the genre of children's fiction encourages sentimentalization, the fate of the passenger pigeon helps us maintain a more sober-eyed perspective on Milne's fiction. Readers only encounter heffalumps obliquely, in description and as the object of terror in Piglet's imagination. And it's a good thing too, because if the moderns had caught a heffalump, they would have likely killed it for sport, or for its ivory, or even perhaps have electrocuted it for profit in a public spectacle. Real elephants met all three of these fates, of course. Roosevelt lists eleven elephants killed by his party (eight of them his) on one of his hunting trips, alongside seventeen lions (nine by the president), twenty rhinoceroses (thirteen at his gun), and dozens of other creatures enumerated in the "List of Game Shot with the Rifle During the

Trip" that concludes his *African Game Trails: An Account of the African Wanderings of an American Hunter-Naturalist* (532–33). The ivory extorted from indigenous Africans by Conrad's Kurtz in *Heart of Darkness* was shipped to Europe to manufacture the billiard balls and piano keys of Victorian ballrooms. Finally, also in 1903, an Asian elephant named Topsy was executed in a for-profit public spectacle at an amusement park on Coney Island (Figure 7). The Edison Film company made a film of the event, which could be viewed in the popular coin-operated kinetoscopes of the period and also provided the technological know-how and the voltage for the gruesome spectacle.

Amazingly, this graphic mode of killing was in fact a "humanitarian" compromise reached after the American Society for the Prevention of the Cruelty to Animals stepped in to protest the animal's owners' original idea of a public hanging. Today, we can watch on YouTube as Topsy is lead to an electrocution platform, chained in place, and subjected to the stiffening force of 6,600 volts passing through her body until she collapses with smoke rising from her feet. To confront these examples forces the uncomfortable proximity of technological progress and horrific

FIGURE 7 Electrocuting an Elephant, *frame shot.*

violence, but this tension is not merely the product of critical retrospection: it is legible even between the lines of *Winnie-the-Pooh*. The name "Winnie," used by Milne for his son's bear, has a militaristic provenance: Winnie was the name of a black bear that was used as a mascot by a Canadian regiment from Winnipeg, and was left behind at the London Zoo, while the original Teddy Bear was invented to mythologize the story of Theodore Roosevelt's refusal to shoot a black bear tied to a tree for sport. In addition to having recently visited the London Zoo, a quintessentially modern environment—Milne's son Christopher appears to have been reading Baden-Powell's *Scouting for Boys*, where pit-traps and deadfalls are discussed in a chapter on "woodcraft," and to have already internalized a violent attitude toward certain aspects of the natural world.

As we have suggested by juxtaposing *Bird in Space* with Martha the passenger pigeon, Topsy the elephant with Milne's heffalump, and Kafka's beetle Gregor Samsa with Toomer's boll weevils, understanding modernism's animals requires a mode of reading that connects the history of ecocide and extinction on the one hand with the innovations of experimental art on the other. Our intention is not to assign blame or point fingers; Theodor Adorno and Max Horkheimer already did so in "Man and Animal," a section of *Dialectic of Enlightenment* first published in 1944, in which the ethical failure of modernity is laid at the feet of the basic division whereby "animal irrationality is adduced as proof of human dignity" (245).

Consider as a counterpoint Yeats's famous poem "The Wild Swans at Coole," in which the poet laments the passage of time and the destructions of the First World War: "The nineteenth autumn has come upon me / Since I first made my count," he writes, but in that time, "All's changed" (131). In the poem's final stanza, the speaker contemplates the upcoming seasonal migration: "But now they drift on the still water / Mysterious, Beautiful; / Among what rushes will they build, / By what lake's edge or pool / Delight men's eyes when I awake some day / To find they have flown away?" (131–32). In the way we are trained to interpret poetry, we might say that the birds here are meant to represent an eternal nature governed by recurrent cycles, oblivious to human concerns such as war or death, and free of the territorial boundaries of Europe's lethal nationalisms. For the ecocritic, however, it is just as important to think seriously about the birds as animals as it is for more traditional formalist critics to identify the poem's rhyme scheme (ABCBDD). In fact, our understanding of the ecological emergency facing wild bird populations at the time of Yeats's writing destabilizes the poem's governing dialectic by raising the specter of extinction. His confidence that the birds will always be free to fly away is an anachronistic fantasy; they are as likely to be slaughtered to supply the millinery shops of London as Lady Gregory's son was to die in the trenches of the Great War.

Coole Park, the estate then owned by Lady Gregory, inhabits a region famed for its turloughs, or vernal pools, which form in the wet limestone karst of the Galway region. Parts of this unique ecosystem have been conserved in what is now the Coole-Garryland Complex Special Area of Conservation, a region specifically known for its importance as a watering site for wintering waterfowl, especially whooper swans and Bewick's swans. Whooper swans in particular are known for elaborate signaling communication within the flock in preparation for taking flight, a phenomenon Yeats notes in the poem: "I saw . . . / All suddenly mount / And scatter wheeling in great broken rings / Upon their clamorous wings" (131). Thus, while we might compare Yeats's swans with the swans in Pyotr Tchaikovsky's *Swan Lake* (premiered by the Bolshoi in 1877), in which the swans belong to an enchanted realm beyond human access, we see that Yeats's poem also encodes species-specific information and thereby participates in nature in the manner of scientific observation.

Finally, another work that bears on extinction in North America is Georgia O'Keeffe's "Cow's Skull: Red, White, and Blue" (1931). In this stark image, a bleached skull floats before a flag of red, white, and blue; a black central stripe descends like a dark tongue along the vertical axis from the broken jaw. The curators of the Metropolitan Museum of Art offer the following gloss: "To O'Keeffe, such bones represented the desert's enduring beauty and the strength of the American spirit, which is alluded to in the striped background" (2018: 52.203). Meanwhile, the animal studies perspective we have cultivated in this chapter suggests that it is also important for "Cow's Skull" to be read alongside the history of factory farming. Modernity was after all, as Döblin writes in *Berlin Alexanderplatz*, "Boomtime in the abattoir, boomboomtime: pigs 11,543, cattle 2,016, calves 920, sheep 14,450, one blow, bop, they lie there.

The pigs, the cattle, the calves, they are all slaughtered. There's no all to think about them. Now, where were we? Eh?" (212). Other contexts for "Cow's Skull" include the systematic, militarized campaign to exterminate the American bison as the lynchpin species of the shortgrass prairie ecology and the economies of the Native American tribes that impeded white settlement and farming in the American West.

At the beginning of the nineteenth century, tens of millions of bison had roamed the Great Plains, maintaining its unique ecosystem; by 1900 fewer than 300 were left in the wild. According to environmental historian William Cronon, "With the arrival of the Union Pacific in Nebraska and Wyoming during the 1860s, followed a few years later by the Kansas Pacific farther south, the railroads drove a knife into the heart of buffalo country." By 1883, he writes, "The great herds had vanished from the face of the plains" (217). Read alongside the slaughter of the bison, we can see how the curatorial gloss quoted earlier willfully misreads O'Keeffe's image in pursuit of an optimistic message. The bleached skull may testify to the "American spirit," but not to its "beauty"; instead, the black line and white bone mark the great extinction at the center of modernity and our nation's history.

One of the final lessons of this chapter is to see modernism's animals not arrayed individually like specimens on display in the cages of a zoo or hunted through the pages of a text, but instead to consider them through an ecosystem approach that reveals a web of interconnected beings, with new connections emerging between writers such as John Muir and Marianne Moore or between Franz Kafka and Jean Toomer, as well as between species such as Woolf's snail and Darwin's earthworms. By combining the granular analysis of specific literary works and specific animals, by focusing sometimes on individual creatures and sometimes on single poems, we hope to have revealed modernism's animals as they appear through an ecocritical lens and an aesthetic one; after all, by Wallace Stevens's estimation, a good modernist needs at least "Thirteen Ways of Looking at a Blackbird."

4

Modernism in the Wilderness

A wilderness, in contrast with those areas where man and his own works dominate the landscape, is hereby recognized as an area where the earth and its community of life are untrammeled by man, where man himself is a visitor who does not remain.
—THE WILDERNESS ACT OF 1964

The wilderness had patted him on the head, . . . and—lo—he had withered.
—JOSEPH CONRAD

Wild and Modern, a Contradiction in Terms?

For readers who come to modernist studies from ecocriticism, particularly for those who self-identify as environmentalists, the inclusion of a chapter on wilderness in this book will hardly need justification, so integral is the term to the environmental movement. The goal of wilderness preservation inspired some of the most significant land protection laws of the twentieth century, including the conservation, under the 1964 US Wilderness Act, of 765 parcels of land covering a total of over 100 million acres, an area larger than the state of California. But the power of wilderness as an idea, and the ideal of pristine ecosystems it embodies, extends far beyond its legal definition or political utility. As activist-novelist Edward Abbey writes in *Desert Solitaire: A Season in the Wilderness* (1968), to environmentalists and outdoor enthusiasts like himself, "the word itself is music. Wilderness, Wilderness . . . we scarcely know what we mean by the term, though the sound of it draws all whose nerves and emotions have not yet been irreparably stunned, deadened, numbed by the caterwauling of commerce, the sweating scramble for profit and domination" (166). Greg Garrard is far more specific and more circumspect, beginning a broad discussion of the topic in *Ecocriticism* (2004) with the claim that "the idea of wilderness, signifying nature in a state uncontaminated by civilization, is the most potent construction of nature available to New World environmentalism" (59). Its aura, and much of its potency as a concept, can be traced back to the gray-haired eminences of American nature writing—Ralph Waldo Emerson, Henry David Thoreau, and John Muir—in whose work the concept of wilderness is elevated to the status of a theological principle. "Wilderness is a necessity," Muir declares in *Our National Parks* (1901), claiming nature as the church of the romantic wanderer (1). Protecting these sacralized spaces has, since the late nineteenth century, been a central component of mainstream environmentalism.

For readers who come to ecocriticism from modernist studies, however, the title of this chapter will likely seem a category mistake, or perhaps a play on words. Modernism's iconic figures, we have learned, are city-dwellers, experimentalists, anti-realists, and iconoclasts; thus, as Jeffrey Mathes McCarthy writes, "A sustained effort to connect the modernist novel with actual physical nature seems for much of modernist studies a contradiction in terms" (2015: 12). In a metaphorical sense—that is, "applied to a place (e.g. a building or town) which one finds 'desolate,' or in which one is lonely or 'lost'" (OED)—the city is modernism's wilderness. We might speak figuratively of Marcel Proust navigating the wilderness of wit in the salons of the Faubourg Saint-Germain, but it's hard to imagine him going camping. In fact, a figurative use of the term was already common enough by 1898 for it to be used in the title of a collection of essays in urban anthropology, *The City Wilderness: A Settlement Study*, authored by and about residents of Boston's South End. The word "wilderness" used in this sense crops up frequently in modernist texts: the urbane Eliot speaks of a "wilderness of mirrors" in the penultimate stanza of "Gerontion" (1920); Wyndham Lewis uses the term in "Enemy of the Stars" (1914), where he proclaims: "Our soul is wild, with primitiveness of its own. Its wilderness is anywhere—in a shop, sailing, reading psalms: its greatest good our destiny" (qtd. in Rainey 181); and Hart Crane's "Chaplinesque" (1922) ends on a note of mock-heroic sublimity when the speaker hears "a kitten in the wilderness."

In this chapter, we make the case that wilderness is more prevalent and more pressing in modernist texts than the field's scholars may expect, though not always in the ways environmentalists may have hoped. Through a series of snapshots and field notes, we explore representations of wild nature in legislation and literature covering roughly the hundred or so years between the creation of the first national park (Yellowstone in 1872) and the passage of the Wilderness Act in 1964. In these readings we track a shift in the normative valence of wilderness as a concept from negative to positive associations, a trend developing alongside new forms of land protection, new modes of recreation, and a new sense of aesthetics. As environmental historian David Brooks observes, this hundred-year interval was a time when "fundamental beliefs about the origin of the earth and of man's place in it were shattered beyond repair; when the approach to nature shifted from the romantic and moral to the scientific; when exploitation gradually began to yield to some thought for the future" (xv). While Brooks's argument implies progress and steady transition, we emphasize the way modernism's relationship to wilderness, like so much else, was characterized by an ethos of experiment and contradiction.

Wilderness: Literary Genealogies

According to the Oxford English Dictionary, the word "wilderness" has Old English roots, formed through a conjunction of *wilde*, or untamed, and the suffix *-nes* denoting place; thus its primary meaning of "uncultivated land." Wilderness is thus defined negatively, as an *un*-place, and this sense of negativity is echoed in the contemporary legal definition of a wilderness area as an ecosystem "unmodified by humanity." Until quite recently in terms of human evolutionary history, wilderness in the sense of uncultivated land comprised the vast majority of the planet. To an imaginary observer in the year

1850, the earth at night would have looked much the same as it did two millennia earlier, during which time the human population had grown at an extremely slow rate from an estimated 150 million before the Common Era to what in retrospect seems a rather modest 1.2 billion people; curves for global population, per capita energy consumption, and global land use had remained relatively flat. Thus, as Thoreau found in the 1850s, he only had to veer slightly off the beaten track, so to speak, to stumble into wilderness. As he wrote, reflecting on his hike to the summit of Mount Katahdin in *Maine Woods* (1864), "It was but a step on either hand to the grim, untrodden wilderness, whose tangled labyrinth of living, fallen, and decaying trees only the deer and moose, the bear and wolf can easily penetrate" (599).

When wilderness is seen as an infinite *great beyond*, it has a transcultural tendency to be regarded as an adversary to be overcome or as a potential resource to exploit. "To the laborer in the sweat of his labor," writes Aldo Leopold in a wonderfully Promethean image from *A Sand County Almanac* (1949), "the raw stuff on his anvil is an adversary to be conquered. So was wilderness an adversary to the pioneer" (264–65). As environmental historian Roderick Nash puts it in *Wilderness and the American Mind*, a pioneering work of ecocriticism, "the largest portion of the energy of early civilization was directed at conquering wildness in nature and eliminating it in human nature" (xii). In a similar vein Peter Coates reminds us that "for the majority of people," wilderness signified "a challenge to surmount and a set of raw materials out of which to wrest a living" (10). Ironically, given his reputation as a conservationist, we can see these attitudes at work in Thoreau's writings, where enjoyment of nature in no way contradicts a desire to penetrate and master it: "The very timber and boards and shingles of which our houses are made," he writes with evident amazement in *Maine Woods*, "grew but yesterday in a wilderness where the Indian still hunts and the moose runs wild. New York has her wilderness within her own borders . . . though the railroad and the telegraph have been established . . . only a few axemen have gone 'up river,' into the howling wilderness which feeds it" (654). Today New York state possesses only a single national wilderness area, on Fire Island, compared to Alaska's forty-nine, from over a million acres in the Aleutian Islands to the staggering nine million acres of Wrangell-Saint Elias, the largest wilderness in the system. Sounding a note similar to Thoreau's, Isabella Bird in 1873 offers a description of Lake Tahoe in a letter to her sister, collected in *A Lady's Life in the Rocky Mountains*:

> I have found a dream of beauty at which one might look all one's life and sigh. Not lovable . . . but beautiful in its own way! A strictly North American beauty—snow-splotched mountains, huge pines, red-woods, sugar pines, silver spruce; a crystalline atmosphere, waves of the richest color; and a pine-hung lake which mirrors all beauty on its surface. . . . There is no sound but the distant and slightly musical ring of the lumberer's axe. (1)

What is striking about these passages to contemporary ears is the way that Thoreau can speak with equal enthusiasm of the "axemen" as of the beauty of the wild-running moose; likewise, Bird can revel equally in her vision of mountain vistas and the "musical ring" of the axe: seemingly infinite nature abounds. More troubling still from an ecological perspective is the way both writers actively valorize projects of resource extraction and landscape transformation as objects of aesthetic beauty while implicitly denigrating the "howling wilderness" (Thoreau) as "not lovable" (Bird). What makes the competing if not mutually exclusive qualities of the beauty of the trees and the beauty of the axe invisible to Thoreau from his promontory in Maine is the fact that despite the advances of the Industrial Revolution, so vast and powerful did the earth seem that he had no way to predict how quickly the "musical ring of the lumberer's axe," when those axes are wielded on an industrial scale, can silence the "howling wilderness." In fact, it is precisely the insignificance of humanity when compared to the vastness of a nonhuman nature that is the primary lesson the wilderness teaches Thoreau: "It was the fresh and natural surface of the planet Earth, as it was made forever and ever. . . . Man was not to be associated with it. It was Matter, vast, terrific—not his Mother Earth that we have heard of," but nature as "vast and drear and inhuman" (645). As Max Oelschlaeger argues, "The journey to Ktaadn's summit was an existential encounter that dealt a death blow to the Emersonian notion that the world existed for humankind," but, at the same time, Thoreau's sense of nature's boundlessness ironically inhibits the idea that such spaces need protection (145).

Not that we didn't do our level best as a species to make incursions into the wilderness. "In the past," however, as Bill McKibben writes,

> We spoiled and polluted parts of... nature, inflicted environmental "damage." But that was like stabbing a man with toothpicks: though it hurt, annoyed, degraded, it did not touch vital organs, block the path of the lymph or blood. We never thought that we had wrecked nature. Deep down, we never really thought we could: it was too big and too old; its forces—the wind, the rain, the sun—were too strong, too elemental. (41)

Prior to the Industrial Revolution, in other words, the idea of human mastery over nature could be seen more in terms of its cultural affects rather than from its environmental effects.

In the English language, the meaning of the term "wilderness"— in particular the lingering sense that wilderness is not only hostile to human habitation but also generally ecologically unproductive—is overdetermined by its use in the King James Bible, a text completed in 1611. "Wilderness," in that text, serves as the preferred term to designate a variety of mostly inhospitable, sparsely settled landscapes encountered by Jews and Christians on their wanderings of exile, exodus, and revelation in the ancient Near East. Because of this usage, wilderness became so synonymous with desert in the minds of the English, writes Nash, that "Samuel Johnson defined it in 1755 in his *Dictionary of the English Language* as 'a desert; a tract of solitude and savageness'" (3). This final flourish, associating wilderness with "savageness," introduces a new and negative normativity, connecting the term to colonialism and empire through its binary understanding of wilderness as the other of civilization.

Puritan colonists and subsequent settlers, meanwhile, brought this biblically inflected and negatively normed view of wilderness to the so-called New World, where early settlers saw themselves surrounded by a "hideous and desolate wilderness" as William Bradford memorably describes coastal Massachusetts in his record of colonial life, *Of Plymouth Plantation*: "What could they see but a hidious & desolate wildernes, full of wild beasts & willd men and what multituds ther might be of them they knew not" (62). In this foundational document, wilderness is seen as a merciless enemy that beset the colonists from all sides. The natural world was regarded not as an Edenic paradise, but as a hostile and unpredictable realm, populated by dangerous creatures both human and nonhuman, inferior in every way to the kingdom of God to which they aspired.

In an essay from *In the American Grain* (1925), William Carlos Williams memorably, if crudely, writes that Puritan women "died shooting children against the wilderness like cannon balls," an image that evokes both the staggeringly high infant mortality rates in the colonies and the colonists' pervasive sense of violent opposition to nature (179). The ripple effects of the biblical usage of wilderness are so strong that James Joyce still refers to the wanderings of "the Jews in the wilderness" in the "Aeolus" chapter of *Ulysses* (108). They also help to account for the way Virginia Woolf links wilderness with madness and danger in *Mrs. Dalloway*: "Human beings have neither kindness, nor faith, nor charity," muses Septimus in a dark, post-traumatic reverie, "they hunt in packs. Their packs scour the desert and vanish screaming into the wilderness. They desert the fallen" (89).

Prejudice against wilderness is particularly clear in genre fiction. Consider, by way of example, the representation of wild nature in J. R. R. Tolkien's *The Hobbit* (1937) and *The Lord of the Rings* trilogy (1954–55), some of the most popular books of all time. In a surface reading, the books appear to offer a clear ecological parable in the contrast between the good, forest-loving elves and the evil, forest-hating enemy—in *The Two Towers* the wizard Saruman even reveals his perfidy by turning Isengard into a dystopian factory and feeding the trees of Fangorn Forest to the forge fires of his war machine. But Tolkien's texts do not celebrate nature in and for itself: instead, the hobbits inhabit a pastoral landscape and the elves practice a form of sustainable silviculture; wild nature—like the forest of Mirkwood—is described as dangerous and ecologically unproductive. Similarly, Arthur Conan Doyle's 1887 novel *A Study in Scarlet* includes a sequence that takes place in the American West. "In the central portion of the great North American Continent there lies an arid and repulsive desert," Doyle writes, identifying there a "mighty wilderness" that "for many a long year served as a barrier against the advance of civilization. From the Sierra Nevada to Nebraska, and from the Yellowstone River in the north to the Colorado upon the south, is a region of desolation and silence . . . barrenness, inhospitality, and misery" (38).

Or consider the way Samuel Clemens, the author better known by his pen name, Mark Twain, describes the Mono Lake wilderness area in California's Sierra Nevada mountains, a region that features in *Roughing It* (1872), a semi-fictionalized account of the writer's travels through the American West and beyond. While at times Clemens writes in a tone reminiscent of Muir or Thoreau in praise of the landscapes of the American West, more often wilderness is associated with biblical desert and wasteland. To Clemens's eye, Mono Lake was "one of the strangest freaks of Nature to be found in any land" (243); it "lies in a lifeless, treeless, hideous desert," a landscape "little graced with the picturesque" (245). Clemens describes Mono Lake as "an unpretending expanse of grayish water, about a hundred miles in circumference, with two islands in its center, mere upheavals of rent and scorched and blistered lava, snowed over with gray banks and drifts of pumice-stone and ashes" (245). For Clemens and his party, Mono Lake and its environs are hardly worth a second look, except insofar as they provide an image of hell. It is hard to imagine Clemens or his readers fighting particularly hard to protect areas like Mono Lake from the effects of human habitation or industrial encroachment. It should thus be no surprise that as fresh water became an increasingly valuable resource in the arid American West, the city of Los Angeles would begin diverting water from the Mono Basin in 1941, sucking down lake levels, oversalinating the water that remained, and destroying riparian habitats. Mary Austin, writing in her 1903 book *The Land of Little Rain* about the fate of Owens Lake, which had already succumbed to the thirst of Los Angeles thirty years before Mono Lake, prophesized with savage irony: "It is the proper destiny of every considerable stream in the West to become an irrigating ditch" (85).

By contrast, the Mono Lake Committee, an organization founded in 1978 to protect the lake from water diversion and restore habitats, describes the same landscape on their website very differently:

> Nestled at the edge of the arid Great Basin and the snowy Sierra Nevada mountains in California, Mono Lake is an ancient saline lake that covers over 70 square miles and supports a unique and productive ecosystem. The lake has no fish; instead it is home to trillions of brine shrimp and alkali flies. . . . Scenic limestone formations known as tufa towers rise from the water's surface. Millions of migratory birds visit the lake each year. (n.p.)

Where Clemens sees a semi-apocalyptic landscape, almost biblical in its evocation of fire and brimstone, we now recognize a vital habitat for migratory birds with a uniquely productive ecosystem. More importantly, this understanding has the force of law: the lake was the subject of extensive litigation in the California water wars, eventually adjudicated in *National Audubon Society v. Superior Court* (1983), which pitted the holders of water rights granted to the Los Angeles Department of Water and Power against those contending that such diversions violated the public trust doctrine—a principle of common law privileging public access to public goods like running water, seashores, and the air—over individual property rights. The recovering landscape now enjoys protected status as a state natural reserve.

In addition to a new understanding of brine shrimp ecosystems and limestone geology, an entirely different attitude toward the natural world pervades the Mono Lake Committee's description of the region when compared to Clemens's account. For Clemens, biodiversity had no value in and of itself; the migratory bird populations celebrated as visitors and accorded legal protections in the 1970s Clemens sees in the 1870s only as game species to be shot for recreation. Clemens describes a wasteland in the same place where the Mono Lake Committee describes picturesque vistas and ecologically productive ecosystems.

In the European literary tradition, an appreciation of nature is most often associated with the pastoral, an artistic mode first practiced by the Ancient Greeks and characterized by idealized representations of rural landscapes and shepherding lifestyles. As Kelly Sultzbach argues, there is always a normative component to pastoral literature, one aimed at critiquing human culture rather than exploring ecology; the pastoral, she writes, is often guilty of "using a kind of magical sense of nature's noble morality to critique the shortsightedness of human greed, as if holding out nature as a looking-glass for humanity's own reflection" (5). From an ecocritical perspective, we can see how the pastoral accounts for both the formal structure and the suggestive force of a poem like Ezra Pound's "In a Station of the Metro" (1913), with its juxtaposition of urban "faces in the crowd" to natural "petals on a wet, black bough." The pastoral concept of nature is even more visible in the poetry of W. B. Yeats. Writing in his autobiography of the inspiration for his early and much celebrated poem "The Lake

Isle of Innisfree" (1890), Yeats describes being in central London, "walking through Fleet Street very homesick" and thinking back to Innisfree, "a little island in Lough Gill," a rural lake in the hill and forest ecosystem of northwest Ireland, where he "had still the ambition . . . of living in imitation of Thoreau" (1994b: 139). In the poem, the speaker declares, "I will arise and go now, and go to Innisfree," and describes the fantasy of pastoral bliss he will create beyond the noise and bustle of modernity. One of the many lessons we can learn from this poem has to do with the way nature is conceived as a retreat, a place visited for therapeutic purposes—even summoned to mind for reassurance "while I stand on the roadway, or on the pavements gray." Like a convenient vacation home, it is preferable for pastoral nature to be within easy striking distance from the city via the modern conveniences of railroad and highway—or, like the Shire of Tolkien's hobbits, safe in the land of imagination.

There are several points to be made about the pastoral tradition from an ecocritical perspective. First, it is crucial to stress that pastoral texts offer not so much an engagement with wild nature as with a fantasy of managed landscapes in which human modifications effected through domesticated livestock, farming, and silvaculture are seen as "improvements" to the natural environment. The environmental humanities teach readers to be more suspicious of the pastoral fantasy that tends to characterize, for example, the Wordsworthian vision of nature—with its pastures, sheep, and hedgerows interspersed with daffodils. Environmental historians similarly teach us how the landscapes of Wordsworth's idylls are actually ecological disasters—landscapes like Tintern Abbey, which is situated at the southern end of the Wye valley only 200 kilometers from London at the edge of a coal mining district. In fact, as Oelschlaeger reminds us, sounding a lot like Conrad's Marlow, "The British Isles, a Roman outpost located at the edge of European civilization, was covered with timber at the beginning of the Middle Ages" (70). The pastoral promises not nature for nature's sake but for the sake of human relaxation, contemplation, and other elite pleasures. Its idea that the utility of wilderness lies in providing opportunities for human recreation, or of valuing nature for its beauty and potential to effect spiritual uplift—however noble one may feel these sentiments to be—seems strikingly anthropocentric when compared to the value of ecosystem health. The pastoral is a far cry from the earth-first ethics articulated by Leopold in *A Sand County Almanac*: "A thing is right when it tends to preserve the integrity, stability, and beauty of the biotic community. It is wrong when it tends otherwise" (224–25).

Second, the pastoral idea that nature would cure humanity from the supposed moral and physical ills of urbanism and industrialism, like religious conceptions of a providential universe and a romantic attitude toward art, is one more false idol modernism will attempt to overturn. "To marvel how beauty outside mirrored beauty within" as the romantic poets and American transcendentalists had done has become impossible, writes Virginia Woolf in the famous "Time Passes" section of *To the Lighthouse* (1927): "The mirror was broken" (134). In its more strident, agonistic forms—as we see among the British Vorticists or Italian Futurists—the breaking of this mirror was fully intentional: "Let's murder the moonlight!" Marinetti crows in the title of one interwar manifesto, declaring war on nature as part of his campaign against traditional aesthetics (Rainey 54). At the same time, however, pastoral rhetoric and aesthetics do play an integral role in establishing land protection programs like the US national parks system.

Wilderness: Legal Genealogies

By the late nineteenth century it was becoming clear to a few that the balance of power between humans and their environment was shifting. An important sign of this transition was the closure of the American frontier, announced in an 1893 paper given to the American Historical Association by Frederick Jackson Turner. The closure of the frontier foretold a new era in political history in North America: "American social development has been continually beginning over again on the frontier" (28), wrote Turner, who saw the exhaustion of appropriable territory as a threat to national dynamism. The closure of the frontier can be read ecocritically as a sign that the distinction between cultivated and uncultivated, inside and outside, foreground and background was in the process of being inverted. Thereafter, wilderness would be confined to fragments, increasingly dependent on legal, political, and economic protection. "Convinced of our own omnipotence," laments William Cronon, "we can imagine nature retreating into small islands—'preserves'—

in the midst of a landscape which otherwise belongs to us" (18). By aiding and abetting this process of enclosure, "We unconsciously affirm our belief that we ourselves are unnatural. Nature is the place where we are not" (18).

The public law establishing the first national park, Yellowstone, signed into law by President Ulysses S. Grant on March 1, 1872, declares that the area "is hereby reserved and withdrawn from settlement, occupancy, or sale under the laws of the United States, and dedicated and set apart as a public park or pleasuring-ground for the benefit and enjoyment of the people." The preservation of Yosemite and the giant sequoias of Mariposa Grove in California, meanwhile, redound in large part to the writing of Frederick Law Olmsted. As a renowned figure in landscape architecture, most famous for the design of Central Park, he has shaped the way hundreds of millions of people perceive and valorize the landscape, and it was his "Yosemite and the Mariposa Grove: A Preliminary Report" of 1865 that spurred Congress to act in protection of the final remnants of old-growth forests of California. "It is the will of the Nation as embodied in the act of Congress," Olmstead argued, "that this scenery shall never be private property, but that like certain defensive points upon our coast it shall be held solely for public purposes" (9). Here environmental protection is sutured to the legal structure enforcing existing forms of militaristic nationalism.

In his book *Wilderness by Design: Landscape Architecture and the National Park Service* (1998), historian Ethan Carr describes the interwar years as the defining era when park development was established as a viable alternative economic engine to the resource extractions for which the forest service and private industry tirelessly lobbied. As Carr argues, Olmsted's plan for a wilderness park at Yosemite bears a close resemblance to his earlier work in Central Park: "The physical development Olmsted proposed for Yosemite derived from the same tradition of landscape park design and management" (29). The encounter with wilderness could, in other words, be modernized and turned into a commodity for enjoyment, as we can see evoked in the iconic 1903 photograph of President Theodore Roosevelt posing with John Muir on Overhanging Rock overlooking Yosemite Falls (Figure 8). There were other proposals to "modernize" environments and they frequently resembled those of William Mulholland, the Los Angeles water baron who fantasizes

FIGURE 8 *Theodore Roosevelt and John Muir at Yosemite Falls.*

about turning Yosemite into a reservoir in a famous moment recorded by Marc Reisner in *Cadillac Desert* (1986), a pioneering work of journalistic ecocriticism: "I'd go in there and build a dam from one side of that valley to the other and *stop the goddamned waste!*" (italics in original, 91–92).

A major shift in ethos from a campaign of park building for human enjoyment to an appreciation of the value of nature for nature's sake can be found in the distinction between parks and wilderness. From a legal perspective, the most important definition of a wilderness area can be found in Public Law 88–577, the "Wilderness Act" of 1964, where wilderness is "recognized as an area where the earth and its community of life are untrammeled by man." The act is necessary, its "statement of policy" explains, "in order to assure that an increasing population, accompanied by expanding settlement and growing mechanization, does not occupy and modify all areas within the United States and its possessions." But wilderness does not include *all* such putatively unmodified areas, only those with "outstanding opportunities for solitude or a primitive and unconfined type of recreation" or "ecological, geological, or other features of scientific, educational, scenic, or historical value"—a broad jurisdiction to be sure, but one firmly and unapologetically anthropocentric in nature.

The purpose of wilderness is thus to promote a distinctive mode of aesthetic consumption or to serve the advancement of scientific knowledge. As Robert Marshall, a forester and activist instrumental in the founding of the American Wilderness Society, writes in "The Problem of the Wilderness" (1930), "The benefits which accrue from the wilderness may be separated into three broad divisions: the physical, the mental and the esthetic" (142). Wilderness, operating as a kind of homeopathic Viagra, restores male potency: "Virile minds, including Thomas Jefferson, Henry Thoreau, Louis Agassiz, Herman Melville, Mark Twain, John Muir and William James," Marshall notes, "have felt the compulsion of periodical retirements into the solitudes" (143). Wilderness satisfies an appetite for adventure "in an age of machinery" in which "only the extremely fortunate have any occasion to satiate this hankering" (143–44). Marshall is clear about the opportunity costs of a wilderness protection policy, which would place so-called natural resources outside the reach of public or private capital; and he concedes that it will be necessary to select only "a few samples of undeveloped territory" with the goal of conserving "enough tracts to insure every one who hungers for it a generous opportunity of enjoying wilderness isolation" (148).

Ontologically and epistemologically, wilderness is defined—and thus produced—by the exclusion of the human. It is predicated on a prior assumption of separation between subject (usually "man") and object (a feminized "nature"). And it reinforces the very notion of human exceptionalism that lies at the root of some of our most destructive ecological practices, as ecofeminist Carolyn Merchant has convincingly argued. For Cronon, "far from bringing people into communion with nature," this way of conceiving the wilderness "creates a false dichotomy that separates them from it, dulling their appreciation of the daily beauty of the world" (43). Additionally, as Kevin DeLuca and Anne Demo argue,

> During its first one hundred years, the environmental movement has been concerned, almost exclusively, with preserving pristine places. This narrow, class- and race-based perspective of what counts as nature leads the environmental movement to neglect people and the places they inhabit, thus isolating the movement from labor and civil rights concerns and rendering it vulnerable to charges of elitism and misanthropism. (257)

The false dichotomy between humans and nature has more than aesthetic implications: humans alone, in this view, are seen as ecological agents—and, in fact, only some humans, since the legal definition of wilderness is based on the empirically false and frequently racist assertion that the farming, hunting, or land-modification projects of indigenous peoples had no impact upon the natural world.

The philosophical exclusion of the human from the wilderness was paralleled by the literal—and forcible—removal of indigenous inhabitants from wilderness areas. The idea of wilderness, as Ursula Heise incisively argues,

> conceals the fact that the apparently transhistorical ideal of *wilderness* only acquired connotations of the sublime and sacred in the nineteenth century and that the cultural valuation of pristine and uninhabited areas led to the displacement of native inhabitants and in some cases to the creation of official parks. Far from being nature in its original state, such wildernesses were the product of cultural processes. The wilderness concept makes it difficult for a political program to conceptualize desirable forms of human inhabitation, relying as it does on the categorical separation of human beings from nature. (2006: 507)

Thinking with Merchant, Cronon, and Heise, it is possible to look back with more skepticism on the paeans to wilderness by Muir and Abbey and to see how they are conditioned by race, class, and gender. They also help us to reexamine the more ambivalent depictions of wilderness at work in high-modernist texts, to which we now turn.

Into the Modern Wilds

Modernism's most canonical foray into the wilderness—and one that lies like a stumbling block in the path of any modernist ecocriticism—is Joseph Conrad's *Heart of Darkness* (1902). In this novella, the word "wilderness" recurs an astonishing twenty-two times—almost as frequently as "ivory" or "darkness," both of which appear thirty-one times counting the latter's use in the novel's title; if we include the cognate "wild" in our word search it brings the number of hits up to fifty-five, dwarfing those of its supposed subject. Through this process of repetition, the novel freights the wilderness with a host of symbolic associations, most of them negative. Marlow, for instance, spends much of his time on his journey up the Congo River contemplating the "mysterious life of the wilderness that stirs in the forest, in the jungles, in the hearts of wild men" (10). Similarly, while awaiting repairs at the Central Station, he describes his impression of "the silent wilderness surrounding this cleared speck on the earth," which "struck me as something great and invincible, like evil or truth, waiting patiently for the passing away of this fantastic invasion" (26). At other times in the novel, wilderness is gendered female, associated with occult knowledge, and conceived as a space of darkness. Frequently, it is anthropomorphized: Kurtz, Ahab-like, calls out to "the invisible wilderness" from his sickbed in diabolical fury, "Oh, but I will wring your heart yet!" (67).

There is no shortage of critical prose on this problematic text; a search of the MLA international bibliography for the terms "Joseph Conrad Heart of Darkness" recalls well over a thousand hits; adding the term "wilderness" to the previous search, however, reduces the yield to seven. Why are Conrad's critics largely silent on a subject of such obvious importance to the novel? Several things are at play: first, despite the frequent appearance of the word "wilderness" in the text, neither the novel nor its characters are terribly interested in the ecology of the Congo basin—the second largest tropical rainforest in the world—except insofar as its resources could be extracted and monetized. The jungle that Marlow faces is a far cry from Muir's Californian idea of a benevolent wilderness. Instead, as McCarthy argues, *Heart of Darkness* "dramatizes modernity's destructive alienation from the natural world against the backdrop of the Congo's ecological collapse" (2009: 620). Ironically, this collapse is invisible to Marlow and the other characters in the story, who read in the vastness of the Congo basin a narrative of nature's invincibility. The idea that humans could prevail over the "jungle" seems absurd to Marlow, as absurd as the French warship he sees shelling the coast:

> The muzzles of the long six-inch guns stuck out all over the low hull . . . in the empty immensity of earth, sky, and water, there she was, incomprehensible, firing into a continent. Pop, would go one of the six-inch guns; a small flame would dart and vanish, a little white smoke would disappear, a tiny projectile would give a feeble screech—and nothing happened. (17)

Second, within modernist studies, scholars have been more drawn to questions of literary forms than to landscape forms, often reading the same lines with different meanings in mind. In his essay "Should We Read *Heart of Darkness*?" the critic J. Hillis Miller, for example, focuses on the formal device of personification when he analyzes Kurtz's dying vow to wring the heart of the wilderness. Describing this personification as the most "ostentatious" stylistic feature of the novel and referring to the trope by its Greek name, *prosopopoeia*, he writes, "in 'Heart of Darkness' *prosopopoeias* are a chief means of naming by indirection what Conrad calls, in a misleading and inadequate metaphor, 'the darkness,' or 'the wilderness'" (120). Miller notes that "more than a dozen explicit personifications of this something, *that is* not really a person but an 'it,' asexual or trans-sexual, impersonal, indifferent, though to Marlow it seems like a person, rhythmically punctuate 'Heart of Darkness' like a recurrent leitmotif" (italics in original, 119).

Miller's argument, however, encourages readers to turn their attention away from the novel's ecological imagination; there is thus a certain irony in the fact that the passage under discussion, with its "invisible wilderness," is very much about the visibility and invisibility of ecology. Wilderness is invisible in *Heart of*

Darkness in at least three senses: first, it is literally invisible to Kurtz, who cannot see anything from his sickbed; second, and more profoundly, the wilderness of the Congo is invisible to the novel, which treats it as an almost purely symbolic space rather than as a functioning ecosystem; and, finally, it has been invisible to many of the novel's readers, though it need not be so to the environmental humanist. Why should we read *Heart of Darkness* ecocritically? Because although it is home to the planet's second largest rainforest, recent studies suggest that the Congo basin will have been almost entirely deforested by the end of this century, largely due to "small-scale forest clearing for agriculture" (Tyukavina n.p.).

There are, of course, reasons other than economic appropriation to enter the wilderness. The theme of nature as a site of restoration and rebirth is perhaps most prominent in Ernest Hemingway's "Big Two-Hearted River" (1925) where protagonist Nick Adams returns from the destruction of the First World War to a town in the Upper Peninsula of Michigan that has been destroyed by fire. As Nick retreats from the town along a road, the landscape inspires him to venture off-road into it:

> He stood with the pack on his back on the brow of the hill looking out across the country, toward the distant river and then struck down the hillside away from the road. Underfoot the ground was good walking. Two hundred yards down the fire line stopped. Then it was sweet fern, growing ankle high, walk through, and clumps of jack pines; a long undulating country with frequent rises and descents, sandy underfoot and the country alive again. (180)

The landscape is both symbolic and literal, serving as a stage for Nick's recollections as the burned-over landscape of Michigan's Upper Peninsula gestures to the battlefields of Europe from which Nick has recently returned. Hemingway's narrative weaves together Nick's return to life after the horrors of the war and the landscape's renewal after the fire.

To environmentalists today, especially to those trained in leave-no-trace practices, Nick is aggressive with his use of the axe and unsentimental in adapting the environment to his desire. Establishing a campsite involves chopping roots with an axe and uprooting a grove of ferns to serve as bedding. Fishing involves reliving the trauma of the war:

> He felt a reaction against deep wading with the water deepening up under his armpits, to hook big trout in places impossible to land them. In the swamp the banks were bare, the big cedars came together overhead, the sun did not come through, except in patches; in the fast deep water, in the half light, the fishing would be tragic. (198)

Like many of Hemingway's characters, Nick seeks to connect with the earth on an intimate, mystical level, but his reverence for the natural world is matched by equally powerful desires to conquer and subdue it. Hemingway, like many of those we might describe as rod-and-gun-club modernists—Conrad and Faulkner among them—deploys predictably gendered conceptions of nature in which wilderness serves, more often than not, as the stage for dramas of masculine self-fashioning. As Glen Love argues, these men engaged with the natural world primarily through "the blood sports, such as hunting and fishing and boxing and bullfighting" (117). As we see it, the challenge for the twenty-first-century ecocritic is both to analyze how these modes of wilderness consumption have been gendered and sexualized and also to track the emergence of nonviolent forms of wilderness recreation and the growing value of nature for nature's sake—a development connected historically and aesthetically to the modernist value of art for art's sake, as we will soon see in our discussion of Wallace Stevens's poem "Anecdote of the Jar."

Indeed, the early twentieth century saw the explosion of sports that substituted what Edward Abbey called "the sweating scramble for profit and domination" with other forms of sweaty scrambles in the wilderness, like hiking, biking, skiing, and mountain climbing. Nash tells the story of the adventurer Joe Knowles, who, in 1913, went "naked and afraid" into the Maine woods and survived for two months in a headline-grabbing act of propaganda; the book he subsequently wrote about his experience, *Alone in the Wilderness*, "sold 300,000 copies, and he toured the vaudeville circuit with top billing" (142). W. H. Auden and Christopher Isherwood wrote a mountaineering drama, *The Ascent of F6* (1936), about an expedition to a distant peak in a fictional British colony, based loosely on Auden's brother's expedition to K2 as a geological surveyor in India. In E. M. Forster's *Howards End* (1910), the Schlegel sisters announce that they have gone on a backpacking trip: "Some ladies do without hotels," Margaret rebukes Henry Wilcox, "Are you aware that Helen and I have walked alone over the Apennines, with our luggage on our backs?" (1996: 153).

In *Skiing into Modernity: A Cultural and Environmental History*, Andrew Denning argues that modernism contributed to the widespread appeal of skiing in the early twentieth century: "In the Alps, modernity arrived on skis . . . the Alps modernized skiing by aligning its practice with spectators' lust for mass cultural spectacles and with the rationalist dictates of modern sports" (9). For Denning, "Alpine skiers believed that their sport allowed them to master time and space by neutralizing the dangers of winter and covering great distances, thus reenchanting an increasingly banal and instrumental world by enabling acts of heroic self-assertion. Simultaneously, skiers claimed to escape the crowds and materialistic concerns of the lowlands by reconnecting with nature in its most arresting form" (12). In D. H. Lawrence's *Women in Love* (1920), Gerald takes to the wilderness in the newly popular sport of alpine skiing, venturing far into the alps:

> Gerald did not come in from his skiing until nightfall . . . he revolted at the thought of finding himself in the world again. He must stay up there in the snow forever. He had been happy by himself, high up there alone, traveling swiftly on skis, taking far flights, and skimming past the dark rocks veined with brilliant snow. (403)

Ultimately, he dies in a mountaineering accident, after nearly strangling his partner, Gudrun, in a paroxysm of domestic violence, connecting the conquest of nature with the violence of erotic conquest.

One of the most surprising naturalists of modernist poetry was the decidedly urban editor and patron of the arts Harriet Monroe, who became a passionate advocate of wilderness preservation. As Anne Raine writes in her chapter on "Ecocriticism and Modernism" in *The Oxford Handbook of Ecocriticism*, "Monroe viewed nature parks as *modern*: she called nature preservation 'the most important . . . spiritual and aesthetic enterprise of our time,' and even declared nature 'the ultimate modern*ist*,' whose untrammeled grandeur would incite American poets to knock down the 'walls and roofs' of literary convention" (98). Monroe promoted the work of poets like Marianne Moore, in whom she saw an original poet of keen descriptive power whose depiction of the natural world, and whose sense of art as "the love of doing hard things," to quote a line from "An Octopus" (1924), would find a ready audience with Monroe's magazine *Poetry: A Magazine of Verse*.

In Moore's poetry, experiential idiom fuses with naturalistic observation as the poet enters the wilderness. In "An Octopus," Moore describes her experience hiking Mt. Rainier, where she adventured as far as the Paradise Park overlook, gazing down on the branching arms of the Nisqually glacier, the octopus of the poem's extended metaphor. Described by the National Parks Service in their website on "Mount Rainer's Glaciers," the Nisqually Glacier is "perhaps the most visited and best surveyed glacier on Mount Rainier" producing a record of expansion and contraction "spanning nearly 150 years. During this time the glacier has retreated and advanced several times, though the general trend has been retreat" (2015: n.p.). We quote these materials in part because of their contextual relevance, but also because Moore herself quotes extensively from National Parks Service materials from her era, teaching park visitors and the poem's readers to recognize "a diversity of creatures" (73): the marmot with its "wild music," and the "miniature cavalcades of chlorophylless fungi" (74). This pedagogic imperative continues as Moore describes the mineral world rich with "calcium gems and alabaster pillars, / topaz, tourmaline crystals and amethyst quartz" (74). Moore directly interpolates scientific discourse and terminology into the stanzas of her poetry alongside more traditional literary references and poetic devices; in this way, she demonstrates how poetry can increase our appreciation of language, and how language can increase our appreciation of nature.

The antinomy between modernism and the wilderness may have seemed especially pronounced for those whose introduction to the modernists was mediated by the new critics, whose approach to textuality was designed to elucidate the self-contained nature of aesthetic objects—to illuminate "the poem as it exists on the page in all its originality and strangeness" as Helen Vendler memorably and movingly describes the enterprise (44). Reading a poem "on the page," however, often comes at the cost of taking the poem *out* of its physical environment. When Vendler offers this description of close reading (a project to which we and many others remain deeply committed), she is setting the stage to discuss "Anecdote of the Jar" by Wallace Stevens, a short poem first published in *Poetry* under Harriet Monroe's editorship in October of 1919. The poem is brief and deserves to be quoted in full because it bears directly on our discussion of the paradoxical nature of wilderness as a concept and modernism's relation to it:

> I placed a jar in Tennessee,
> And round it was, upon a hill.
> It made the slovenly wilderness
> Surround that hill.
>
> The wilderness rose up to it,
> And sprawled around, no longer wild.
> The jar was round upon the ground
> And tall and of a port in air.
>
> It took dominion everywhere.
> The jar was gray and bare.
> It did not give of bird or bush,
> Like nothing else in Tennessee. (76)

At this point in our book, we hope that readers will find it perfectly natural to read "Anecdote of a Jar" as a form of nature writing—one that contains a valuable ecological parable even if we allow that its main referent might not rise to the level of an ecological emergency. It is worth noting, however, that to read the poem ecocritically is to diverge significantly from the critical consensus. For Robert Buttell, the poem echoes the compositional practices of still life painting in the European tradition (166). At the same time, and more radically, Stevens's poem "could be describing the creation of a readymade," as Glen MacLeod argues, comparing Stevens's jar to Duchamp's art of the found object. More recently, for Joshua Schuster, the "poem's attention to human and nonhuman interactions, and how concepts and forms affect environs, articulates a distinctly modern view of ecology. Representation happens at the moment of human contact with the landscape" (xi).

With the exception of Schuster's recent intervention, "Anecdote of the Jar" is widely regarded (and highly praised) as a "writerly" text in Roland Barthes's sense of that term: a difficult and self-referential work that demands intertextual analysis on the part of the reader in order to assemble its meaning—a quintessentially new critical work. Vendler, for example, begins her discussion of the poem with the confident declaration that "*Anecdote of the Jar*, as various critics have seen, is a commentary on Keats's *Ode on a Grecian Urn*. Though this is nowhere said by Stevens, the poem is not comprehensible, in matter or manner, unless it is taken to be centrally about Keats's poem" (45). Despite her avowed commitment to the poem on the page, Vendler sees Stevens's poem as an act of literary criticism rather than ecocriticism—the poem is "a vow to stop imitating Keats" rather than a meditation on the effect of the relationship between the modern industrial subject and its environments (46).

Returned to its hillside in Tennessee, the text holds at least two alternate meanings, reflecting two successive phases in ecocriticism. One trajectory emerges through a form of surface reading, when we see leaving a jar on a hill for what it is if you don't pick it up again: an act of littering. The second involves examining the relational, mutually constitutive encounter between nature and culture: an act of making. In this way, we can see how each of the poem's three stanzas rework the same basic premise, showing the reader how the presence of a single manufactured item, one artifact of human culture—and a rather ordinary jar at that—has the power to utterly to transform the landscape and the speaker's relation to it. What is striking for the ecocritical reader—perhaps even alarming—is the fact that the speaker appears to bring a host of negative preconceptions about humans and their relationship with nature along with him to the hill in Tennessee, and thus into the poem's first quatrain. "Slovenly," in other words, precedes "wilderness" in more than just word order. Compared to the ambiguous implications of the poem's gnarled syntax (what does it mean to be "of a port in air"? or to "give of bird or bush"?) the poem's attitude toward the natural world is clear: in the first stanza, the geometrical regularity and manufactured precision of the jar makes the wilderness seem "slovenly" by comparison, echoed by the way, in the second stanza, the natural world seems to "sprawl" in disorder around the Euclidean lines of the jar.

This "rage for order," as Stevens puts it in "The Idea of Order at Key West" (1934), is a distinctly modernist prejudice, hinging on the decidedly modernist concept of form (130). Toward the beginning of

The City of Tomorrow and Its Planning, an instant classic of modernist architectural theory and urban planning upon its publication in 1929, Le Corbusier derisively compares disordered nature with intentional human design in a way that echoes Stevens's poem:

> Nature presents itself to us as a chaos; the vault of the heavens, the shapes of lakes and seas, the outlines of hills. The actual scene which lies before our eyes, with its kaleidoscopic fragments and its vague distances, is a confusion. There is nothing there that resembles the objects with which we surround ourselves, and which we have created. (18)

The sense that nature was dirty, chaotic, and excessive echoes attitudes chronicled by the Austrian intellectual Stefan Zweig in *The World of Yesterday*, in which he argues that embracing the modern often meant believing that, by contrast, "what was natural was dirty . . . *naturalis sunt turpia*," an attempted pun that inverts a once familiar adage attributed to Virgil, *naturalis non sunt turpia* (nothing natural is evil), passed down to modernity via medieval natural philosophy (91).

Wilderness, in the poem's conception of the term, also appears to be highly vulnerable to degradation through human action. From the speaker's perspective, the jar has a quasi-religious magnetism, a curious power to focalize that enacts violence upon the natural world culminating in the "dominion" proclaimed in the final stanza. "Dominion" carries at least two meanings. In characteristically indeterminate modernist fashion, it gestures toward the biblical trope of man's dominion over nature, and at the same time, it names a model of glass jar produced in great quantities at that time of the poem's publication by the Ball Jar company—a "Dominion Wide-Mouth Special," as Roy Harvey Pearce has plausibly argued (65). Once we learn this, the jar becomes something other than a piece of mass-produced trash or a monument to the human ingenuity of modern times. It becomes instead an object of knowledge for archaeology, a potsherd of modernity that thrusts us into the future, when archaeological historians might use it to reconstruct and understand our lifeworld, which will doubtlessly be as foreign to them as Keats's was to the urn he contemplated.

But the poem also and more subtly points to a revaluation occurring within the idea of wilderness itself. The pejorative connotation of the term that we see in the poem's first stanza in the "slovenly wilderness," with its unmistakable tone of moral judgment, has changed by the end of the poem, which moves from its matter-of-fact beginnings to a melancholic conclusion. By the final stanza the speaker has revised their assessment of the human artifact: rather than the natural world, it is "the jar [that] was gray and bare." If the jar facilitates representation by serving as a focal point, it is also clear by the end of the poem that this vision of cultural production comes at the cost of biological reproduction, with the sterility of the human artifact shown to be at odds with the world of living things, the "giving" world of birds and bushes that constitutes the background fecundity of nature, a force pushing back against the lifeless objects of industrial modernity.

Conclusions

In the Anthropocene, wilderness does not exist. At best, it is a legal fiction. By the time the Wilderness Act was voted into law in 1964 with the intention of protecting those vestiges of wild nature in the United States and its territories "untrammeled" by humanity, no such spaces could truly be said to remain on earth. By the 1960s, after centuries of industrial fossil fuel use and decades of nuclear testing involving hundreds of warheads, the signatures of the Anthropocene—our carbon footprints, the traces of our radioactive waste, particles of plastics and chemical pesticides—were already ubiquitous in even the most remote and trackless regions where no literal footprints might be found. By the time Hillary and Norgay set foot on the summit of Everest in 1953, our ecological footprints were already there. In the era of the Anthropocene, we are learning that we *are* even where we *are not*, and within the regime of this new logic familiar binaries like nature and culture, civilization and wilderness lose their supposed autonomy, giving rise to new and murky hybrids.

Once upon a time, or so the story goes, wilderness in the sense of untrammeled nature *did* exist; at least until 5:29 a.m. on July 16, 1945. It was then that the first detonation of a nuclear weapon, code-named Trinity, was carried out at the newly created White Sands Proving Ground in the deserts of central New Mexico, part of what is now the largest property owned by the US military. While climate change has taken center stage in contemporary environmental discourse, it is clear that with the splitting of the atom and the detonation of the first atomic bomb something profound changed in the relationship between humans and the biosphere on both a symbolic level, with the usurpation of god-like powers over life and death, and on the physical level, with the release of radioactive isotopes. W. Robert Oppenheimer recalled his thoughts during the test in a 1965 interview for the documentary *The Decision to Drop the Bomb*. He "remembered the line from the Hindu scripture, the *Bhagavad-Gita*. . . . 'Now I am become Death, the destroyer of worlds.'"

Radioactive fallout and the threat of nuclear war is, however, only one index of the Anthropocene. In the century and a half between Thoreau's writing and the present day the human population has grown by approximately six billion; world energy consumption has increased from less than 40 exajoules per year to more than 400; we have detonated approximately 2,000 nuclear devices (the vast majority by the United States and the Soviet Union). We live on the steep slopes of what climatologist Jerry Mahlman described as the "hockey stick curves" of the Great Acceleration, and all of the numbers continue to rise at nosebleed-inducing speed.

Andreas Malm argues that the dissolution of binaries such as nature and culture or wilderness and civilization constitutes one of the hallmarks of our ongoing postmodernity. Discussing Frederic Jameson's definition of the postmodern as involving the primacy of "categories of space" over "categories of time," Malm calls attention to how something fundamental has changed between "us" and "them"—between a postmodern "we" and a modern "they"—that hinges on what he describes as "the eradication of nature":

> In the modern era, vast fields of old nature remained spread out between the bustling new centres of factory and market. A short drive would take the modernist back to the rural village where she was born. . . . It was this contrast that made the modernists *feel* the movement of time—from the old to the new, towards the future—that so fundamentally structured their culture. Now the foil is gone. (2)

Writing not on the distinction between modernism and postmodernism but between Holocene and Anthropocene,

McKibben makes a similar point: "Beginning with the invisible releases of radiation, and then the toxic pollutants like DDT, and then the by-products of large-scale industrialization like acid rain . . . we began to alter even the places where we were not" (xix). Climate change, McKibben goes on, "represents the largest imaginable such alteration: by changing the very temperature of the planet, we inexorably affect its flora, its fauna, its rainfall and evaporation, the decomposition of its soils. Every inch of the planet is different; indeed, the physics of climate change mean the most extreme changes are going on at the North and South poles, farthest from human beings" (xix). McKibben calls this transformation "the end of nature"; for us, the end of the wilderness unexpectedly might mark the end of modernism.

There is nothing particularly modernist about the desire to preserve beautiful places from the pressures of industrialization, just as a desire to strip-mine a mountainside is not an inevitable mark of the avant-garde, and yet we face our current ecological crisis in a world where protected lands, let alone ecosystems substantively undisturbed by human activity, are mere fragments shored against our ruins, to borrow from the closing lines of T. S. Eliot's *The Waste Land*. Protectedplanet.net, a site managed by the UN Environment World Conservation Monitoring Center, reports that approximately 15 percent of the planet's land area and 8 percent of its marine area were protected as of 2015. According to E. O. Wilson and the Half-Earth Project, however, these fragments are not enough:

> The formula widely agreed upon by conservation scientists is to keep half the land and half the sea of the planet as wild and protected from human intervention or activity as possible. This conservation goal did not come out of the blue. Its conception, called the Half-Earth Project, is an initiative led by a group of biodiversity and conservation experts. (Wilson n.p.)

But even if the vision of the Half-Earth Project were to be realized, the half of earth that fell under the protection of conservation would not be a wilderness in the early twentieth-century sense of the word. It would be something more like a "rambunctious garden," to borrow the title of Emma Marris's 2011 book, a natural resource whose status as "wilderness" would have to be carefully curated as a resource for human flourishing: not a "restoration ecology" but an "intervention ecology," in the terms of Rickard J. Hobbs, Eric S. Higgs, and Carol Hall (qtd. in Heise 2016, 11). Nor would it partake of Arne Naess's "deep ecology," with its insistence that "intervention in nature should be guided primarily by the need to preserve biotic integrity rather than the needs of humans" (Guha 2). Rather, as Heise argues, "moving beyond established decline narratives to a new, future-oriented conceptualization of environmentalism" will entail a regrounding of environmentalist politics in something other than "the idea of minimal human presence and impact" (2016: 10–11). What needs to be rethought, in a rethinking of the concept of wilderness, is our sense of what human needs really are and what human flourishing really means, and the extent to which those concerns are bound to the flourishing of the earthly biotic community. For once nature is bounded for our benefit, it is no longer a nature distinct from human culture. As we've learned, that distinction was never as clear in reality as it was insisted upon in theory; and all life, human included, might be better off without it.

5

The Climate of Modernism

Everyone knows it shouldn't be this hot.
—ZADIE SMITH

Scientifically speaking, the flesh was melted off the world.
—VIRGINIA WOOLF

Our final chapter is dedicated to exploring some of the ways that modernism represents weather and climate. Here, however, we no longer confine our discussion to high modernism, but instead wholeheartedly adopt an expansive and expanding understanding of what might be read as modernist. In an obvious sense, modernism undeniably persists in many of the cultural movements that have since declared themselves its inheritors—like ecomodernism—or its usurpers—like postmodernism. But the persistence of modernism is, as we intend to show in this final chapter, a matter of more than just nominalism. As Timothy Wienstzen argues, echoing critics like Susan Stanford Freidman, "To be modern is to exist within a system of relationships that is both spatially extensive (i.e. global) and which collapses incommensurate scales of human and geological time (i.e. planetary)" (Wienstzen n.p.). The new modernist studies is "no longer animated," according to Aarthi Vadde, "by strict formal markers or periodized boundaries," but rather by a more loosely defined "attitude or temperament, a system of literary world-making, or a set of relationships with modernity" (Vadde n.p.). This is what Paul Saint-Amour champions as a weak theory of modernism, whose very weakness has the paradoxical effect of strengthening the field; the result is a "more conjectural, more conjunctural" understanding of modernism (41). Among other things, this means that we might read for an atmosphere of modernism or, as Jesse Oak Taylor calls it, a climatic modernism.

In what follows, we utilize a weak theory of modernism in the interest of highlighting the fraught conjunction between modernism and environmentalism. Modernist forms have influenced and been influenced by the environmentalist turn of the 1970s, and they continue to inform environmental thinking in the twenty-first century. As we will argue, the naming of a new geological epoch in the wake of anthropogenic global warming, the Anthropocene, has led to a wholesale revaluation of modernity that, in many cases, has meant a renewal of modernist modes, styles, and techniques. At the origins of modernism sits the history of the sciences of meteorology and climatology; we recount that history here, asserting its importance alongside some of the more standard stories about modernism's origins, such as the standardization of time and the colonization of space. From these emergent disciplines and discourses the modernists seized on abstract forms like the grid and the spiral. These forms signified powerfully in the high-modernist period and beyond it; they gave the self-styled Land Artists of the 1970s in the United States a template for their outdoor modernist monuments, into whose making and meaning they incorporated the weather and the climate.

We pursue suggestive connections between high-modernist texts and twenty-first-century texts through their relationship to the weather and climate. Danish artist Olafur Eliasson cites Edvard Munch's *The Scream*, which we examined in our Introduction as an example of modernism's attention to its environment, as a key inspiration for the artificial red sun he built for his 2003 installation at the Tate Modern, *The Weather Project*. The London heat wave that oppressed Virginia Woolf's characters in *Mrs. Dalloway* in 1923 prefigures another London heat wave in 2010, as represented in Zadie Smith's *NW*. And in Kate Tempest's epic poem *Let Them Eat Chaos* (2016), a dramatic thunderstorm, ambiguously a harbinger of catastrophic global warming, briefly unites a group of lonely Londoners. The texts we examine in this chapter describe a modernist legacy of thinking about and representing the environment over more than a century; connecting them here contributes to a newly conjunctural understanding of modernist studies.

The Weather Project

The Tate Modern's website introduces Olafur Eliasson's 2003 art installation *The Weather Project*, an image of which we chose for the cover of this volume, with an observation made by the English man of letters Samuel Johnson in 1758: "It is commonly observed, that when two Englishmen meet, their first talk is of the weather; they are in a haste to tell each other, what each must already know, that it is hot or cold, bright or cloudy, windy or calm" (qtd. in "About the Installation" n.p.). Talking about the weather serves a valuable phatic function in language; it offers a way to socialize without saying or doing anything of consequence, a mode of interacting that implies and requires no transacting, or at least serves as a polite prelude to transacting. This is the function of weather talk that Johnson has in mind, since as he points out, both parties in this conversation "already know" what the weather is. As such, talking about the weather is, according to Francis Ferguson, "the most egalitarian topos in the social repertoire" (qtd. in Martin 128). Though phatic conversation about the weather is by definition banal, it was never pointless. In the era of anthropogenic climate change, however, talking about the weather is losing its phatic function; it has become, instead, anxious and politically charged. The weather has changed, and so has the way we talk about it.

For six months in 2003, one of the hottest years on record in the UK, Eliasson's *The Weather Project* occupied the Turbine Hall in the Tate Modern Museum. The installation created an uncanny sense of outdoor weather indoors using a giant orange "sun" made of monofrequency lamps, and humidifiers that pumped out a fine mist made of sugar and water. The ceiling was covered with a mirror that traversed its 500-foot length and 75-foot width, effectively doubling the hall's perceived height. Eliasson, whose work frequently addresses the theme of climate change, wrote in the *Guardian* in 2018 that the central idea for *The Weather Project* was "the idea of creating a sun. . . . I was thinking of the way the sun sets against the sea, or the reflections in Edvard Munch's paintings" (Eliasson n.p.). The connection Eliasson makes between *The Weather Project* and Munch's red skies in *The Scream* (1893) and *Anxiety* (1894), or his brilliant white sun in *The Sun* (1909), reveals a mutual interest in the dramatic light effects of sunset and the kinds of feelings evoked by them. The scream of nature that inspired *The Scream*, which, as we saw in our Introduction, may or may not have been a representation of the atmospheric effects of the catastrophic eruption of the Krakatoa volcano, evoked a dreadful anxiety in Munch. *The Weather Project* traffics in the same ambiguity and the same dread: Does this big red sun mark some catastrophic weather event? Is it linked somehow to the record-breaking heat outside? Should we, experiencing it, feel dread?

Eliasson began with the idea of "playing" with the weather, and he ended up "stripping away from this idea until all I had left was the idea of creating a sun" (Eliasson n.p.). The artistic genesis of *The Weather Project* was a surrender of weather to climate. It was a simulation of the experience of climate change, in which anxious uncertainty about whether any given weather event constitutes an experience of climate change is itself one of the defining experiences of climate change. Under normal circumstances, as Tobias Boes and Kate Marshall observe, climate change "can never be experienced—only local changes in weather patterns can.... Climate change can instead only be explained (rather than known) through the statistical methods of the natural sciences" (61). Or as Theodore Martin puts it in his *Contemporary Drift: Genre, Historicism, and the Problem of the Present*, "Weather is anecdotal, and climate is statistical; there is no middle ground between the two" (129). Eliasson had in effect taken up the oft-repeated warning not to confuse weather and climate and understood it as a challenge for art: to represent climate in a way that can be directly felt and experienced. He created an indoor simulation of what climate change might feel like, thereby avoiding both the uncertainty of the anecdote and the sterility of the statistic.

In color photographs of *The Weather Project*, one is struck by the intense redness of the artificial sun's glow; it suggests the end of something, something more than just the day—maybe the end of days. Time was stopped in the Turbine Hall; the sun never moved. For the six months that *The Weather Project* was displayed, it was always—maybe—apocalypse o'clock. But that anxious mood did not put off visitors. Instead they frequently lay down on the floor and gazed up at their reflections in the mirrors above them, enjoying the immersive experience, a phenomenon which added to the apocalyptic effect a suggestion of rapture. In 2003, gazing up at themselves in the mirrored ceiling, visitors to Turbine Hall saw, instead of the heavens, themselves bathed in the light of the end: an allegory, and perhaps a rather heavy-handed one, of the Anthropocene, enacted by both artist and audience. If *The Weather Project* offers any kind of a spur to environmentalist action, however, it is not primarily extended to the visitors we observe taking selfies in images of the installation. We see them enjoying themselves in an environment that seems to spell doom; they are as much a part of the installation's apparatus as the artificial sun and the mirror. They have been scripted, or conscripted, into playing the role of the Anthropos in Anthropocene. We observe their complacency in the photographs and ask ourselves how we might act otherwise.

Anthropocene Modernism

The stuck time of *The Weather Project* reminds us that our conception of time and the weather are intimately related. In the 1930s, while Walter Benjamin was roaming Paris and taking notes for his *Arcades Project*, he jotted down a reminder to himself to meditate on "the double meaning of the term *temps* in French" (106). The French word *temps* means both weather and time, and may be a linguistic vestige of the way, before clocks and calendars, humans gauged the passage of time—beyond the unit of the day— by the length and repetition of seasonal weather. Because time was measured by the changing seasons, weather was the index of time's passing—*temps* is of course related to *tempo*, to rhythm. For Benjamin, the "working of the weather on humans" was a "most intimate and mysterious affair," and he was affronted by the fact that, in modern times, it "should have become the theme of their emptiest chatter" (102). But what happens when the weather patterns change and the seasons no longer arrive and depart with predictable regularity; when the sun never sets; when, to filter Hamlet's famous line through Benjamin, the *temps* are "out of joint"? For the kinds of terrestrial life that depend on environmental cues for things like migration and breeding, climate change poses a significant threat. "The timing of key life events (phenology) is a critical part of nearly every important ecological relationship," writes Madeleine Rubenstein of the US Geological Survey. "Climate change therefore has the potential to desynchronize . . . critical relationships" (Rubenstein n.p.). Scientists studying climate change refer to growing "phenological 'mismatches'"—such as birds migrating thousands of miles only to have missed a crucial hatch of insects, which now occurs weeks earlier in a warming arctic (Visser and Gienapp 879). Climate change disrupts and transforms the time of life on earth.

How, then, might climate change alter the time of humanity? In 2003, when *The Weather Project* was on display, mainstream culture had fairly recently come to new terms with the issue of anthropogenic global warming. Those new terms were set down in an audacious act of naming that was also an act of periodizing; it had, and continues to have, profound ramifications for our understanding of modernity and modernism. In a brief paper in the May 2000 edition of the *International Geosphere-Biosphere Programme Newsletter*, Paul J. Crutzen and Eugene F. Stoermer proposed that the earth had entered a new geological epoch they called the Anthropocene: an epoch driven by human interventions in the earth's biosphere, principally through the burning of hydrocarbons as energy fuels, which release by-product carbon dioxide into the atmosphere. This process results in warming air, melting icecaps, rising oceans, and extreme weather events. Before Crutzen and Stoermer coined the term "Anthropocene," the geological consensus was that we were living in the Holocene epoch: the short (in geological terms) 11,000 year period—encompassing all of historical humanity since the invention of writing, plus another 5,000 or so years—which was characterized by unusual climate stability compared to other, much more volatile epochs. With the Anthropocene, Crutzen and Stoermer crystallized, in a word, the deep paradox of the present; the moment it was discovered that humanity had the power to transform the entire planet, it was also revealed that such transformation threatened the environmental foundations of human flourishing.

Soon after their article appeared, Crutzen and Stoermer's term became shorthand for a metanarrative about the folly, precarity, and tragedy of human civilization. The Anthropocene was neither the first nor the only proposal for renaming the present geological epoch in which humans became a driving geological force. But the Anthropocene, both as a term and as a concept, caught on like no other in the discourses of environmentalism. It edged out several other contenders, among them Michael Soulé's "Catastrophozoic," Michael Samways's "Homogenocene," and Daniel Pauly's "Myxocene," from the Greek "myxos" meaning "slime" (Kolbert

107). These and other proposed renamings suggest the range of debates raging around the concept. From the humanities, Donna Haraway proposed both the Chthulucene, inspired by the hybrid monsters in the fiction of H. P. Lovecraft, and the Plantationocene, which takes the scene of imperial labor relations (slavery) and resource extraction as its starting point (162). Jason Moore insists that the Anthropocene is no more than a polite euphemism for what is better understood as the *Capitalocene*, wherein capitalism, not humanity, is the primary agent in anthropogenic global warming.

Other critics, like Kathryn Yusoff in *A Billion Black Anthropocenes or None*, argue that the Anthropocene concept "erases histories of racism that were incubated through the regulatory structure of geologic relations" (Preface, n.p.). In his *Slow Violence: The Environmentalism of the Poor*, Rob Nixon argues that the Anthropocene suggests, in its evocation of a general humanity or anthropos, that all humans are equally responsible for global warming—a false premise that willfully obscures the gross structural inequalities between those humans who burn the greatest amounts of fossil fuels, and those who suffer the most and the soonest from the climatological consequences. In the introduction to their edited volume *Postcolonial Ecologies: Literatures of the Environment*, Elizabeth DeLoughrey and George B. Handley cite statistics gathered by the UN's Global Humanitarian Forum of deaths caused by climate disruption: "300,000 deaths a year due to increased drought, flooding, and other environmental consequences," of which "ninety-eight percent" are "occurring in postcolonial nations" (26). For them, the Anthropocene concept has "made it possible for countless individual perpetrators of environmental wrong to hide their actions in the midst of the complexity and collectivity of global processes and thus escape accountability" (26). In contrast to these critiques of the Anthropocene, Dipesh Chakrabarty argues in "The Climate of History: Four Theses" that the term is useful because, even when it does hide structural inequality, it also marks the necessity for a unified, global approach to reducing carbon emissions and to providing support for those most immediately affected by global warming. Even if not all humans are responsible for causing global warming, all humans are responsible for curtailing it (or not), and adapting to it (or not); and to the extent that an inclusively conceived notion of humanity can also justly redistribute responsibilities and entitlements, such a traditional humanist conception might finally fulfill its long-disappointed promise, in the shadow of the threat of species extinction.

The Anthropocene concept has at least two distinct consequences for historiography. The first is a new division between the time before humans began burning fossils fuels for energy on a large scale, and the time since then. This raises some difficult questions for students and scholars of modernism specifically: as cultural critics, how does the fact that the modernist period occurs within the Anthropocene change the way we interpret modernism? What should we make of the fact—which we discussed in great detail in Chapter 1—that the "general energizing" that characterizes the modernist period was one of the great driving forces of global warming in the twentieth century? The second consequence concerns a new historical division between the time before human beings were fully *aware* that their burning of fossil fuels was the most significant driver of the fastest warming trend in global atmospheric temperatures in millions of years, and the time after that. And that historical moment must be dated somewhere between when Crutzen and Stoermer coined the "Anthropocene" in 2000 and when it reached media saturation over the next decade. This consequence directly concerns cultural historians and theorists of the twenty-first century; it marks a new kind of human consciousness about our relationship with the natural world as well as our own vulnerability as a species.

If humanity entered a new geological epoch when it fired up the first steam engine, then it entered a new cultural moment when it came to understand the calamitous environmental consequences of its fossil fuel use. The *cultural* era of the Anthropocene, to put it simply, bears a belated relationship to the *geological* epoch of the Anthropocene. Mark McGurl has suggested a name for the cultural era of the Anthropocene: the exomodern, which "positions itself strategically outside of rather than after the modern or postmodern, displacing postmodernism's notorious pillaging of past historical styles by trying to imagine what lies beyond or alongside style" (381). While suggestive, it is nevertheless telling that the exomodern, like the postmodern, should be so unshakably beholden to the modern for its definition, even or especially as it attempts to enact a break from it. Nevertheless, the naming of the Anthropocene caused the humanities to reevaluate their periodizing schemas such that modernity and modernism came under a new kind of scrutiny, providing another, and for a time separate, rationale for expanding the definition of what counts as modernism. Though postmodernism had already lost much of its currency as a periodizing schema, the Anthropocene concept helped demote it to a subcategory of modernism as opposed to a wholly new cultural paradigm. At about the same time, the new modernist studies expanded the boundaries of the kinds of cultural artifacts and works of art that could be considered modernist. And ecocriticism propounded new methods for performing environmentalist readings of texts and artworks that appeared uninterested in environmentalism or even violently opposed to it. These new methods opened up high modernism—for so long considered simply anti-environmentalist—to ecocritical analysis, and opened up late-, post-, and exo-modernist cultural artifacts to investigation within a newly broadened definition of modernist studies.

Atmospheric Science

The narrative of the Anthropocene is in part dependent upon the discoveries of the atmospheric sciences of meteorology and climatology that have made it possible to identify the phenomenon of global warming through data gathering and system modeling. Their disciplinary histories, as we will see, were roughly simultaneous with other key developments of modernity that are well rehearsed within literary and cultural studies, like the International Meridian Conference of 1884 that divided the world into twenty-four-hour time zones and, in the same year, the Berlin Conference where the European powers mapped, divided, and claimed the entire territory of continental Africa as their imperial property. But it is not often in modernist studies that the disciplinary histories of climatology and meteorology are taken up by critics to help think through cultural texts. With the rise of ecocriticism, however, the significance of these sciences to culture, as much as physics, biology, and mechanical engineering, is becoming clearer.

Meteorology was one of the first sciences to declare itself as fundamentally "planetary," and therefore deeply imbricated with the schemes of global time and imperial territory laid out in 1884 as well as with incipient notions of ecology. For meteorology to work as science, it needed a global network of scientists making observations and communicating with one another to build an understanding of the global climate system. In its early days, the Meteorological Society of London counted as one of its members the cultural critic John Ruskin. In the published "Transactions of the Meteorological Society of 1839," Ruskin contributed a piece called "Remarks on the Present State of Meteorological Science," in which he stressed the necessarily global scale and reach of a science that was still in its infancy. "There is one point, it must now be observed, in which the science of meteorology differs from all others" (209). It is that meteorology needs a global network:

> A Galileo, or a Newton, by the unassisted workings of his solitary mind, may discover the secrets of the heavens, and form a new system of astronomy ... but the meteorologist is impotent if alone; his observations are useless; for they are made upon a point, while the speculations to be derived from them must be on space. . . . The Meteorological Society, therefore, has been formed, not for a city, nor for a kingdom, but for the world. (209–10)

Meteorology would need to build itself into a "vast machine," to make its contributions to scientific knowledge, a machine that could "know, at any given instant, the state of the atmosphere on every point of its surface" (Ruskin 210). It demanded a mastery of time and space that corresponded with the institution of Greenwich Mean Time, and with the imperial mapping of the colonial territories. It was a cosmopolitan enterprise underwritten in part by imperial ideology. Proof of this point can be seen in Ruskin's lecture, which wantonly conflates knowledge and power. With international cooperation, made possible by the telegraph and by standardized nomenclatures, units, and measures, meteorology would be a "multitudinous power ... capable of solving the most deeply hidden problems of Nature" (210).

The practical application of theoretical meteorology took form in 1859 when Robert Fitzroy first used the term "forecasting" to rationalize weather predictions made by meteorologists. Fitzroy chose his term deliberately, according to Katharine Anderson in *Predicting the Weather: Victorians and the Science of Meteorology*, in order to distinguish it from "the distasteful connotations of 'prophecy' or 'prognostications,'" which he considered unscientific and unreliable (180). Fitzroy's outline for implementing what he called "storm warnings" was published the same year as Charles Darwin's *The Origin of Species*, and represented almost as much of an affront to the religious worldview—wherein extreme weather events were understood, as they still are today in the world of insurance underwriting, as unpredictable "acts of God"—as Darwin's theory of evolution. Fitzroy's weather forecasts were controversial (not to mention inaccurate), but they launched the quest to predict the weather by scientific means. The forecast evolved over the course of the nineteenth century into a form of imperial control, its accuracy improving in step with an administrative awareness of the power that would come with foreknowledge. In the British Raj meteorologists used their developing science to institute a cyclone warning service and "long-term monsoon forecasts, which gave an estimate of the general character of rainfall for the following four months," and thereby helped predict regional droughts. In India, meteorological research proved that it "could control the anarchy of the weather just as the Raj controlled its chaotic and immense possessions" (Anderson 284).

By the 1880s, the Meteorological Society's efforts were beginning to pay off, though the really big leaps in short- and long-term accuracy would not come until the later twentieth century in the wake of computerization. But by the turn of the nineteenth century, the weather forecast, accurate or not, had become a fixture of everyday life in Europe and the United States. According to Alexandra Harris, in Britain weather "forecasts appeared in the newspapers from 1879 and by the 1920s regional detail was available" (Loc 5879). Weather bulletins were broadcast by radio in the 1920s, and then on television in the 1950s. Since then, as Harris muses in her book *Weatherland: Writers and Artists under English Skies*, the weather forecast has become "a regular feature of our lives, a soothing institution . . . a form of ceremony as we bear witness to the moving isobars and hear this particular day's permutation of the old repeated phrases: rain clearing northwards, fog slow to lift" (Loc 6409– 15). The ritual of the forecast, because it was a ritual, redoubled the feeling of security in knowing what the weather would bring. Its taken-for-grantedness, and even the contempt expressed for it by many, indexed the enormity rather than the minuteness of the change it effected in everyday life.

The weather forecast plays an important role in a number of modernist texts. Robert Musil begins his *The Man Without Qualities* (1930) with a weather report:

A barometric low hung over the Atlantic. It moved eastward toward a high-pressure area over Russia without as yet showing any inclination to bypass this high in a northerly direction. The isotherms and isotheres were functioning as they should. The air temperature was appropriate relative to the annual mean temperature and to the aperiodic monthly fluctuations of the temperature. The rising and setting of the sun, the moon, the phases of the moon, of Venus, of the rings of Saturn, and many other significant phenomena were all in accordance with the forecasts in the astronomical yearbooks. The water vapor in the air was at its maximal state of tension, while the humidity was minimal. In a word that characterizes the facts fairly accurately, even if it is a bit old-fashioned: It was a fine day in August 1913. (3)

Until the colon, it is as though a meteorologist were narrating the novel. What kind of novelistic atmosphere is created by this introductory discourse of atmospherics? The meteorological terminology here appears soaringly dramatic in the way it allows access to a continent-spanning aerial perspective, while at the same time it feels mired in the unpoetic, technical vocabulary of the sciences. The punch line—that all of this meteorological data can be summed up by the folksy banality "it was a fine day"—could mean either that the meteorological is superfluous to straightforward, everyday description, and therefore comical; or that the meteorological language is beautiful, and therefore superior to the economical but uninteresting description that follows. Moreover, the weather forecast, a barometric low and a high-pressure area heading towardcollision, predicts a great storm over Europe; the Great War, as Musil knew, was only a year away from this "fine day in August 1913."

In Joyce's "The Dead," the last story in his short story collection *Dubliners* (1914), the forecast turns poetic. Mary Jane says at the dinner party that she "read in the papers that the snow is general all over Ireland" (240), and the protagonist Gabriel, in the final scene, stares out his hotel window ruminating on his life and riffing on Mary Jane's words:

> Yes, the newspapers were right: snow was general all over Ireland. It was falling on every part of the dark central plain, on the treeless hills, falling softly upon the Bog of Allen and, farther westward, softly falling into the dark mutinous Shannon waves. . . . His soul swooned slowly as he heard the snow falling faintly through the universe and faintly falling, like the descent of their last end, upon all the living and the dead. (250–51)

The weather forecast gives Gabriel a trope through which to imagine the regions of his country, Ireland, as a kind of organic whole, reconstituted from the division through which he previously conceived it by a simple, everyday weather forecast.

In Virginia Woolf's *To the Lighthouse* (1927), it is bad weather (or the threat thereof) that derails James's dreamed-of excursion. "Yes, of course, if it's fine tomorrow" (3), Mrs. Ramsay reassures her son in the novel's famous opening line, before his father crushes the boy's hopes by delivering a weather report: "There wasn't the slightest possible chance that they could go to the lighthouse tomorrow, Mr. Ramsay snapped out irascibly . . . not with the barometer falling and the wind due west" (31–32). For the rationalist Mr. Ramsay, meteorology proves the victory of science over sentiment; for the plot of the novel, the promise of better weather to come finally enables the family, ten years later, to complete the promised voyage at the novel's end. Musil begins a modernist epic with a weather report; Joyce ends his novella about Irish identity with one; and Woolf emplots her novel with a trip deferred ten years by heeding one. These examples demonstrate both the ordinariness of the weather forecast as a daily mass-cultural occurrence and its momentousness as an emergent technology of weather prediction.

Meteorology insisted in its early years that the science required a global effort of data collection and coordination. Climatology, which specialized in meteorology over much longer time spans, found its seminal expression in 1883, when the Austrian meteorologist Julius von Hann published his *Handbook of Climatology*. According to Paul N. Edwards, Hann's book "would remain the standard textbook in theoretical climatology for 50 years" (63). In it Hann defined climate as the "sum total of the meteorological conditions insofar as they affect animal or vegetable life" (qtd. in Edwards 63). He was one of the first to theorize the climate as a total system, as evidenced in the title of one of his later monographs from 1896, *The Earth as a Whole: Its Atmosphere and Hydrosphere*. The global effort toward the construction of meteorological knowledge led, perhaps inevitably, to Hann's construction of a global object for climatology: the climate. In the 1880s, the time of the world, the space of the world, and, finally, the weather of the world were forged into disciplines and regimes that could make them knowable and exploitable, up to and including the future. The table was set for the modernist revolution of cultural conventions and cultural forms.

Quadrats, Grids, and Spirals

A certain version of modernity—the one that coincides with modernism—began with the standardization and universalization of time and space. At the most abstract level, the cultural forms that corresponded to these developments were the grid and the spiral. As Rosalind Krauss argues in a now-classic essay, the grid emerged in the early part of the twentieth century as "a structure that has remained emblematic of the modernist ambition within the visual arts ever since" (50). It emerges from the governmental technologies of the modern imperial system: from the longitudinal division of rationalized time zones; from the surveyed territorial lines that mark the boundaries between the claims of European empires; and from the newly introduced electrical grids supplying the metropoles. The grid was a way of knowing things that actively changed those things; it forced them into conformity with the tool being used to comprehend them. It was the opposite of the organic, its straight regular lines contrasting sharply with the designs of nature. But the modernists embraced it with wildly creative results. The modernist grid, Krauss states flatly, "is what art looks like when it turns its back on nature" (50). "It is not just the sheer number of careers that have been devoted to the exploration of the grid that is impressive," she writes, "but the fact that never could exploration have chosen less fertile ground" (50). Indeed, that very infertility turned fecund in the vision of modernist painters like Piet Mondrian, who started his career painting organic forms like trees and ended it with a series of abstract grid paintings restricted to three primary colors that made his reputation as a kind of arch-modernist. Likewise, the penciled grids of Agnes Martin's canvases demonstrated, by sheer repetition, the power of the grid form to offer unexpected multiplicities and differences within its surface uniformity.

The spiral often served as the grid's antithesis. Like the grid, the spiral carried multiple and often contradictory meanings, but one thing it did reliably was serve its proponents as an alternative to the perceived sterility and standardization of the grid. In his *Spirals: The Whirled Image in Twentieth-Century Literature and Art* (2017), Nico Israel argues that the spiral form was integral to the self-conception of the high modernists; that critics of high modernism have largely failed to comment on the phenomenon; and that critics not only might reevaluate the high modernists through the spiral trope but also might use it "as a new way of thinking about modernism after modernism" (19). One suggestive way of looking at the spiral, in the context of climate and weather, might be as the shape of a tropical storm or a tornado—as the recognizable shape of the powerful and destructive weather events that meteorology was, and still is, learning to predict.

Of course a storm system is only one of the things that the spiral signified for the modernists. The spiral, unlike the grid, is a form inspired by nature; spirals could be observed in air currents and wave motions as well as biological shapes like mollusk shells, among other things. Beautiful mathematical formulae could be derived from these natural phenomena, and those formulae could be made to drive scientific discovery, as in climatology and meteorology, and technological innovation, as in the design of motors, turbines, and other kinds of dynamos. Conversely, the spiral could also figure the second law of thermodynamics, also known as entropy, which guarantees the eventual heat-death of the universe. W. B. Yeats famously used the spiraled figure of the gyre in his 1921 poem "The Second Coming" to invoke the inevitable degeneration of human civilization: "Turning and turning in the widening gyre / The falcon cannot hear the falconer; / Things fall apart; the centre cannot hold; / Mere anarchy is loosed upon the world" (187). More benignly, Yeats used the figure of the gyre in *A Vision* (1925) to imagine the intimate workings of the human mind. Both the Futurists and the Vorticists envisioned the spiral as a kind of energy vortex whose technological analogue was the dynamo. The spiral denoted the furious energy of modern times, an energy that Futurists and Vorticists celebrated, and that was connected in their theories to terrible violence and war.

Grids and spirals continued to fascinate artists after 1945. In the 1970s, as the environmentalist movement was coalescing in the United States, two artists identified with the American land art movement—Walter De Maria and Robert Smithson—inscribed these modernist hieroglyphs into the landscape of the American southwest on a grand scale. Walter De Maria's *The Lightning Field* (1977) is an installation of 400 stainless steel poles arranged in a 1-mile by 1-kilometer rectangular grid in Catron County, New Mexico. The poles are uniformly spaced 250-feet apart, and vary in length from 14 feet to 27 feet. The variation in length accounts for the unevenness of the ground in which they are stuck, so that at their skyward tips, the poles are level with each other, forming what novelist and essayist Geoff Dyer calls a "level plane of invisible flatness." "Given the precision of all the distances involved," Dyer wonders whether "this place was a tribute to the God of *measuring*" (Loc 777–82). But that is Dyer's characteristically wry humor—and a nod back to Krauss—more than it is his verdict on the work. The work's machine-like exactitude produces—counterintuitively perhaps—a profound aesthetic effect on, and aestheticized affect in, the perceiver. Acknowledging the work to be "rigorously atheistic" and "geometrically neutral," he asserts that the experience of De Maria's land art somehow transcends the terms of its making. It "takes the faith and vaulting promise of modernism into the wilderness," where it not only exposes itself to the weather but integrates with it (Loc 832). Unlike the grids of the high modernists like Mondrian, De Maria's grid does not "turn its back on nature," as Krauss argued the modernists did. De Maria himself insisted that "the land is not the setting for the work but a part of the work" (52).

The Lightning Field is not, by definition, transportable; De Maria chose its location with several criteria in mind. "Desirable qualities of the location included flatness, high lightning activity and isolation" (De Maria 52). "High lightning activity" can be misconstrued. Though many officially licensed photographs of *The Lightning Field* depict it in the middle of a spectacular lightning storm, of which there are, statistically speaking, many more than most other places in the world, and for which the stainless steel poles serve as powerful attractors and conductors, the fact is that the vast majority of people who travel to Catron to see the work do not see a lightning storm during their stay. Dyer did not see one, but that did not diminish his experience of *The Lightning Field*. For him it was "not a piece of art to be seen," but "an experience of space that unfolds over time" (Loc 837).

Robert Smithson's *Spiral Jetty* (Figure 9) is perhaps the most well-known artwork to come out of the land art movement. Smithson oversaw the project's construction in 1970—the same year that saw the celebration of the first Earth Day. Situated on the northeastern shore of the Great Salt Lake in Utah, the jetty is a 15-foot-wide, 1,500-foot-long sculpture made of rocks and mud. When the water

FIGURE 9 Spiral Jetty, *Robert Smithson.*

level is just right, the jetty resembles a primitive footpath leading from the shore in a straight line out into the shallows of the lake before curving left and coiling in on itself. Viewed from the air, according to Israel, it "resembles a giant stuck drain" (165).

If *The Lightning Field* used the weather as part of its compositional materials, *Spiral Jetty* similarly used the climate or, more properly, climate change. Smithson knew that the water level on the lake would not remain constant. He knew that the jetty would sometimes hide under the water line, sometimes appear to lead from the shore into the water, and sometimes become landlocked when water levels dropped dramatically. When the structure was built water levels were low, which was convenient for its construction. Three years later the whole structure was under water and mostly invisible from land or air, the result of higher than average snowmelt from the surrounding mountains. Almost thirty years later in 1999, a severe drought in the southwest region evaporated so much water from the lake that its banks contracted, leaving the jetty entirely stranded on shore. It reemerged from its decades-long mineral bath in a "newly resurrected form," which Dyer imagines as covered in "pristine glittering white" salt crystals (Loc 883). But by the time Dyer visited the jetty, "the magical coating of white crystal was largely gone, rubbed off, presumably, by people like us tramping all over it" (Loc 968).

All these transformations through time were the main point of *Spiral Jetty* in particular and the land art movement in general. Smithson's idea was to construct an artwork that would become part of nature, change with it, and eventually succumb to it. Entropy was also for Smithson at the heart of the spiral design chosen for the jetty, much like Yeats's notion of the "widening gyre." *Spiral Jetty* does not defy time or space; it embraces them both, and thus embraces its own mutability. The time evoked by *Spiral Jetty* is beyond the scale of the human. Most of us alive now will not be alive when *Spiral Jetty* subsides into the landscape, when it becomes unrecognizable as a human intervention on it. The counterclockwise curve of its spiral suggests a "rejection of clock time"—to those of us still attuned to analog clocks anyway—"in favor of a notion of time in which extreme past, present, and future interpenetrate" (Israel 168–69). It evokes geological time, or evolutionary time— time measured in millennia and wrought by wind, water, and fire. The spiral itself suggests the indifferent and awesome forces of nature: a tropical cyclone or a tornado, or even the tectonic drift of continents.

Spiral Jetty and *The Lightning Field* are both precursors to Eliasson's *The Weather Project*. Smithson counted on long-term changes in the level of the lake—climate—to transform his work slowly and continually. De Maria counted on low-odds extreme events—weather—to make his work live up to its title. Thirty years later, Eliasson constructed, in the turbine hall of a decommissioned power plant, an artificial weather event whose proximate cause could be inferred to be climate change, and whose ultimate cause, like the construction itself, was human. These installation artists drew inspiration from the most abstract of modernist forms to make the most concrete of statements about the climate of modernism.

Atmospheric Readings

Unlike the preceding examples of modernist land art, narrative fiction is often not particularly good at representing climate change, or even just normal weather. "It was a dark and stormy night," the opening line of Edward Bulwer-Lytton's 1830 novel *Paul Clifford*, has become, according to Kathryn Schulz, "by broad consensus, the worst sentence in the history of English literature" (105). In fact novelists have often enough evinced open contempt for the weather, denying its importance to the kinds of stories they were telling. In 1892, Mark Twain announced in his novel *The American Claimant* that "no weather will be found in this book" in the interest of avoiding narrative "delays on account of the weather" (qtd. in Schulz 105). Twain implies that as far as fiction is concerned the weather is nothing but decorative setting, entirely superfluous to the action of the story, which in realist fiction chiefly involves individuals vying with each other for position in the social world. The dignity of highbrow literature was above the use of the pathetic fallacy, Bulwer-Lytton's unpardonable offense.

There are exceptions to this general rule about fiction and weather, and those exceptions are proliferating in the era of accelerating global warming, as we will see in the final section of this chapter. But for the moment we turn to a different set of literary texts, in order to ask how a literary critic can draw out the ecological implications of weather and climate in texts where they seem to remain in the background as a passive, stable setting. In this way we might gain insight into what Lawrence Buell refers to, as we discussed in our Introduction, as a text's environmentality. We therefore take up two interwoven modernist fictions whose plots do not directly concern weather or climate, published eighty-seven years apart. Both Zadie Smith's 2012 novel *NW* and Virginia Woolf's 1925 novel *Mrs. Dalloway* are set in London in the midst of a heat wave. They both qualify as modernist, though in different ways: *Mrs. Dalloway* in the strict sense of high modernism, and *NW* in the loosened sense of what David James and Urmila Seshagiri have called metamodernism, a mode of contemporary fiction that styles its "twenty-first-century literary innovations as explicit engagements with the innovation of early-twentieth-century writing" (87). Both novels make note, without making much, of the unusual weather. In *Mrs. Dalloway* the heat wave is significant enough to make the news cycle. "Since it was a very hot night and the paper boys went by with placards proclaiming in huge red letters that there was a heat wave," the narrator of *Mrs. Dalloway* reports, "wicker chairs were placed on the hotel steps and there, sipping, smoking, detached gentlemen sat" (161). It is significant enough that it becomes a motif in the novel, as Clarissa thinks repeatedly of a line from Shakespeare's *Cymbeline*, "fear no more the heat of the sun," treating it as a kind of memento mori. It appears in the phatic conversation between Ellie Henderson and Richard Dalloway during Clarissa's party, as an obvious marker of the awkward fact that they have nothing, really, to say to one another:

> "Well, Ellie, and how's the world treating you?" he said in his genial way, and Ellie Henderson, getting nervous and flushing and feeling that it was extraordinarily nice of him to come and talk to her, said that many people really felt the heat more than the cold.
> "Yes, they do," said Richard Dalloway. "Yes."
> But what more did one say? (169–70)

If this had been set in contemporary times, no doubt we would have been treated to a lively discussion between Ellie and Richard about rising sea levels and record-setting heat waves. But in the universe of *Mrs. Dalloway*, Londoners experience a heat wave as a statistical anomaly; as news media; as a pleasure or as a discomfort;

as, in the Shakespeare line, a momentary death anxiety; or as empty small talk. There is, however, in all this chatter a background note of existential terror that becomes unbearably amplified in Septimus Smith's broken mind: "Why could he see through bodies, see into the future, when dogs will become men? It was the heat wave presumably, operating on a brain made sensitive by eons of evolution. Scientifically speaking, the flesh was melted off the world" (68). Septimus's thoughts are drawn from his traumatic experience of mass death in the Great War. They are aggravated by the heat, and then inspired by it, which conjures his apocalyptic vision of flesh "melted off the world": an uncanny echo of the apocalyptic visions conjured by global warming at the other end of the twentieth century.

That background note of weather-related terror in Mrs. Dalloway is brought to the foreground in Smith's NW, where a London heat wave in April 2010 is represented as a source of barely suppressed, generalizable existential dread. "Everyone knows it shouldn't be this hot," thinks Leah Hanwell to herself as she lounges in a hammock in the garden of her basement flat in a council housing estate in Northwest London, flipping through a magazine and listening to the radio (1). Leah's lounging may be less a decision to take the day off than an effect of the ominous and oppressive heat she is simultaneously experiencing and thinking about—the lugubrious somnolence of simply being too hot to do anything but lie around. Most of us have had the same thought at one time or another, and most of us do exactly what fictional Leah Hanwell does as soon as she has it: nothing. On the surface, most of us know exactly what Leah means by "everyone knows it shouldn't be this hot." She means that this heat wave is not a statistical anomaly, as it was in Mrs. Dalloway; that something is different, and wrong, about the weather; and that this wrongness is intuited not by her alone but, she imagines, by everyone—even if no one, including Leah, is talking about it.

Even thinking about it is fraught. Just after thinking "everyone knows it shouldn't be this hot," Leah's mind begins listing some circumstantial evidence for global warming to support her initial intuition: "Shriveled blossom and bitter little apples. Birds singing the wrong tunes in the wrong trees too early in the year" (1). But that catalog of clues is jarringly interrupted by someone shouting, "Don't you bloody start!" as if merely thinking about the phenological evidence for global warming were enough to conjure forth an angry censor. On the page the source of this outburst is unclear—deliberately unclear, a narrative technique pioneered in high-modernist fiction. A few phrases later it is revealed to be Leah's upstairs neighbor shouting into her Bluetooth headset at someone else, but the shock and uncertainty of the interruption, the frustration of our need to know where it came from generated in the gap between its occurrence on the page and our understanding of its place in the narrative, force the reader to wonder: Who has shouted? Is the shout perhaps part of Leah's thoughts, a remembered conversation in which someone is talking about global warming and someone else is refusing to listen? Or, even once we've understood that they are part of someone else's cell phone conversation, isn't it still possible that Leah hears them and feels them as if they were an angry response to her thoughts about global warming, just as we readers did for a moment?

What is in any case unambiguous is that "don't you bloody start!" functions *textually* through its ambiguity as a rejoinder to the initial thought, "Everybody knows," such that, even though the words turn out to be unrelated to Leah's thought about global warming, both Leah and the reader are made to react to them initially as if they were. This is one of the semantically productive effects of modernist ambiguity and difficulty. It is also a marker of the way conversations about global warming—even the one we all occasionally have in our own heads—meet with a series of subjective and intersubjective impasses: emotional trauma, intellectual stupefaction, political conflict. The anger and the threat in "don't you bloody start" embody what Paul Krugman, referring specifically to climate change denialism in a recent *New York Times* editorial, called "the special rage of those who knowingly act in bad faith." And that rage works, in *NW*, to put an end to Leah's thinking about climate change.

What Leah Hanwell thinks that everyone already knows is every day being confirmed not only by professional phenological observation but also by computer modeling. How do scientists know that megastorms and heat waves are caused by anthropogenic global warming? In the subfield of climatology known as "event attribution," according to Andreas Malm in *The Progress of This Storm: Nature and Society in a Warming World* (2018), "Simulation of recent storms is contrasted to models of what the weather would have been like in the absence of human influence. That is how the historical imprint is detected" (30–31). The speculative fictions generated by the computers are "now confirming the common intuition"—like the speculative fiction of Leah Hanwell's stream of consciousness—"that all of this extreme weather would not have happened without" human causation. "The experience is becoming well-nigh universal," Malm goes on, "a majority of the human population has been exposed to abnormally warm weather over the past decade" (4). Whether "everyone knows" or not, everyone "has been exposed" (4). In the words of the editors of *N+1*, words that echo and amplify Leah's: "No one can plausibly claim ignorance. You either know and know, or you know and deny, or you don't even know you know, but have absorbed the knowledge through subtler means, whether collective anxiety or just something in the air" (n.p.).

In other words, global warming is in the air, literally and figuratively. Kate Tempest's crossover epic poem and hip-hop album *Let Them Eat Chaos* tells the story of seven struggling Londoners, unknown to one another, who are awoken at 4:18 one morning by a window-rattling peal of thunder. A large storm—not a megastorm, not even an obviously exceptional or especially mediagenic storm—whips through the city and unifies, for a moment, the otherwise isolated and isolating narratives of each character. Simultaneously they step out of their flats into the empty streets to gawk at the damage, but instead encounter each other. Tempest devotes a song near the middle of the album called "Don't Fall In" to the voices of the storm itself: "We came from the four corners," the storm says, "We are the raw waters that course" (39). But this storm is not *the* storm, the one that we all dread and also, perversely, long for, the notional "big one" that will announce the definitive moment when human civilization falls before the advancing deluge of its own making: "We are not the dread storm that will end things / We're just your playful / Gale-force friend / In the end times / Come to remind you / That you're not an island" (43). Tempest's album was released in October 2016, a few months after the Brexit vote; the storm in "Don't Fall In" suggests the logical impasse or short circuit between the global issue of climate change and the isolationist, nationalist populism of the Leave campaign. But it also suggests that global warming might finally bring people together in a common cause.

The political causes and consequences of climate change are a central theme in *Let Them Eat Chaos*. By contrast, after Leah

Hanwell's first thoughts in NW, the topic of climate change is abandoned. Indeed, the episode doesn't appear to ramify in NW beyond this passage. The novel's plot is not *about* global warming, but global warming is all about, around, and in the novel. Global warming is the environment of NW, in the precise sense of one of the earliest, now obsolete, uses of the word "environment" to mean "the action of circumnavigating, encompassing, or surrounding something," or "the state of being encompassed or surrounded." The *Oxford English Dictionary* cites two nineteenth-century uses of "environment" to describe military actions and situations: one from 1843 announces the "strict environment of the city" by a rebel army, and another from 1888 warns of the possible capture of a naval vessel by "a close environment of heavy guns." To the extent that the military use of "environment" threatens physical harm from all sides, global warming can be said to be the environment of NW, even though NW is not, as we said, about global warming.

There are other, less etymological, more theoretical ways to say this. Set in a time and place witnessing the accelerating and intensifying effects of global warming, along with a growing public awareness and certainty about it, NW is, from its very first page, permeated and saturated with global warming, slimed in its viscous goo. And we mean "slimed in its viscous goo" in a technical sense. Ecocritic and philosopher Timothy Morton identifies global warming as what he calls a hyperobject—a thing that is "massively distributed in time and space relative to humans," and that has "a significant impact on human social and psychic space" (2013: 1). Morton goes on to describe five properties that belong to hyperobjects, the first of which is their viscosity, "which means that they 'stick' to beings that are involved with them" (1). Here in Leah's thoughts his description of global warming rings absolutely true: as something whose scale is too vast, too "massively distributed" to be fully comprehended in Leah's stream of consciousness; as something that nevertheless occupies a lot of "social and psychic space" in her stream of consciousness; and finally, as something that, despite not becoming a plot point exactly, nevertheless "sticks" to the dramatic atmosphere evoked throughout NW.

Of course, to speak of the "dramatic atmosphere" of a novel is to speak through a metaphor so worn down by long overuse as to have become a cliché, which is to say that it is rarely if ever noticed that the vehicle of the metaphor of a "dramatic atmosphere" is the weather. Bulwer-Lytton's old gothic saw, "it was a dark and stormy night," becomes "everyone knows it shouldn't be this hot." In *NW* the metaphor of dramatic atmosphere is made freshly aware of itself, re-literalized in Leah's first thoughts about the unseasonable heat. Ecocritic Jesse Oak Taylor is one of the first to theorize what he calls "atmospheric reading," a critical practice whose aim is to draw out the meanings of literary representations of the environment. "One of the consequences of atmospheric reading," for Taylor, "is the doing away with the notion that setting is by definition passive, a mere container in which events take place, while nominally human characters provide narrative action. Instead, settings, atmospheres, and environments can become agents in their own right" (36).

Taylor's atmospheric reading changes the way we understand literary periods because it reinserts them into larger scales of time, granting us a perspective from which we can see changes in cultural forms as parts of larger ecologies. Some modernists were themselves atmospheric thinkers. Virginia Woolf was one of them, and in her 1928 novel *Orlando* she launched a bold experiment in what Taylor calls "climatic modernism," which he defines as "a condition in which modernity refigures our relationship to deep time, making any moment at once immediate and radically dispersed on scales that exceed human memory" (189). The eponymous protagonist of *Orlando* lives a biblical time span through several distinctive historical periods, from the Elizabethan period to the 1920s, fluidly changing sex along the way. Each successive period is sharply defined by climatic variations that must pass unobserved in a single realistic lifetime. *Orlando* allows us to notice them because Orlando lives long enough to pass through successive climatological periods. The novel presents a superhuman perspective on time in which climate change can be perceived—as in Eliasson's *The Weather Project*—as opposed to deduced, calculated, and recorded.

Signs of the Times

Our comparison of *Mrs. Dalloway* and *NW* allows us to see the ecologies of modernity and modernism in both flux and continuity. Like *Mrs. Dalloway*, *NW* is set in London, but in another neighborhood a few miles away from Bloomsbury: a working-class neighborhood as opposed to a well-to-do neighborhood; a neighborhood populated by Irish, Caribbean, South Asian, and African immigrants, not MPs and old monied Anglo-Saxon families. The plot of *Mrs. Dalloway* unfolds on a June day in 1923; *NW*'s over the late spring and summer of 2010. Like *Mrs. Dalloway*, *NW* captures the lived experience of urban street life in those neighborhoods. And Like *Mrs. Dalloway*, *NW* anchors its narrative in the tragic death of a sympathetic young man—Septimus in *Dalloway*, Felix in *NW*—whose story-arc only mediately intersects with the main female protagonists via overheard conversations or the news on TV. Set in very different times and spaces, and focalized through very different characters, the two novels nevertheless attempt to characterize the same concept: the city of London, insofar as "London" can be said to persist as the same thing through the years and from different points of view. This is very much a modernist obsession: the character of the city, or the city as a character.

In the opening pages of *Mrs. Dalloway*, Clarissa is walking along Piccadilly Street when "the sound of an aeroplane bore ominously into the ears of the crowd" and "everyone looked up" (20). The sound of airplanes was relatively rare in London in 1923 and would, moreover, be associated with aerial warfare. But though the plane drops "dead down," it is not diving to bomb the city but to bombard its population with advertisements for commodities. As Paul Saint-Amour writes of this well-studied scene, "Given the military origins and potential of skywriting, one might argue that the airplane's significance in *Mrs. Dalloway* is not exclusively commercial or military but a new alloy of the two . . . placing [the reader] among war survivors in a scene of high-stakes reading" (115). So the moment is fraught: filled with excitement about a technological novelty, and, if only for a split second, with the threat of death from above. Contrast this moment to the opening pages of *NW*, which is set during the eruption of Eyjafjallajökull, a volcanic ice cap in Iceland whose particulate discharge reddened the skies and, for six days in April of 2010, grounded all Northern European air traffic, stranding millions of travelers. Leah Hanwell thinks, "The skies are empty and silent" (55). One could say the silence "bore ominously" into her ears, and the ears of twenty-first-century

Londoners like her. When air traffic resumes, Leah thinks, "The planes are back in the sky. Work is work. Time has ceased being uncanny" (62). This is one measure of the distance traveled in the history of modern urban experience, from *noticing* when you hear an airplane and stopping in your tracks to gaze wonderingly up at it, to noticing, not airplanes, but the *absence* of airplanes, that is, noticing when you no longer hear the sound of airplanes as part of the background dynamo-drone of modern urban life. Instead, one is left, in the uncanny red-skied silence, with a reminder of the vast inhuman scale of geological—volcanic—time, and of the fragility of the things, like airplanes, that make us modern.

The difference between noticing a plane in 1923 and noticing the absence of planes in 2010 is a neat illustration of the difference between modernism and metamodernism. For the moderns, urbanization was an ongoing transformative process. Rural life still persisted; nature was a short distance from the metropolis, pressing against urban encroachment, as powerful and threatening to modernization as modernization was to nature. But by 1991, when Fredric Jameson published *Postmodernism, or, the Cultural Logic of Late Capitalism*, it was hard to find nature amid the grids of urbanization and suburbanization. And this, more than anything else, defined for Jameson the difference between modernism and postmodernism: "Postmodernism is what you have when the modernization process is complete and nature is gone for good" (vii). High modernism saw itself locked in a struggle against nature, a conflict in which both sides appeared more or less equally formidable. Under the condition of postmodernity, nature appears to have been eradicated from daily human existence. But that, it turns out, was a momentary delusion born of human hubris. Once everyone knows about the Anthropocene, nature returns in spectacular fashion. The representation of the eruption of Eyjafjallajökull in *NW* marks this new post-postmodern understanding of the relationship between nature and the modern built environment. It is both metamodernist, insofar as it uses the techniques of modernism to narrate, and exomodernist, insofar as it narrates geological time coming up against the time of modernity. A volcanic eruption that turns the sky red is exactly the kind of weather event that might have made Edvard Munch imagine in 1882 "a vast, endless scream" passing "through nature." It is also exactly the kind of weather event that for Amitav Ghosh would have to be considered too improbable to make good material for a realist novel. As Ghosh writes in his 2016 *The Great Derangement: Climate Change and the Unthinkable*, "The calculus of probability that is deployed within the imaginary world of a novel is not the same as that which obtains outside it; this is why it is commonly said, 'If this were in a novel, no one would believe it'" (23). If Eyjafjallajökull had not really erupted in 2010, it would not have been believable in *NW*. It would not be imagined or imaginable in a standard literary, realist, or literary-realist fiction. What happens in a realist novel must, according to Ghosh, be *more probable* than what happens in real life. If it is not, it will be read as unrealistic. That realist fiction has a lower tolerance for the improbable than reality is the second half of a two-part problem concerning fiction's relationship to climate and weather: first, that talking about the weather is too boring for fiction; and second, that representing extreme weather events is too unrealistic for fiction. Realist fiction only exists, according to these arguments, in a surprisingly narrow, fragile band between the boring and the extreme.

It is not only realist fiction that has difficulty representing climate change, however. The impasse is part of the larger story of Enlightenment thought which, in attempting to construct an ideal human will that operated independently of nature, banished the idea that weather could operate as a determining force on human events. "Bad weather was a scandal to the modern constitution," writes Jonathan Bate in *The Song of the Earth*. "The Enlightenment was one long attempt to repress the weather, to dispel the clouds of unknowing" (Bate 100). That Enlightenment attitude in turn favored a gradualist view of natural history. As Ghosh puts it, "Through much of the era when geology—and also the modern novel—were coming of age, the gradualist (or 'uniformitarian') view held absolute sway and catastrophism was exiled to the margins" (20).

For George Perkins Marsh, one of the founders of ecology in the nineteenth century, nature as a whole existed in a state of near absolute equilibrium or stasis. In *Man and Nature Or, Physical Geography as Modified by Human Action* (1864), he insisted that "nature, left undisturbed, so fashions her territory as to give it almost unchanging permanence of form, outline, and proportion" (29). That "almost" gives Marsh just enough room to accommodate

Darwin's natural selection, which acknowledged change through time in a gradualist paradigm. But "unchanging permanence" was mostly wishful thinking, even as it became one of the founding assumptions of early ecology. As Ghosh puts it, "Nature does certainly jump, if not leap. The geological record bears witness to many fractures in time, some of which led to mass extinctions and the like: it was one such, in the form of the Chicxulub asteroid, that probably killed the dinosaurs" (20).

Many ecologists have since moved away from early ecological notions of equilibrium and balance. The Anthropocene is itself a major challenge to the gradualist model of earth history. Cultural forms like the novel are changing as global warming ushers in a new relationship to weather and climate, both in reality and in the imaginative work of art. The old conventions for the novel must weaken, as we are "confronted suddenly with a new task: that of finding other ways in which to imagine the unthinkable beings and events of this era" (Ghosh 33). There are some precedents for this imaginative shift in the history of the modernist novel, but they tend to fit in subgenres like magical realism rather than in realist literary fiction. Woolf's *Orlando* makes an interesting example. Macondo, the fictional setting of Gabriel García Márquez's *One Hundred Years of Solitude* (1967), is destroyed at the end of the novel by a supernatural hurricane. Citing a more realist example, Ghosh singles out John Steinbeck's *The Grapes of Wrath* (1939) as a modernist experiment—often not credited with modernist experimentalism—that "grapples with climate change *avant la lettre*" by attempting to narrate the experience of the severe drought and dust storms that ravaged the Dustbowl region of the Great Plains in the 1930s, causing massive crop failures, and the mass migration of tens of thousands of people (80). Stylistically, that experiment manifests itself in the way the novel's chapters alternate between a narrative focused on the migration of the Joad family and discrete narratives of other, often unnamed characters. Another example is Zora Neale Hurston's *Their Eyes Were Watching God* (1937), which narrates the 1928 Okeechobee hurricane that claimed 2,500 lives in Florida alone.

In the contemporary moment, a new genre dubbed "cli-fi" or "climate fiction" has emerged to represent—and sometimes it seems, more cynically, to commodify—our fears about climate change and our possible futures within it. Many of these texts are comfortingly framed as science fiction—such as Kim Stanley Robinson's *Science in the Capital* series (2004, 2005, 2007) and Cixin Liu's *The Three-Body Problem* (2010)—or are pitched to young adult audiences, such as Octavia Butler's *Parable of the Sower* (1993), Saci Lloyd's *The Carbon Diaries: 2015* (2009), and Paolo Bacigalupi's *The Water Knife* (2015). Other recent texts disrupt these categories entirely, such as Barbara Kingsolver's *Flight Behavior* (2012), Margaret Atwood's *MaddAddam* trilogy (2003, 2009, 2013), David Mitchell's *The Bone Clocks* (2014), Annie Proulx's *Barkskins* (2016), and Richard Powers's *The Overstory* (2018). As climate change proceeds, and as extreme weather events become more and more frequent and more and more normal, the line between cli-fi and literary fiction is likely to become thinner and thinner.

Meanwhile, writers like Zadie Smith and Kate Tempest undertake the transformation of realist fiction by their recognition of anthropogenic climate change and through their uses of modernist modes, styles, and techniques. By enumerating the similarities between *Mrs. Dalloway*, on the one hand, and *NW* and *Let Them Eat Chaos*, on the other, we mean to suggest that they are all, despite the eighty-seven years between their publications, modernist texts. What distinguishes them is less their form and their methods—stream-of-consciousness narrative technique, formal experimentation—than their conception of their respective environments. For Woolf, the environment is composed of the newest things of modernization: airplanes, limos, buses, streets, clocks, store-bought flowers, and so on. For Smith, the things of modernization are old news; what's new is an ambient cultural and subjective awareness of the mutability of those things, as well as the environmental and human consequences wrought by them. In *Mrs. Dalloway* modernity confidently and spectacularly dominates and domesticates nature, while in *NW*, for a few days at least during the volcanic event, nature spectacularly dominates modernity. *NW* doesn't make much of Leah's environmentalist thought; the novel's plot carries on in a completely unrelated direction. But it doesn't have to make much of its characters' anxious awareness of global warming in order to demonstrate that those characters are different from the characters in *Mrs. Dalloway*, in part simply because they carry that anxious awareness of the changes in their climate: the mark of the Anthropocene.

The age of anthropogenic climate change presents a new challenge to the literary common sense that saw weather as either too banal to be represented or too extreme to be believed. What can be the meaning today of the literary "mistake" of the pathetic fallacy in a time when humanity's actions are, in reality, reflected in climatic conditions like shifting seasonal tempos; sea level rise; and storms, floods, droughts, and fires of increasing intensity and frequency? There is no "innate melodrama left in meteorology," writes Kathryn Schulz, "weather is, instead, at the heart of the great drama of our time" (110). That drama's origins, as we have demonstrated throughout this volume, can be traced in the contours of high-modernist forms, forms that persist and evolve as artists and writers from the late twentieth century to the present struggle to represent the drama of weather and climate in ways that offer new kinds of understanding, resolve, and resolution.

WORKS CITED

Abbey, Edward. *Desert Solitaire: A Season in the Wilderness*. New York: Touchstone, 1968.
"About the Installation." "The Unilever Series: Olafur Eliasson: The Weather Project." *Tate Modern Online*. https://www.tate.org.uk/whats-on/tate-modern/exhibition/unilever-series/unilever-series-olafur-eliasson-weather-project-0. Accessed June 10, 2019.
Adams, Henry. *The Education of Henry Adams: An Autobiography*. New York: Library of America, 2010.
Adorno, Theodor W. and Max Horkheimer. *Dialectic of Enlightenment*. Trans. John Cumming. New York: Verso, 1997.
Agamben, Georgio. *The Open: Man and Animal*. Trans. Kevin Attell. Stanford: Stanford University Press, 2004.
Albert, Dan. *Are We There Yet? The American Automobile Past, Present, and Driverless*. New York: W.W. Norton, 2019.
Anderson, Katharine. *Predicting the Weather: Victorians and the Science of Meteorology*. Chicago: University of Chicago Press, 2005.
Armstrong, Philip. *What Animals Mean in the Fiction of Modernity*. New York: Routledge, 2008.
Armstrong, Tim. *Modernism, Technology, and the Body: A Cultural Study*. Cambridge: Cambridge University Press, 1998.
Asafu-Adjaye, John, Linus Blomqvist, Stewart Brand, Barry Brook, Ruth Defries, Erle Ellis, Christopher Foreman, David Keith, Martin Lewis, Mark Lynas, Ted Nordhaus, Roger Pielke, Jr., Rachel Pritzker, Joyashree Roy, Mark Sagoff, Michael Shellenberger, Robert Stone, and Peter Teague. "An EcoModernist Manifesto." *ecomodernism.org*, 2015. http://www.ecomodernism.org/manifesto. Accessed June 6, 2019).
Auden, W.H. *Collected Poems*. Ed. Edward Mendelson. New York: Vintage, 1991.
Austin, Mary. *The Land of Little Rain*. New York: Penguin, 1997.
Baker, Steve. *The Postmodern Animal*. London: Reaktion Books, 2000.
Barnes, Djuna. *Nightwood*. New York: New Directions Books, 2006.
Batchelor, Ray. *Henry Ford, Mass Production, Modernism, and Design*. Manchester: Manchester University Press, 1994.
Bate, Jonathan. *The Song of the Earth*. London: Picador, 2000.

Bateman, Benjamin. *The Modernist Art of Queer Survival*. Oxford: Oxford University Press, 2017.
Baudelaire, Charles. *The Painter of Modern Life and Other Essays*. Trans. Jonathan Mayne. London: Phaidon Press, 1964.
Baudelaire, Charles. *Paris Spleen*. New York: New Directions, 1970.
Beer, Gillian. *Darwin's Plots: Evolutionary Narrative in Darwin, George Eliot, and Nineteenth-Century Fiction*. Cambridge: Cambridge University Press, 2000.
Benjamin, Walter. *The Arcades Project*. Trans. Howard Eiland and Kevin McLaughlin. Cambridge: Harvard University Press, 1999.
Benjamin, Walter. *Charles Baudelaire*. London: Verso, 1997.
Berger, John. *Why Look at Animals?* New York: Penguin, 2009.
Berman, Jessica. *Modernist Commitments: Ethics, Politics, and Transnational Modernism*. New York: Columbia University Press, 2011.
Berman, Marshall. *All That Is Solid Melts into Air: The Experience of Modernity*. New York: Penguin, 1982.
Besant, Annie. "Vegetarianism in the Light of Theosophy." *International Vegetarian Union*. www.ivu.org/congress/wvc57/souvenir/besant.html. Accessed June 28, 2019.
"The Best of a Bad Situation." By the Editors. *N+1*. 33 (Winter 2019). https://nplusonemag.com/issue-33/the-intellectual-situation/the-best-of-a-bad-situation. Accessed June 1, 2019.
Bilger, Burkhard. "The Eternal Seductive Beauty of Feathers." *The New Yorker*, September 25, 2017: 68–77.
Bird, Isabella. *A Lady's Life in the Rocky Mountains*. New York: J.P. Putnam's and Sons, 1893.
Bishop, Elizabeth. *The Complete Poems, 1927–1979*. New York: Farrar, Strauss, and Giroux, 1983.
Boes, Tobias and Kate Marshall. "Writing the Anthropocene: An Introduction." *Minnesota Review* 83 (2014): 60–72.
Bowen, Elizabeth. *Look at All Those Roses*. London: Jonathan Cape, 1941.
Bradbury, Malcolm. "The Cities of Modernism." In *Modernism 1890–1930*. Ed. Malcom Bradbury and James McFarlane. New York: Penguin, 1976. 96–104.
Bradford, William. *Of Plymouth Plantation: 1620–1627*. New York: Modern Library, 1967.
Brazeau, Robert and Derek Gladwin, eds. *Eco-Joyce: The Environmental Imagination of James Joyce*. Cork: Cork University Press, 2014.
Brecht, Bertolt. *Brecht on Theatre: The Development of an Aesthetic*. Trans. John Willett. New York: Hill and Wang, 1992.
Brief Encounter [Film]. Dir. David Lean. London: Eagle-Lion Distributors, 1945.

Brinkley, Douglas. *The Wilderness Warrior: Theodore Roosevelt and the Crusade for America*. New York: Harper Collins, 2010.
Brooks, David. *Speaking for Nature: How Literary Naturalists from Henry Thoreau to Rachel Carson Have Shaped America*. Boston: Houghton Mifflin, 1980.
Brooks, Peter. *Reading for the Plot: Design and Intention in Narrative*. Cambridge: Harvard University Press, 1992.
Brox, Jane. *Brilliant: The Evolution of Artificial Light*. Boston: Houghton Mifflin Harcourt, 2010.
Buck-Morss, Susan. *Dreamworld and Catastrophe: The Passing of Mass Utopia in East and West*. Cambridge: MIT Press, 2000.
Buell, Frederick. "A Short History of Oil Cultures: Or, the Marriage of Catastrophe and Exuberance." *Journal of American Studies* 46.2 (2012): 273–93.
Buell, Lawrence. *The Future of Environmental Criticism: Environmental Crisis and Literary Imagination*. Malden: Blackwell, 2005.
Buttel, Robert. *Wallace Stevens: The Making of Harmonium*. Princeton: Princeton University Press, 1967.
Carr, Ethan. *Wilderness by Design: Landscape Architecture and the National Park Service*. Lincoln: University of Nebraska Press, 1998.
Cavalieri, Paola. "Consequences of Humanism, or, Advocating What?" In *Species Matters: Humane Advocacy and Cultural Theory*. Ed. Marianne DeKoven and Michael Lundblad. New York: Columbia University Press, 2012. 49–74.
Chakrabarty, Dipesh. "The Climate of History: Four Theses." *Critical Inquiry* 35 (2009): 197–222.
Clarke, Deborah. *Driving Women: Fiction and Automobile Culture in Twentieth-Century America*. Baltimore: The Johns Hopkins University Press, 2007.
Cleary, Mary Kate. "'But Is It Art?' Constantin Brancusi vs. the United States." *Inside/Out*, July 24, 2014. MoMa/PS1 Blog. www.moma.org/explore/inside_out/2014/07/24/but-is-it-art-constantin-brancusi-vs-the-united-states/. Accessed June 28, 2019.
Coates, Peter. *Nature: Western Attitudes since Ancient Times*. Berkeley: University of California Press, 1998.
Coetzee, J.M. *Disgrace*. New York: Penguin, 2000.
Coetzee, J.M. *Elizabeth Costello*. New York: Penguin, 2003.
Coolidge, Calvin. "Address before the Annual Convention of the American Farm Bureau Federation, Chicago, Ill." December 7, 1925. Online by Gerhard Peters and John T. Woolley. The American Presidency Project. www.presidency.ucsb.edu/ws/?pid=480.
Corton, Christine L. *London Fog: The Biography*. Cambridge: Harvard University Press, 2017.

Crawford, Robert. *The Savage and the City in the Work of T.S. Eliot*. Oxford: Clarendon Press, 1987.
Cronon, William. *Nature's Metropolis: Chicago and the Great West*. New York: Norton, 1991.
Danius, Sarah. *The Senses of Modernism: Technology, Perception, and Aesthetics*. Ithaca: Cornell University Press, 2002.
Davis, Mike. *Planet of Slums*. London: Verso, 2006.
Debeir, Jean-Claude, Jean-Paul Deléage, and Daniel Hémery. *In the Servitude of Power: Energy and Civilisation through the Ages*. London: Zed Books, 1991.
DeLoughrey, Elizabeth and George B. Handley. "Introduction: Toward and Aesthetics of the Earth." In *Postcolonial Ecologies: Literatures of the Environment*. Ed. Elizabeth DeLoughrey and George B. Handley. Oxford: Oxford University Press, 2011. 3–42.
DeLuca, Kevin Michael and Anne Teresa Demo. "Imaging Nature: Watkins, Yosemite, and the Birth of Environmentalism." *Critical Studies in Media Communication* 17.3 (2000): 241–60.
Denning, Andrew. *Skiing into Modernity: A Cultural and Environmental History*. Berkeley: University of California Press, 2015.
Derrida, Jacques. *The Animal That Therefore I Am*. Trans. David Willis. Ed. Marie-Louise Mallet. New York: Fordham University Press, 2008.
DeWitt, John. *Cool Cars, High Art: The Rise of Kustom Kulture*. Oxford: University Press of Mississippi, 2002.
Dickens, Charles. *Bleak House*. Hertfordshire: Wordsworth Editions, 1993.
Döblin, Alfred. *Berlin Alexanderplatz*. Trans. Michael Hofmann. New York: New York Review of Books, 2018.
Dos Passos, John. *1919*. New York: Harcourt, 2013.
Doyle, Arthur Conan. *Sherlock Holmes: The Complete Stories*. Hertfordshire: Ware, 1996.
Dreiser, Theodore. *Sister Carrie*. New York: Norton, 2006.
Duffy, Enda. "High-Energy Modernism." In *Moving Modernisms: Motion, Technology, and Modernity*. Ed. David Bradshaw, Laura Marcus, and Rebecca Roach. Oxford: Oxford University Press, 2016. 83–97.
Duffy, Enda. *The Speed Handbook: Velocity, Pleasure, Modernism*. Durham: Duke University Press, 2009.
Dyer, Geoff. *White Sands: Experiences from the Outside World*. New York: Penguin, 2017.
Edwards, Paul N. *A Vast Machine: Computer Models, Climate Data, and the Politics of Global Warming*. Cambridge: MIT Press, 2010.
Eliasson, Olafur. "How We Made Olafur Eliasson's The Weather Project." *The Guardian*. October 2, 2018. https://www.theguardian.com/ar tanddesign/2018/oct/02/how-we-made-olafur-eliasson-the-weather-pr oject. Accessed June 10, 2019.

Eliot, T.S. *T.S. Eliot: The Collected Poems, 1909–1962*. Orlando: Harcourt, 1968.

Ellison, Ralph. *Invisible Man*. New York: Vintage, 1995.

Ellmann, Maud. *Nets of Modernism: Henry James, Virginia Woolf, James Joyce, and Sigmund Freud*. Cambridge: Cambridge University Press, 2010.

Esty, Jed. *A Shrinking Island: Modernism and National Culture in England*. Princeton: Princeton University Press, 2009.

Faulkner, William. *As I Lay Dying*. New York: Vintage, 1990.

Faulkner, William. *Go Down, Moses*. New York: Vintage, 2011.

Fikke, Svein, Jøn Kristjánsson, and Øyvind Nordli. "Screaming Clouds." *Weather* 72 (2017): 115–21.

Fisher, Rudolph. "The City of Refuge." In *The New Negro*. Ed. Alain Locke. New York: Touchstone, 1992.

Foley, Jonathan A., Ruth DeFries, Gregory P. Asner, Carol Barford, Gordon Bonan, Stephen R. Carpenter, F. Stuart Chapin, Michael T. Coe, Gretchen C. Daily, Holly K. Gibbs, Joseph H. Helkowski, Tracey Holloway, Erica A. Howard, Christopher J. Kucharik, Chad Monfreda, Jonathan A. Patz, I. Colin Prentice, Navin Ramankutty, and Peter K. Snyder. "Global Consequences of Land Use." *Science* 309.570 (2005): 570–74.

Ford, Henry. *Ford Ideals: Being A Selection from "Mr. Ford's Page" in The Dearborn Independent*. Dearborn: Dearborn Publishing Company, 1922.

Forster, E.M. *Howards End*. New York: Penguin, 2000.

Forster, E.M. *The Machine Stops and Other Stories*. New York: Deutsch, 1997.

Forster, E.M. *Maurice*. London: Andre Deutsch, 1999.

Foster, Hal. "Prosthetic Gods." *Modernism/modernity* 4.2 (1997): 5–38.

Freud, Sigmund. *Civilization and Its Discontents*. Trans. James Strachey. New York: Norton, 1961.

Friedman, Susan Stanford. *Planetary Modernisms: Provocations on Modernity Across Time*. New York: Columbia University Press, 2015.

Gandhi, Mohandas. *The Story of My Experiments with Truth*. New York: Dover, 1983.

Garrard, Greg. *Ecocriticism*. New York: Routledge, 2004.

Garrard, Greg. "Worlds Without Us: Some Types of Disanthropy." *SubStance* 41.1 (2012): 40–60.

Gartman, David. *From Autos to Architecture: Fordism and Architectural Aesthetics in The Twentieth Century*. New York: Princeton Architectural Press, 2009.

Ghosh, Amitav. *The Great Derangement: Climate Change and the Unthinkable*. Chicago: University of Chicago Press, 2016.

Ghosh, Amitav. "Petrofiction: The Oil Encounter and the Novel." *The New Republic*, March 2, 1992: 29–34.
Gibbons, Luke. "Ghostly Light: Specters of Modernity in James Joyce's and John Huston's The Dead." In *The Blackwell Companion to James Joyce*, Ed. Richard Brown. London: Blackwell, 2008. 360–61.
Glotfelty, Cheryll. *An Ecocriticism Reader: Landmarks in Literary Ecology*. Ed. Cheryll Glotfelty and Harold Fromm. Athens: The University of Georgia Press, 1996. xv–xxxvii.
Guha, Ramachandra. "Radical American Environmentalism and Wilderness Preservation: A Third World Critique." *Environmental Ethics* 11.1 (1989): 71–83.
Hall, Stephanie. "The Life and Times of Boll Weevil." *Folklife Today*, December 11, 2013. Library of Congress Blogs. blogs.loc.gov/folklife/2013/12/the-life-and-times-of-boll-weevil/. Accessed June 28, 2019.
Haraway, Donna. "Anthropocene, Capitalocene, Plantationocene, Chthulucene: Making Kin." *Environmental Humanities* 6 (2015): 159–65.
Haraway, Donna. "Species Matters, Humane Advocacy: In the Promising Grip of Earthly Oxymorons." In *Species Matters: Humane Advocacy and Cultural Theory*. Ed. Marianne DeKoven and Michael Lundblad. New York: Columbia University Press, 2012. 17–26.
Harris, Alexandra. *Weatherland: Writers and Artists under English Skies*. London: Thames and Hudson, 2001.
Harvey, David. *The Condition of Postmodernity: An Inquiry into the Origins of Cultural Change*. Cambridge: Blackwell, 1989.
Heck, Christian and Rémy Cordonnier. *The Grand Medieval Bestiary: Animals in Illuminated Manuscripts*. New York: Abbeville Press, 2012.
Heise, Ursula K. *Imagining Extinction: The Cultural Meanings of Endangered Species*. Chicago: University of Chicago Press, 2016.
Heise, Ursula K. "The Hitchhiker's Guide to Ecocriticism." *PMLA* 121.2 (2006): 503–16.
Hemingway, Ernest. *The Nick Adams Stories*. New York: Scribner, 1972.
Henderson, Linda Dalrymple. "Etherial Bride and Mechanical Bachelors: Science and Allegory in Marcel Duchamp's 'Large Glass.'" *Configurations* 4.1 (1996): 91–120.
Hensley, Nathan K. and Philip Steer. *Ecological Form: System and Aesthetics in the Age of Empire*. New York: Fordham University Press, 2019.
Herrick, Robert. *The Gospel of Freedom*. New York: Macmillan, 1898.
Howard, Ebenezer. *Garden Cities of To-morrow*. Cambridge: The MIT Press, 1965.
Huber, Matthew T. *Lifeblood: Oil, Freedom, and the Forces of Capital*. Minneapolis: University of Minnesota Press, 2013.

Hugo, Victor. *Les Misérables*. Trans. Lee Fahnestock and Norman MacAfee. New York: Penguin, 1987.
Huntington, Ellsworth. *Civilization and Climate*. New Haven: Yale University Press, 1915.
Hurston, Zora Neale. *Their Eyes Were Watching God*. Chicago: University of Illinois Press, 1991.
Huysmans, Joris-Karl. *Against Nature*. Trans. Margaret Mauldon. Oxford: Oxford University Press, 1998.
Israel, Nico. *Spirals: The Whirled Image in Twentieth-Century Literature and Art*. New York: Columbia University Press, 2015.
Jacobs, Jane. *The Death and Life of Great American Cities*. New York: Random House, 1993.
James, David, and Urmila Seshagiri. "Metamodernism: Narratives of Continuity and Revolution." *PMLA* 129.1 (2014): 87–100.
Johnson, Bob. *Mineral Rites: An Archaeology of the Fossil Economy*. Baltimore: Johns Hopkins University Press, 2019.
Joyce, James. *Dubliners*. New York: Penguin, 1996.
Joyce, James. *A Portrait of the Artist as a Young Man*. New York: Penguin, 1992.
Joyce, James. *Ulysses*. Ed. Hans Walter Gabler et al. New York: Vintage Books, 1986.
Kafka, Franz. *The Metamorphosis*. Trans. Stanley Corngold. New York: Norton, 1996.
Kander, Astrid, Paolo Malanima, and Paul Warde. *Power to the People: Energy in Europe over the Last Five Centuries*. Princeton: Princeton University Press, 2013.
Kenner, Hugh. *The Mechanic Muse*. Oxford: Oxford University Press, 1987.
Kern, Stephen. *The Cultures of Time and Space, 1880–1918*. Cambridge: Harvard University Press, 2003.
Kolbert, Elizabeth. *The Sixth Extinction: An Unnatural History*. New York: Henry Holt, 2014.
Kolocotroni, Vassiliki, Jane Goldman, and Olga Taxidou. *Modernism: An Anthology of Sources and Documents*. Chicago: University of Chicago Press, 1998.
Koolhaas, Rem. *Delirious New York*. New York: The Monacelli Press, 1978.
Krauss, Rosalind. "Grids." October 9, 1979: 50–64.
Krugman, Paul. "The G.O.P.'s Climate of Paranoia." *New York Times*, August 20, 2018. https://www.nytimes.com/2018/08/20/opinion/trump-republican-truth-climate-change.html. Accessed June 20, 2019.
Lacivita, Alison. *The Ecology of* Finnegans Wake. Gainesville: University Press of Florida, 2015.

Lawrence, D.H. *Lady Chatterley's Lover*. New York: Penguin, 2010.
Lawrence, D.H. *The Rainbow*. Cambridge: Cambridge University Press, 1989.
Lawrence, D.H. *Women in Love*. New York: Penguin, 2007.
Le Corbusier. *The City of Tomorrow and Its Planning*. Trans. Frederick Etchells. New York: Dover, 1987.
LeMenager, Stephanie. *Living Oil: Petroleum Culture in the American Century*. New York: Oxford University Press, 2014.
Lenin, Vladimir. *Collected Works, Vol. 31: April–December 1920*. Trans. Julius Katzer. Moscow: Progress Publishers, 1966.
Leopold, Aldo. *A Sand County Almanac: With Other Essays on Conservation from Round River*. New York: Ballantine, 1970.
Lewis, Wyndham. *BLAST*. Santa Rosa: Black Sparrow Press, 2002.
Love, Glen. *Practical Ecocriticism: Literature, Biology, and the Environment*. Charlottesville: University of Virginia Press, 2003.
Lundblad, Michael and Marianne Dekoven. "Introduction: Animality and Advocacy." In *Species Matters: Humane Advocacy and Cultural Theory*. Ed. Marianne Dekoven and Michael Lundblad. New York: Columbia University Press, 2011. 1–16.
MacLeod, Glen. *Wallace Stevens in Context*. Cambridge: Cambridge University Press, 2016.
Malm, Andreas. *The Progress of This Storm: Nature and Society in a Warming World*. London: Verso, 2018.
Mao, Douglas and Rebecca L. Walkowitz. "The New Modernist Studies." *PMLA* 123.3 (2008): 737–48.
Marc, Franz. "How Does a Horse See the World?" In *Theories of Modern Art: A Source Book by Artists and Critics*. Ed. Herschel B. Chipp. Berkeley: University of California Press, 1968.
Maria, Walter De. "The Lightning Field." *Artforum* 18.8 (1980): 52.
Marinetti, F.T. "Founding and Manifesto of Futurism." In *Futurism: An Anthology*. Ed. Lawrence Rainey, Christine Poggi, and Laura Wittman. New Haven: Yale University Press, 2009. 49–53.
Marinetti, F.T. "The New Religion-Morality of Speed." In *Futurism: An Anthology*. Ed. Lawrence Rainey, Christine Poggi, and Laura Wittman. New Haven: Yale University Press, 2009. 224–29.
Marris, Emma. *Rambunctious Garden: Saving Nature in a Post-Wild World*. New York: Bloomsbury, 2011.
Marsh, George Perkins. *Man and Nature Or, Physical Geography as Modified by Human Action*. Cambridge: Harvard University Press, 1965.
Marshall, Robert. "The Problem of the Wilderness." *The Scientific Monthly* 30.2 (1930): 141–48.
Martin, Theodore. *Contemporary Drift: Genre, Historicism, and the Problem of the Present*. New York: Columbia University Press, 2017.

Masterman, C.F.G. *The Conditions of England*. London: Methuen & Co., 1909.
McCarthy, Jeffrey Mathes. "'A Choice of Nightmares:' The Ecology of *Heart of Darkness*." *Modern Fiction Studies* 55.3 (2009): 620–48.
McGurl, Mark. "The New Cultural Geology." *Twentieth Century Literature* 57 (2011): 380–90.
McKenzie, R.D. "The Ecological Approach to the Study of the Human Community." *American Journal of Sociology* 30.3 (1924): 287–301.
McKibben, Bill. *The End of Nature*. New York: Random House, 1989.
McNeill, J.R. "Energy, Population, and Environmental Change since 1750: Entering the Anthropocene." In *The Cambridge World History Vol. VII: Production, Destruction, and Connection, 1750—Present, Part 1: Structures, Spaces and Boundary Making*. Ed. J.R. McNeill and Kenneth Pomeranz. Cambridge: Cambridge University Press, 2015. 51–82.
McNeill, J.R. and Kenneth Pomeranz. "Production, Destruction, and Connection, 1750-Present: Introduction." In *The Cambridge World History Vol. VII: Production, Destruction, and Connection, 1750—Present, Part 1: Structures, Spaces and Boundary Making*. Ed. J.R. McNeill and Kenneth Pomeranz. Cambridge: Cambridge University Press, 2015. 1–49.
Metropolis [Film]. Dir. Fritz Lang. Berlin: Parufamet, 1927.
Miller, J. Hillis. "Should We Read Heart of Darkness?" In *Joseph Conrad's Heart of Darkness*. Ed. Harold Bloom. New York: Infobase, 2008. 115–30.
Milne, A.A. *The Complete Tales of Winnie-the-Poo*. New York: Dutton, 2016.
Moore, Jason W. "The Capitalocene, Part 1: On the Nature and Origins of Our Ecological Crisis." *The Journal of Peasant Studies* 44.3 (2017): 594–630.
Moore, Marianne. *The Complete Poems of Marianne Moore*. New York: Macmillian, 1981.
Morton, Timothy. *Being Ecological*. Cambridge: The MIT Press, 2018.
Morton, Timothy. *Hyperobjects: Philosophy and Energy after the End of the World*. Minneapolis: University of Minnesota Press, 2013.
Muir, John. *Nature Writings*. Ed. William Cronon. New York: Penguin, 1997.
Mumford, Lewis. *Technics and Civilization*. New York: Harcourt, 1934.
Mumford, Lewis. *The Culture of Cities*. London: Secker & Warburg, 1946.
Musil, Robert. *The Man Without Qualities*. Trans. Sophie Wilkins and Burton Pike. New York: Knopf, 1995.
Nabokov, Vladimir. *Nabokov's Butterflies: Unpublished and Uncollected Writings*. Trans. Dimitri Nabokov. Ed. Brian Boyd and Robert Michael Pyle. Boston: Beacon, 2000.

Nash, Roderick. *Wilderness and the American Mind*. New Haven: Yale University Press, 1967.
National Parks Service. "The Glaciers of Mount Rainier." 2015. www.nps.gov/mora/learn/nature/mount-rainier-glaciers.htm. Accessed June 1, 2019.
Neuman, Justin. "Anthropocene Interruptions: Energy Recognition Scenes and the Global Cooling Myth." In *Anthropocene Reading: Literary History in Geologic Times*. Ed. Tobias Menely and Jesse Oak Taylor. University Park: Penn State University Press, 2017.
Nye, David E. *When the Lights Went Out: A History of Blackouts in America*. Cambridge: MIT Press, 2010.
Oelschlaeger, Max. *The Idea of Wilderness: From Prehistory to the Age of Ecology*. New Haven: Yale University Press, 1991.
Olmsted, Frederick Law. *Yosemite and the Mariposa Grove: A Preliminary Report*. Fresno: Yosemite Association, 1993.
Olson, D., R. Doescher, and M. Olson. "When the Sky Ran Red: The Story behind *The Scream*." *Sky Telescope*, 2004. 107.2: 29–35.
Orwell, George. *The Road to Wigan Pier*. New York: Harcourt, 1985.
Park, Robert E. "The City: Suggestions for the Investigation of Human Behavior in the Urban Environment." In *The City*. Ed. Robert E. Park and Ernest W. Burgess. Chicago: The University of Chicago Press, 1925. 1–46.
Pearce, Roy Harvey. "'Anecdote of the Jar': An Iconological Note." *The Wallace Stevens Journal* 1.2 (1977): 65.
Perloff, Marjorie. *The Poetics of Indeterminacy: Rimbaud to Cage*. Evanston: Northwestern University Press, 1981.
Prata, Fred, Alan Robock, and Richard Hamblyn. "The Sky in Edvard Munch's *The Scream*." *Bulletin of the American Meteorological Association* July (2018): 1377–90.
Proust, Marcel. *Against Sainte-Beuve and Other Essays*. Trans. John Sturrock. New York: Penguin, 1988.
Rae, Douglas. *City: Urbanism and Its End*. New Haven: Yale University Press, 2008.
Raine, Anne. "Ecocriticism and Modernism." In *The Oxford Handbook of Ecocriticism*. Ed. Greg Garrard. Oxford: Oxford University Press, 2014. 98–117.
Rainey, Lawrence. *Modernism: An Anthology*. Malden: Blackwell, 2005.
Reisner, Marc. *Cadillac Dessert: The American West and Its Disappearing Water*. New York: Penguin, 1986.
Rohman, Carrie. *Stalking the Subject: Modernism and the Animal*. New York: Columbia University Press, 2009.
Roosevelt, Theodore. *African Game Trails: An Account of the African Wanderings of an American Hunter-Naturalist*. New York: Syndicate, 1910.

Roosevelt, Theodore. "Nature Fakers." *Everybody's Magazine* 17.3 (1907): 427–30.
Rosenberg, Aaron. "Nitrogen Fixations: From Waste to World War." *Modernist Studies Association Annual Conference*, November 17–20, 2016, Pasadena, California. Unpublished Conference Paper. Courtesy of the author, 2019.
Rosner, Victoria. *Modernism and the Architecture of Private Life*. New York: Columbia University Press, 2005.
Roth, Henry. *Call It Sleep*. New York: Picador, 1991.
Rubenstein, Madeleine. "When Timing Is Everything: Migratory Bird Phenology in a Changing Climate." *USGS News*, February 10, 2017. https://www.usgs.gov/center-news/when-timing-everything-migratory-bird-phenology-a-changing-climate. Accessed June 20, 2019.
Rubenstein, Michael. "City Circuits: 'Aeolus' and 'Wandering Rocks.'" In *The Cambridge Companion to Ulysses*. Ed. Sean Latham. Cambridge: Cambridge University Press, 2014. 113–27.
Rubenstein, Michael. *Public Works: Infrastructure, Irish Modernism, and the Postcolonial*. South Bend: Notre Dame University Press, 2010.
Ruskin, John. *The Works of John Ruskin*. Ed. E.T. Cook and Alexander Wedderburn. New York: Longmans, Green, and Co., 1903.
Sandburg, Carl. *The Complete Poems of Carl Sandburg*. San Diego: Harcourt, 1970.
Schulz, Kathryn. "Writers in the Storm: How Weather Went from Symbol to Science and Back Again." *The New Yorker*, November 15, 2015. 105–10.
Schuster, Joshua. *The Ecology of Modernism: American Environments and Avant-Garde Poetics*. Tuscaloosa: The University of Alabama Press, 2015.
Scott, Bonnie Kime. "Ecocritical Woolf." In *A Companion to Virginia Woolf*. Ed. Jessica Berman. Baltimore: Johns Hopkins University Press, 2016. 319–31.
Scranton, Roy. "Learning How to Die in the Anthropocene." *The New York Times*, November 10, 2013. https://opinionator.blogs.nytimes.com/2013/11/10/learning-how-to-die-in-the-anthropocene. Accessed June 10, 2019.
Seton, Ernest Thompson. *Wild Animals I Have Known, and 200 Drawings*. New York: Grosset & Dunlap, 1898.
Seymour, Nicole. *Bad Environmentalism: Irony and Irreverence in the Ecological Age*. Minneapolis: University of Minnesota Press, 2018.
Shprintzen, Adam D. *The Vegetarian Crusade: The Rise of the American Reform Movement, 1817–1921*. Chapel Hill: The University of North Carolina Press, 2013.
Simmel, Georg. *On Individuality and Social Forms*. Chicago: The University of Chicago Press, 1971.

Smith, Zadie. *NW*. New York: Penguin, 2012.
Soddy, Frederick. *Matter and Energy*. Cambridge: Cambridge University Press, 1912.
Soddy, Frederick. *Wealth, Virtual Wealth and Debt: The Solution of the Economic Paradox*. New York: Dutton, 1926.
Steffen, Will, Wendy Broadgate, Lisa Deutsch, Owen Gaffney, and Cornelia Ludwig. "The Trajectory of the Anthropocene: The Great Acceleration." *The Anthropocene Review* 2.1 (2015): 81–98.
Stevens, Wallace. *The Collected Poems of Wallace Stevens*. New York: Knopf, 1990.
Stierli, Martino. *Montage and the Metropolis: Architecture, Modernity, and the Representation of Space*. New Haven: Yale University Press, 2018.
Strauss, Lewis. "Remarks Prepared by Lewis L. Strauss, Chairman, United States Atomic Energy Commission, For Delivery at the Founders' Day Dinner, National Association of Science Writers, On Thursday, September 16, 1954, New York, New York." *nrc.gov*. https://www.nrc.gov/docs/ML1613/ML16131A120.pdf. Accessed June 6, 2019.
Sultzbach, Kelly. *Ecocriticism in the Modernist Imagination: Foster, Woolf, and Auden*. Cambridge: Cambridge University Press, 2016.
Szeman, Imre. *On Petrocultures: Globalization, Culture, and Energy*. Morgantown: West Virginia University Press, 2019.
Szeman, Imre and Dominic Boyer. "Introduction: On the Energy Humanities." In *The Energy Humanities Reader*. Ed. Imre Szeman and Dominic Boyer. Baltimore: Johns Hopkins University Press, 2017. 1–14.
Taylor, Jesse Oak. *The Sky of Our Manufacture: The London Fog in British Fiction from Dickens to Woolf*. Charlottesville: University of Virginia Press, 2016.
Tempest, Kate. *Let Them Eat Chaos*. London: Picador, 2016.
Thoreau, Henry David. *Henry David Thoreau: A Week, Walden, The Maine Woods, Cape Cod*. Ed. Robert F. Sayre. New York: The Library of America, 1985.
Tichi, Cecelia. *Shifting Gears: Technology, Literature, and Culture in Modernist America*. Chapel Hill: The University of North Carolina Press, 1987.
Toomer, Jean. *Cane*. New York: Liveright, 1951.
Turner, Frederick Jackson. *The Significance of the Frontier in American History*. New York: Unger, 1963.
Twain, Mark. *Roughing It*. Berkeley: University of California Press, 1996.
Tzara, Tristan. *Seven Dada Manifestos and Lampisteries*. Trans. Barbara Wright. London: John Calder, 1977.
Vadde, Aarthei. "Scalability." *Modernism / Modernity Print Plus* 4, Cycle (2019). https://modernismmodernity.org/ forums/posts/scalability. Accessed September 30, 2019.

Valéry, Paul. *The Outlook for Intelligence*. Trans. Denise Folliot and Jackson Mathews. New York: Harper & Row, 1962.
Valéry, Paul. *Regards sur le monde actuel*. Paris: Librarie Stock, Delamain et Boutelleau, 1931.
Vendler, Helen. *Wallace Stevens: Words Chosen Out of Desire*. Cambridge: Harvard University Press, 1984.
Visser, Marcel E. and Phillip Gienapp. "Evolutionary and Demographic Consequences of Phenological Mismatches." *Nature Ecology & Evolution* 3 (2019): 879–85.
von Hofmannsthal, Hugo. *Selected Tales*. Trans. J.M.Q. Davies. London: Angel Books, 2007.
Waldau, Paul. *Animal Studies: An Introduction*. Oxford: Oxford University Press, 2013.
Warde, Paul, Libby Robin, and Sverker Sörlin. *The Environment: A History of the Idea*. Baltimore: Johns Hopkins University Press, 2018.
Wells, H.G. "The Future in America: A Search of its Realities—The End of Niagara." *Harper's Weekly* 40 (July 21, 1906): 1019.
Wells, H.G. *The Sleeper Awakes*. New York: Penguin, 2005.
Wenzel, Jennifer. "Introduction." In *Fueling Culture 101: Words for Energy and Environment*. Ed. Imre Szeman, Jennifer Wenzel, and Patricia Yaeger. New York: Fordham University Press, 2017. 1–16.
Wharton, Edith. *The House of Mirth*. New York: Scribner, 1997.
Wienstzen, Timothy. "Not a Globe but a Planet: Modernism and the Epoch of Modernity." *Modernism / Modernity Print Plus* 4, Cycle 3 (2019). https://modernismmodernity.org/ forums/scale-and-form. Accessed September 30, 2019.
Williams, Raymond. *The Country and the City*. Oxford: Oxford University Press, 1973.
Williams, Raymond. "Culture Is Ordinary." In *Raymond Williams on Culture and Society: Essential Writings*. Ed. Jim McGuigan. Los Angeles: Sage, 2014. 1–19.
Williams, William Carlos. *The Collected Poems of William Carlos Williams, Volume 1: 1909–1939*. Ed. A. Walton Litz and Christopher MacGowan. New York: New Directions, 1986.
Williams, William Carlos. *In the American Grain*. New York: New Directions, 1956.
Willmott, Glenn. "Cat People." *Modernism/modernity* 17.4 (2010): 839–56.
Wilson, E.O. "The 8 Million Species We Don't Know." *The New York Times Sunday Review*, March 3, 2018. https://www.nytimes.com/2 018/03/03/opinion/sunday/species-conservation-extinction.html. Accessed June 29, 2019.
Woolf, Virginia. *Between the Acts*. New York: Harcourt, 2008.

Woolf, Virginia. *The Complete Shorter Fiction of Virginia Woolf*. Ed. Susan Dick. New York: Harcourt, 1989.
Woolf, Virginia. *Mrs. Dalloway*. Orlando: Harcourt, 2005.
Woolf, Virginia. *To The Lighthouse*. New York: Harcourt, 1981.
Wright, Frank Lloyd. *The Disappearing City*. New York: W.F. Payson, 1932.
Wright, Richard. *Native Son*. New York: Harper Perennial, 1940.
Yaeger, Patricia, Laurie Shannon, Vin Nardizzi, Ken Hiltner, Saree Makdisi, Michael Ziser, and Imre Szeman. "Editor's Column: Literature in the Ages of Wood, Tallow, Coal, Whale Oil, Gasoline, Atomic Power, and Other Energy Sources." *PMLA* 126.2 (2011): 305–26.
Yeats, W.B. *The Collected Poems of W.B. Yeats*. Ed. Richard J. Finneran. New York: Scribner, 1996.
Yeats, W.B. *The Collected Works of W.B. Yeats, Volume V: Later Essays*. Ed. William H. O'Donnell. New York: Scribner, 1994a.
Yeats, W.B. *The Collected Works of W.B. Yeats, Volume III: Autobiographies*. Ed. William H. O'Donnell and Douglas N. Archibald. New York: Scribner, 1994b.
Yergin, Daniel. *The Quest: Energy, Security, and the Remaking of the Modern World*. New York: Penguin, 2011.
Young, A. B. Filson. *The Complete Motorist: Being an Account of the Evolution and Construction of the Modern Motor-Car, with Notes on the Selection, Use, and Maintenance of the Same, and on the Pleasures of Travel upon the Public Roads*. New York: McClure, 1905.
Yusoff, Kathryn. *A Billion Black Anthropocenes or None*. Minneapolis: University of Minnesota Press, 2019.
Zweig, Stefan. *The World of Yesterday*. Trans. Anthea Bell. Lincoln: University of Nebraska Press, 2009.

INDEX

Abbey, Edward   116, 133
Adams, Henry   19
aesthetics
  of modernism   6, 28, 51, 67, 117, 125
  and modernist studies   3, 15
  urbanization   61
agriculture   51. *See also* Haber-Bosch process
Anand, Raj   69–70
Anderson, Katharine   152–3
animals
  bears   96, 112
  birds   97, 101–2, 106, 113
  boll weevil   102–3
  cats   93–4
  dogs   94–5
  elephants   110–11
  farm animals   95–6
  passenger pigeons   100–1
  rats   93
  wolf   100
animal studies   104–8. *See also* ecocriticism; speciesism
Anthropocene. *See also* climate change; extinction; population
  definition of   147–51
  energy   27–8
  and Kafka   92–3
  and literature   171–2
  and modernity   144
  wilderness   139–41

architecture   72–3, 80. *See also* Eiffel Tower; Le Corbusier; Wright
Armstrong, Philip   99, 108
Ascent of F6, The (Auden & Isherwood)   133
Association for the Study of Literature and Environment (ASLE)   9–11. *See also* ecocriticism
Auden, W. H.   99, 133
Austin, Mary   122
automobile   7–8, 45–7, 82–3. *See also* fossil fuels; oil
avant-garde   5–6, 60, 96, 107, 117, 141

Banham, Raynor   32
Barnes, Djuna   94
Bate, Jonathan   170
Baudelaire, Charles   32, 75
Beard, Thomas   53
beauty
  animal life   113–14
  technology   31, 89
  wilderness   119, 124–5, 141
Bell, Clive   17
Benjamin, Walter   61, 72, 147
Benton, Thomas Hart   29
Berger, John   107–8
Berman, Marshall   6, 61, 79
Beston, Henry   33–4
Bird, Isabella   118–19
Bishop, Elizabeth   54–5

Bloomsbury Group 7, 17, 59
Boccioni, Umberto 90–1, 96
Bowen, Elizabeth 83
Bradbury, Malcolm 60
Bradford, William 120
Brancusi, Constantin 97, 100, 103–4
Brooks, Peter 32
Buell, Frederick 28, 40, 43
Buell, Lawrence 13–14, 18, 162

capitalism 32, 44–5, 104, 128, 149. *See also* Anthropocene; communism
Carson, Rachel 8
Cather, Willa 95
Chakrabarty, Dipesh 27, 149
Chernobyl 32
Chicago School (sociology) 77–8
climate change. *See also* Anthropocene
  Anthropocene 144–51
  environmentalism 7
  and literature 160–73
  and modernist studies 3–4
  preservation 141
  urbanization 81–2
climate fiction 171–2. *See also* petrofiction
coal 17, 36–7, 43–6, 63. *See also* fossil fuels
Coetzee, J. M. 94, 105
communism 32. *See also* Marxism; Trotsky; USSR
Conrad, Joseph 52. *See also Heart of Darkness*
conservation 106, 109–10, 141–2. *See also* environmentalism; National Parks; preservation
Coolidge, Calvin 95
Corton, Christine L. 84
Crane, Hart 117

Cronon, William 79, 114, 125–6, 129
cubism 71, 96

Dada 5, 6
Darwin, Charles 97–9, 153
de Maria, Walter 158–61. *See also* Land Art
Denning, Andrew 134
Derrida, Jacques 94, 107
Dickens, Charles 66–7
Döblin, Alfred 74–5, 96, 113
Doyle, Arthur Conan 121
Dreiser, Theodore 64, 75
Duchamp, Marcel 31, 97, 136
  The Bride Stripped Bare by her Bachelors, Even (The Large Glass) 47–8
Duffy, Edna 47, 53, 82
Dufy, Raoul 29, 31
Duncan, Isadora 16
Dyer, Geoff 23, 158–60

ecocriticism 2–3, 9–18. *See also* animal studies; environmental humanities
ecomodernism 19–20, 39, 143
Eiffel Tower 72–3
Einstein, Albert 53
electricity 31–7, 53. *See also* grid
  and Joyce 34–7
Eliasson, Olafur 145–8, 161, 167
Eliot, T. S. 4, 61, 93
  "Gerontion" 116–17
  "The Love Song of J. Alfred Prufrock" 66–7, 68, 93
  "The Waste Land" 60, 67, 93
Ellison, Ralph 85, 86–7
Emerson, Ralph Waldo 32
energy. *See also* coal; electricity; nuclear energy; oil
  and culture 36–40
  electricity 29–34

in Joyce   34–6
modernization   42–3, 52–4
technology   18–20, 25–7
energy humanities   40–2
environment
  definition of   4–7, 109
environmental humanities   8, 12, 16, 83–6. *See also* ecocriticism
environmentalism   3, 6–8, 13, 20. *See also* conservation; preservation
environmentality   14, 18, 162. *See also* Buell, Lawrence
Environmental Protection Agency   8
exomodernism   150–1, 169. *See also* Anthropocene; McGurl
extinction   100–4, 106, 112–14. *See also* Anthropocene

Faulkner, William   95, 96
fauvism   96
film   58–9, 62, 70–1, 101–2, 111. *See also The Life and Death of Colonel Blimp*; *Metropolis*
Fisher, Rudolph   85–6
Fitzroy, Robert   152–3
flâneur   75
Ford, Henry   7–8, 82
formalism
  ecocriticism   14, 112–13
  in modernist art   17, 144, 157, 161; *See also* grid
Forster, E.M.   19
  Howards End   42, 46, 134
  Maurice   46
fossil fuels   38–43, 45, 48–50. *See also* coal; oil; pollution
Foster, Hal   37
Freud, Sigmund   32, 99–100

Friedman, Susan Stanford   9
frontier   125–6
Futurism   5, 90. *See also* Marinetti

Gág, Wanda   94
Gandhi, Mohandas   70, 104–5
Garrard, Greg   10–11, 116
gasoline   48–9. *See also* fossil fuels; oil
Ghosh, Amitav   41, 52, 54, 170–1
Glotfelty, Cheryll   9–10
Gramsci, Antonio   6
Grant, Ulysses S.   126
grid   35, 64, 156–8. *See also* electricity; urbanization

Haber-Bosch process   51–3. *See also* agriculture; nitrogen; Rosenberg
Haraway, Donna   109, 149
Harvey, David   60
Heart of Darkness (Conrad)   111, 115, 130–2
Heise, Ursula K.   12, 129, 142
Hemingway, Ernest   132–3
Hofmannsthal, Hugo von   93
Hoover Dam   31
Howard, Ebenezer   79–80
Hugo, Victor   70
Huntington, Ellsworth   7
Hurston, Zora Neale   94–5, 171

impressionism   17, 67, 96
infrastructure   37, 62–3, 77, 79–80. *See also* rail; transportation; urbanization
Israel, Nico   157, 160

Jacobs, Jane   62, 78, 79
Jameson, Frederic   140, 169
Joyce, James   11, 19

Cats of Copenhagen 94
"The Dead" 35–6, 154–5
Portrait of the Artist as a Young Man 34–5, 69–70
Ulysses 34, 59, 70, 93, 105, 121

Kafka, Franz
 The Metamorphosis 92–3, 104, 112, 114
 The Trial 94
Kenner, Hugh 3–4, 35, 67
Krakatoa 2, 146
Krauss, Rosalind 156, 158

Land Art 144, 158–60. *See also* de Maria; Smithson
Lawrence, D. H. 96
 Lady Chatterley's Lover 44, 54
 The Rainbow 95
 Women in Love 45–6, 134
Le Corbusier 71, 78, 80, 81–2, 138. *See also* architecture
LeMenager, Stephanie 45
Lenin, Vladimir 32–3
Leopold, Aldo 118, 125
Lewis, Wyndham 96, 117
Life and Death of Colonel Blimp, The (film) 101–2
London 64–9, 110, 168
London, Jack 94, 110

McCarthy, Jeffrey Mathes 11, 15, 116, 131
McGurl, Mark 150
McKenzie, R. D. 77
McKibben, Bill 120, 141
McNeill, J. R. 26–7
Malm, Andreas 140, 164–5
Malthus, Thomas 51
Man Without Qualities, The (Musil) 49–50, 77, 78–9, 154, 155

Marc, Franz 96, 108
Marinetti, F. T. 89–90, 125. *See also* Futurism
Márquez, Gabriel García 171
Marsh, George Perkins 170–1
Marshall, Robert 128
Martin, Agnes 157
Marxism 104. *See also* communism; Trotsky; USSR
metamodernism 162, 169–70. *See also* postmodernism; Smith
meteorology 151–6
Metropolis (Lang) 58–9, 62, 71, 76
Miller, J. Hillis 131
Milne, A. A. 96, 110–12
mimesis 2, 67. *See also* realism
minimalism (design) 16
modernism
 definition of 4–5, 8–9, 143–4
Modernist Studies Association (MSA) 8–9, 11
modernization 34, 69, 95, 169, 172. *See also* urbanization
Mondrian, Piet 156–7, 158
Monet, Claude 67–8
Monroe, Harriet 134–6
Moore, Marianne 96, 106, 114, 135
Morris, William 19
Morton, Timothy 17, 166
Moses, Robert 79–80
Muir, John 16, 101, 110, 114, 116, 126–7
Mumford, Lewis 33, 63
Munch, Edvard 1–2, 144–6, 169
Musil, Robert 49–50, 77, 78–9, 154, 155

Nabokov, Vladimir 92
Naess, Arne 16, 142
narrative 52, 99, 151, 161, 164, 172

Nash, Roderick   118, 120, 133
National Parks   126–8. *See also*
    conservation; preservation
naturalism   7–8, 67
natural selection   98–9
nature. *See also* conservation;
    environment; pastoral;
    preservation
  Darwin   97–9
  definition of   7, 10, 40, 138
  nature writing   13–15, 18,
    118–19
  and postmodernism   12, 169
  and technology   19, 31, 120–1
nature fakers controversy
    109–10. *See also* Roosevelt
Neuman, Justin   44
nitrogen   51–3. *See also* Haber-
    Bosch
Nixon, Rob   16–17, 49, 149
nuclear power   32
nuclear weapons   139–40
Nye, David   3, 63

oil   41–3, 45, 50, 54–5. *See also*
    fossil fuels
O'Keeffe, Georgia   90, 113–14
Olmsted, Frederick Law   126
Orwell, George   44, 46
  Animal Farm   92
outdoor recreation   117, 124,
    133–4. *See also* National
    Parks

Parade (ballet)   71–2
Park, Robert E.   77–8
passenger pigeons   100–1, 110,
    112
pastoral   123–5
Perloff, Marjorie   47
petrofiction   41–2, 46, 48, 54.
    See also climate fiction
Phillips, Dana   13–14
Picabia, Francis   29–31, 48

pollution. *See also* fossil fuels;
    waste
  coal   44
  electricity   37
  and environmental
    justice   83–4
  in London   65–9
  urbanization   61, 63, 73,
    82–83
population   50–1, 64–6, 72, 118.
    See also Anthropocene
postmodernism   12–13, 140–1,
    143, 150–1, 169
post-postmodernism   169
Pound, Ezra   8, 89, 94, 123
preservation   115–16,
    118–19, 122–3, 126–8.
    See also conservation;
    environmentalism; National
    Parks
Proust, Marcel   15, 48–9

racism
  alienation   85–7
  environmental justice   83–5
  naturalism   7–8
rail   33, 62, 72, 73, 75
Raine, Anne   134
realism   52, 67, 161, 170–2.
    See also mimesis
Rivera, Diego   29
Roosevelt, Theodore   109–11,
    112, 126–7. *See also* nature
    fakers
Rosenberg, Aaron   51–2. *See also*
    Haber-Bosch; nitrogen
Roth, Henry   21
  Call it Sleep   25, 76, 84, 86
Rousseau, Henri   96–7
Rubenstein, Michael   70, 86
Ruskin, John   152

Saint-Amour, Paul   143, 168
Sandburg, Carl   73–4

Schuster, Joshua   5, 14–15, 126
science fiction   52, 71
Scream, The (Munch)   1–2, 144–6, 169
sculpture   31, 47, 90–1, 97. *See also* Boccioni; Duchamp; Land Art
Seton, Ernest Thompson   109–10
Seymour, Nicole   17
Simmel, Georg   76
Sinclair, Upton
  The Jungle   95–6
  Oil!   45
Singer, Peter   104
skyscraper   62, 71–3, 82, 86. *See also* infrastructure; urbanization
Smil, Vaclav   40–1, 63
Smith, Zadie   143, 162, 163–70, 172
Smithson, Robert   158–61. *See also* Land Art
Soddy, Frederick   27, 39, 50–1
Sōseki, Natsume   94
speciesism   106–10, 142. *See also* animal studies
Stevens, Wallace   22, 114
  "Anecdote of the Jar"   136–9
suburbs   79, 81–3. *See also* modernization; urbanization
Szeman, Imre   41–7, 54

Taylor, Jesse Oak   144, 167
Tempest, Kate   144, 165, 172
Third Man, The (film)   70–1
Thoreau, Henry David   118–19
Tolkien, J. R. R.   68, 121, 124
Toomer, Jean   53–4, 102–4, 112
transportation   58, 62–3, 72, 82–3. *See also* infrastructure
Trotsky, Leon   27

Turner, Frederick Jackson   125
Twain, Mark   121–3
Tzara, Tristan   6

urbanization   59, 61–5, 73–5, 79, 81–2, 169. *See also* grid; infrastructure; modernization; suburbs
USSR   27, 32. *See also* communism; Marxism; Trotsky

Vadde, Aarthi   143
Valéry, Paul   25–6, 27, 28, 29, 31, 32–3, 40, 50, 51, 52
Van Gogh, Vincent   1
vegetarianism   104–5
Vollman, William T.   52

Waldau, Paul   104, 107
war
  weapons   51–2, 140
  World War I   18–19, 50, 93, 132–3
waste   68–71. *See also* pollution
Wells, H. G.   39, 52, 59
Wenzel, Jennifer   38
West, Rebecca   96
Wharton, Edith   76
Whitman, Walt   32
Wienstzen, Timothy   143
Wilde, Oscar   67, 94
wilderness
  definition of   116–18, 120, 128–9
Wilderness Act (1964)   115–17, 128, 139
Williams, Raymond   38–40, 60–1
Williams, William Carlos   6, 8, 121
Winnie-the-Pooh (Milne)   96, 110–12
Woolf, Virginia   4, 6, 11, 76, 78
  Between the Acts   69, 95

Flush 94
"Kew Gardens" 108–9
Mrs Dalloway 34, 60, 69, 85, 121, 144, 162–3, 167–9, 172
Orlando 67, 171
A Sketch of the Past 15–16
To the Lighthouse 125, 155
Wordsworth, William 66, 124
Wright, Frank Lloyd
 Broadacre City 18, 81
 The Disappearing City 80–1
Wright, Richard 84–5

Yaeger, Patricia 42
Yeats, W. B.
 "The Lake Isle of Innisfree" 123–4
 "The Second Coming" 157, 160
 "The Wild Swans at Coole" 112–13
Young, A. B. Filson 19
Yusoff, Kathryn 149

Zola, Emile 32, 44
Zweig, Stefan 6, 138

www.ingramcontent.com/pod-product-compliance
Ingram Content Group UK Ltd.
Pitfield, Milton Keynes, MK11 3LW, UK
UKHW021901220326
469204UK00008B/117

WAVEFORMS
BULL ISLAND HAIKU

WAVEFORMS
BULL ISLAND HAIKU

Pat Boran

ORANGE CRATE BOOKS

Waveforms: Bull Island Haiku
is first published in 2015 by
Orange Crate Books,
Dublin, Ireland.

orangecratebooks@gmail.com

Text and photographs
copyright © Pat Boran, 2015, 2021

ISBN 978 0 9931726 0 1

All rights reserved. No part of this publication may be
reproduced in any form or by any means without the
prior permission of the publisher.

Orange Crate Books
are available through
Dedalus Press
www.dedaluspress.com

Printed in Dublin
by Print Dynamics

for Lee and Luca,
dreamers, explorers, guardians

CONTENTS

✵

About Bull Island / 9

✵

Waveforms: Bull Island Haiku / 13

✵

Afterword / 107
About the Photographs / 118
About the Author / 120

ABOUT BULL ISLAND

Bull Island (properly North Bull Island) is a landmass some 5km in length and 800m in width, running more or less parallel to the shore in Dublin Bay, north of the mouth of the River Liffey. Stretching from Clontarf and the North Bull Wall at its most southerly point to the area of Sutton Creek to the north-east, the island is less than 200 years old. Its existence is a direct result of changes in currents in the bay following the construction of the North Bull Wall (1820-25). The island is a Special Area of Conservation under the EU Habitats Directive and, since 1981, a UNESCO Biosphere Reserve, the only one in the world within the boundaries of a capital city. It is also a hugely popular recreational area for Dubliners and visitors alike.

First, a mystery,
the absence of things. And then?
Then the land, the sea …

※

Out of nothingness,
on a whim, a stir of air,
scarcely more than breath …

※

Grain by tumbling grain,
the world forms before our eyes,
and may fade again.

This. Then this … and this …
A lone crab scuttles between
islands of stillness.

※

Incredibly smooth,
morning's newly washed-up stones –
like fresh eggs, or fruit.

※

The world at our feet,
scraps of wood with flaking paint –
dream cartographies.

Salt wort breaks the wind
and the grains accumulate.
Thus a dune begins.

✤

One for every year,
the small beads of knotted wrack –
calendars of air.

✤

When the Vikings came
there was nothing here. A breeze
is the wind of change.

Riddle of the sands:
lugworms casting question marks
linked by ampersands.

❉

As the tide retreats,
plans are made, sandcastles built …
History repeats.

❉

Poor old Captain Bligh,
never guessed what was to come –
bounty by and by.

First up, the skylark
looking for the early worm.
Whistle while you work.

✭

Small dogs running free;
fitful, feigning, doubling back –
the sea on its leash.

✭

Light-headed or not –
hills of swaying marram grass
rooted to the spot.

Listen to the bridge
shudder softly as you cross.
Lover, make a wish.

⁂

Sleepers, nuts and bolts;
and, between the gaps, the air
in which this world floats.

⁂

Sunday traffic jam:
line of cars behind a tot
pushing a toy pram.

The sky and the sea.
And that faint line in between,
drawn as if for me.

✲

Walking the mudflats,
I pass a stranger. We nod.
And leave it at that.

✲

As precise as words
on a page, in the fresh mud –
the language of birds.

Things the sea gives up:
plastic, nappies, the handle
of a china cup …

✺

Empty at first sight,
unless that *is* the message –
a bottle of light.

✺

It's all about light –
bird song, child's play, plankton bloom,
the weed's dizzy height …

Difficult to tell:
angel wings carved out of stone
or a cockle shell?

※

Poolbeg's twin towers,
equally ambiguous:
Peace, friend or *Up yours?*

※

The world's axis shifts:
from a garden in Clontarf
cherry blossom drifts.

Look what we've just found,
something religions yearn for –
the sky on the ground.

※

When the sky turns red
the fish in the bucket stops –
and backs out again.

※

Two boys with a kite
made from twigs and plastic bags.
Wind shrugs: "Oh, all right."

Man in a canoe
gliding past, his oar a brush,
painting white on blue.

※

Sand dunes, then the sea
and, beyond it, Wales – those peaks
calling back to these.

※

On a windy day
sand gets in your eyes, your teeth,
makes grass of your hair.

The bright-painted hull
of a fishing boat appears.
Cue applause of gulls.

✻

Gem anemone –
warty, green, with pink punk hair:
You looking at me?

✻

Twenty-legged fools,
common shrimp are commonly
stuck in some rock pool.

Jesus, he might be,
that long-haired kite-surfer dude
walking on the sea.

※

Human suffering:
a child's balloon carried off,
its long string dangling.

※

In the swirl of tide
half a dozen see-through fish
gliding side by side.

Studying bird song
on my iPhone while songbirds
gamely sing along.

✻

Sudden smell of hops
from a city worlds away –
distances collapse.

✻

James is Cool. Who knew?
James, for one; and, well, his dad –
all you need is two.

Maps drawn and redrawn,
the tide inching in around
the unmoved heron.

※

"Glad we had this talk,"
my self whispers to himself.
(Never just a walk.)

※

A two-person tent
pitched in the dunes. Young lovers?
Kids without the rent.

Blackbird on a pole
watching sanderlings charge past:
air traffic control.

※

Unseen things recoil
when you lift a twig, a shell;
the sand rich as soil.

※

Bivalves, molluscs, worms …
Underfoot, deep in the mud,
the wheel of life turns.

When I was a boy
we drove out here once, these dunes
like the ruins of Troy.

※

It was our world then,
us midlander boys and girls –
islanders again.

※

Dew-damp, the long grass,
balancing small globes of light,
trembles as I pass.

Picnic on the beach?
A dog with a bag of chips,
two crows with one each.

※

Polish? Latvian?
Laughter carried on the wind
needs no translation.

※

Smell that? Camping gas
fulfilling the primal dream:
beer, bunburgers, grass.

Having a few beers
in the dunes, two head-the-balls,
shoulders like red meat.

※

Grasses wave like flame,
or crowds in the Hogan Stand
for the Sunday game.

※

Maids from Cabra West,
Painted Lady butterflies
up from Marrakech …

Sirens on the shore:
tipsy teenage girls strip off.
Garda out in force.

※

Picking through the scraps,
magpies think they own the beach –
till a toddler claps.

※

Holding there, so still,
the kestrel – out of this world,
then in for the kill.

Someone's had enough.
Latest gangland victim or
drunk sleeping it off?

※

Thus it comes to pass,
bottle emptied, back he goes
to doze in the grass.

※

The Bull Island Blues:
"Well I woke up this morning,
the sea got my shoes."

Young lad on the phone –
"I've got other things to do!" –
stood there, skimming stones.

※

A robin redbreast
settles on my toe. Can't breathe.
Not yet, not just yet.

※

Small kids playing war,
rifles raised in the long grass,
bullets made of air.

Slowly drifting by
under sail, a fragile craft —
one cloud in the sky.

※

By my floating hand,
pushing head-down through the waves —
beetle in the sand.

※

"Bee orchid, I know
you're here somewhere, but it's late.
Soon I'll have to go."

Alien attack:
shoals of jelly-fish washed up.
The empire strikes back.

✭

Dracula himself —
the cormorant drying off,
great black wings outspread.

✭

Seal's head in the sea.
Like a passing astronaut.
And his eye on me.

Sharing cigarettes,
old man sitting on the wall
with his former self.

✻

"Mornings, without fail,
rain or shine, on Dollymount.
And then, one fine day …"

✻

Named for Dolly, wife
of the local landlord, this
stunning afterlife.

Waves themselves, their wings
flashing silver when they turn
as one – the starlings.

✸

Evening. An old crow.
Who said magpies have sole rights
on loss and sorrow?

✸

Just about alive,
in staggered V formation
the brent geese arrive.

The sun's dying rays
single out an average rock
for singular praise.

✭

In his high-vis vest
the bicycle courier
pauses to reflect.

✭

(As the buddhists sing
to the ice-cream man, *Make me
one with everything.*)

Like a polar bear
creeping up on nesting birds –
the photographer.

✱

A container ship –
city skyline on the move –
gives the docks the slip.

✱

Dollymount selfie:
five Italian girls, three dogs,
endless kites – and me.

The first drops of rain
strike the concrete bathing hut –
colour once again.

✯

The skull of a bird,
like a seashell, whispers *is* –
always the same word.

✯

Brent geese, hooded crows,
curlews, godwits, sanderlings ...
Lengthening shadows.

The killer's technique –
herring gull plays cool, a crab
struggling in its beak.

✻

Not rust after all
or paint from a paintball gun –
lichen on the wall.

✻

Let the day recur;
to the watercolourist
everything's a blur.

Turning in circles –
the L-driver learning to
credit miracles.

※

Eating fish and chips,
two old sisters gently dab
ketchup from their lips.

※

Ferry heading out
into the unknown, no time
to admit to doubt.

Power-walking past,
ladies of uncertain age –
the years go so fast.

※

Old man in his car
staring out to sea, Tosca
singing from the heart.

※

When my best friend died
I came here and sat for hours.
The gulls cried. They cried.

Into the chill sea,
flock of dunlin wading out:
… *deep deep deep, deep deep …*

*

A New Year's promise,
hardy locals bare their teeth,
part smile, part grimace.

*

History begins
with two swimmers, statuesque
in their marbled skin.

All alone at last –
the crab in the pool beside
the pool full of crabs.

✤

Jogger with a light
strapped onto his arm, its glow
stitching through the night.

✤

Last time we came here
some dog took off with your hat.
And the seagulls jeered.

On a rusty pole
two girls tape a bunch of flowers.
The sea looks so cold.

※

Each wearing one glove
here they come now, hand in hand –
teenagers in love.

※

Virgin on her plinth
stares into the distance. Some
junkie's left his syringe.

All day by the sea,
meeting my own footprints now
out to look for me.

※

Late introspection:
curlews quietly wading out
on their reflections.

※

Now my dog is dead
paw-prints in the concrete path
follow me instead.

Darkness drawing near;
slowly – a porch light left on –
the moon re-appears.

※

It's the moon you've caught
in your bucket, little boy,
budding astronaut.

※

Where the angler fell
to his death, the sea remains
inconsolable.

The day almost done,
the sun's golden robes slipped off,
city lights all on.

※

See, the full moon floats,
and the wooden bridge becomes
the deck of a boat.

※

There's our own selves there
in the water, looking up,
moonlight in our hair.

Homewards? Wait, there's still
movement yet, a few last gulls
riding the thermals …

✻

Somewhere in the dark –
lovers, gangsters, the headlights
of a Garda car …

✻

Youngsters, left alone,
huddled in a concrete hut,
laughing, getting stoned.

Badger, owl and fox,
creatures just beyond our sight;
rats among the rocks.

✺

Forest of seaweed
lifted by the rising tide,
gentled out of sleep.

✺

Even as we sleep
the island grows. Pause here now,
your eyes closed, and dream …

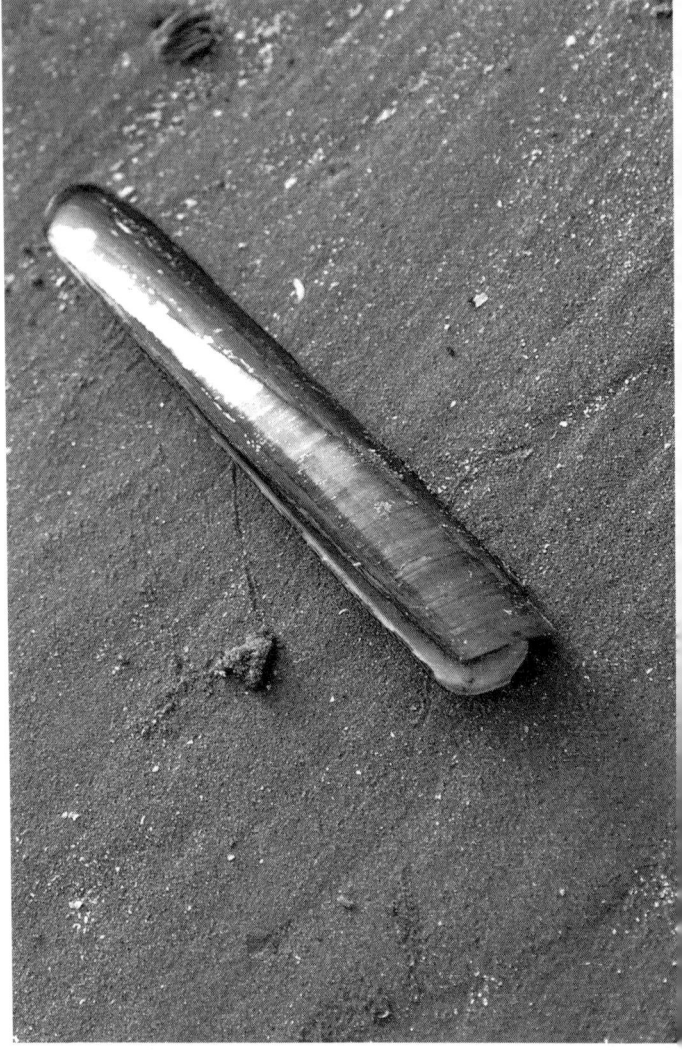

Dream it starts again:
a first, a second, a third breath,
the countless following.

※

Dream the sand's alive —
moving, shifting, never still;
the grains multiply …

※

Dream that you are dead —
flash of darkness, the kestrel
passing overhead.

Nights you cannot sleep,
imagine yourself out here,
walking in bare feet.

✯

Shells and dust of shells.
Evolution got it right:
no us without them.

✯

Tattoo of small wings,
shudder of grass-stalks, grass heads,
and then the settling.

The metal handrail
whistles as the breeze picks up.
Hard to pull away.

❈

A cell phone ringing,
a gull screeching overhead.
No one answering.

❈

What is it we say
with this sweep of light, or words?
We are here today.

Marram grass is tough.
Sometimes that is everything,
and still not enough.

※

Nothing stays the same
from one minute to the next.
New life stakes its claim.

※

They lead to nothing,
the steps at the bathing hut;
then the tide comes in.

Any morning now
the first tender buds will show,
pushing clear somehow.

✺

On the wooden bench
last night's frost starting to melt –
almost time for lunch.

✺

Maps of worlds like this:
when they're drawn, where we stand now
doesn't yet exist.

Taxi driver sat
on the bonnet of his car –
steam cloud from his flask.

※

You ask: "Are you free?"
"We are all *born* free," he says,
turning from the sea.

※

Then it's home again,
stars like grains of sand, the sky
tide-washed overhead.

AFTERWORD

Despite having written a large number of haiku in recent times (far more than eventually gelled together to make this small book), I don't consider myself a haiku poet, certainly not in the traditional sense.

Haiku writers these days have their own journals, their own websites, their own apparently inward-looking world. Poets working in other forms may dabble in haiku, but there is often the sense that this is but a brief dalliance, and not to be taken as seriously as their other (almost by definition) larger work.

However, it seems to me that, rather than being harmed by them, traditions of all sorts may be refreshed and reaffirmed by occasional encounters with difference. These haiku will have to find their way in the world as what they are, what almost all of the things and creatures in the world are:

as hybrids, compromises between intention and accident, between skill and luck, and, in the case of poems, between words and the invisible stuff they try to make visible.

While many of these haiku are concerned with the traditional subjects and themes of the form – nature, time, the seasons, our place in the world – their tone owes at least as much to the West as to the East (to borrow a simplistic notation). Indeed it has often seemed to me that the Shakespearean sonnet's closing couplet might have more in common with the haiku than first seems evident.

In general, English-language writers of haiku do not stick rigidly to the 17-syllable, 3-line stanza that the name still suggests to the average reader. Delicious, jazz-flavoured haiku by Jack Kerouac among many others have influenced a generation of writers for whom the name now suggests more an attitude and general approach than a rigid form. This 'opening' of the form seems to me a good thing, though a certain amount of resistance is indispensable when it comes to testing what ideas or new formulations may be worthwhile. Indulgence is, after all, the artist's enemy; the doubting, second-guessing imperatives of form can both supply a necessary distraction or diversion and also provoke occasional resolve.

Haiku sometimes rhyme, but generally they are not built for that purpose. Rhyme is an accident of a given language: some languages are more blessed (or cursed) than others. (In Italian, for instance, where rhymes are almost as common in daily language as they are in verse, it might be argued that they add little real extra weight to poetic forms. In English, their comparative rarity might be said to confer an added potency or concentration.)

For my part, I like the way rhyme (both 'full' or partial) works to close and seal an idea, to unite the lines it spans, even as the spirit of the verse (poem or haiku), attempts to reach beyond. The expectation of rhyme is a tension, and a provocation to attention and memory, and it can produce a small electrical charge in the language, a charge that often brings with it some degree of surprise and illumination.

From the outset, therefore, it seemed important that these resolutely three-line forms should chime or ring out briefly, that they should take root on the page almost like the marram grass of the island itself, being stitched down by their own system of roots or stays. I liked the notion of the first and third lines rhyming, the way, out on the shore on a clear day, the sky and sea might be said to rhyme with one another, with the horizon, that third distinctive line in the middle, acting as both separation and, sometimes, as mirror. Poems that would not fit the general run of the sequence (for a kind of narrative emerges whether intended or not) I worried about for a time; in the end I had to abandon many I felt had promise: the cruel masters of chance, rhyme and metre add an element of randomness that is worth any (haiku) poet's time; and disappointment seems to me the first opportunity to step back from any creative work long enough to see if it might warrant further time and exploration.

Haiku are often viewed as self-contained, even mutually isolated poems of momentary insight (hopefully with enduring implications). But as well as acting like this on their own, they can also be brought together in a variety of patterns and sequences, adding up, one hopes, to something more than the sum of their parts.

The first Japanese haiku (then called *hokku*) date from the mid-17th century and were conceived as the opening sections of longer works, often by many hands, that included 5-line forms *(tanka)* and even passages in prose *(haibun)*. A form that combined both haiku and painting – known as *haiga* – would seem to be a direct predecessor of haiku-photo compositions such as this one. The many traditional arrangements and permutations are beyond the scope of a note such as this; and what has happened to haiku in the age of the internet, the cellphone and Twitter on its own would make a fascinating full-length essay by someone better qualified than myself. Suffice to say that the picture is, as usual, more complicated than it first appears. The spirit of haiku inspires some, the form inspires others, and a great many poets have taken either impulse, or both, down paths previously untrodden, overthrowing the received notion that haiku is something that belongs in the distant (Japanese) past.

What does invite brief discussion, however, is the haiku sequence (or *rensaku)*, an increasingly popular form that offers the poet the opportunity to explore subjects if not in greater depth then over a longer period of time and from a variety of angles. Elements that haiku normally omit (including overt narrative) are brought within reach, the gaps between linked verses allowing (if not in fact suggesting) narrative progress in the reader's mind.

Interestingly, one of the essential ingredients of traditional haiku (alongside the presence of the *kigo,* or seasonal reference) is the quality known as *kiru*, which loosely translates as 'cutting'. The idea is that the haiku poet should cut between two ideas, thereby recognising them as clear and distinct, but at the same – by the decisive energy of the transition – drawing attention to the deeper connections between them. In *rensaku,* this 'cutting' effect is intensified, and a modern reader, brought up on a diet of television and cinema, should be quite at home with a sequence of brief images, animated by a jump-cut technique that anticipates the film editing suite by a couple of hundred years.

In this small book, I have followed a generally chronological (that is seasonal) line throughout (an essential aspect of the tradition in most of its variations). However, on many occasions I have allowed a given haiku's position in the whole to speak for itself, not wishing to introduce more 'signposts' than seemed necessary. The sequence does not take place over a single day, or even over a single year, but a certain coherence is, I hope, achieved by those occasional temporal and seasonal references. Once established in any text, place and time continue to exert an influence until they are revised or re-rendered before the reader's eyes: it is the nature of human experience (and the human experience of nature) than we read it as such.

Finally, in any regular composition, there may be a moment when the plan is called into question, when something like a random mutation begins to emerge, for better or worse, with its own set of threats if also new possibilities. When it came to the rhythm of these lines, I wanted something that was as close as possible to everyday speech, but also something that wouldn't push against the haiku's natural division into three lines and, usually, two linked images or ideas. After some experimenting I found that a predominantly trochaic (i.e. heavy-light / heavy-light …) rather than iambic (light-heavy / light-heavy …) metre was the most comfortable fit. I point this out here only because the iambic is often seen as the default measure of English language verse, being the basis of the sonnet's iambic pentameter, Shakespeare's blank verse, and so much more. It may be that the trochee works well in the haiku because it makes the most of those opening and closing syllables of each line, helping to recreate some of the feel of the *kiru* or 'cutting' effect that the form so often depends on. In any case, in the end it felt to me that a kind of prevailing wind was blowing through the text as a whole, connecting the individual verses with each other on an aural as well as on an imagistic level.

My own attitude to haiku has changed considerably in the course of writing and compiling this volume. Though I have long read and admired haiku (and find it a wonderful way of stepping outside of the sometimes often complicated syntax of some other forms – if only for the proverbial 'breath of fresh air' – the form itself seemed too proscriptive, insisting that too much of what I might call the noise of the world be excluded in the search for essence. Whatever worth this book might have, it has opened again for me the small aperture of this venerable form, and shown me how haiku has the power to render a world I recognise in a way both precise and suggestive, a way that I am certain will bring me back to it again.

ABOUT THE PHOTOGRAPHS

Of the photographs there is little to be said. I took them and a good number of others over the course of a year or so, almost every day when visiting or passing along the roadway beside the island. Drawn to the ever-changing colours of the mudflats, the grasslands and dunes, originally I thought of doing a little book of haiku with a few colour plates. In the end I compromised by including a much smaller number in their black and white incarnations. (Perhaps some of the colour images will some time serve a function somewhere else.) As it turns out, losing some of the beauty of the images (by which I mean the striking colours rather than the dubious artistic merits) gives more 'space' to the poems, which is just as well. How it works, precisely, may not be for the practitioner to figure out – on any given day there are tasks and deadlines, practical challenges to be met – but on occasion the call of poetry is to engage with some specific subject over an extended period of time rather than in the single intense burst of the lyric moment. Haiku seems well placed to reflect such engagement, reminding us through both its simplicity and its brevity of form that much of what we know (or think we know) is assembled from vivid, discrete impressions, and did not come to us all at once or ready-made. Indeed it may take some of us (myself included) an inordinately long time to see how, like drifting or wind-borne grains of sand, perhaps, they may join with each other to form something far greater than the sum of their parts.

ABOUT THE AUTHOR

Pat Boran is an Irish poet, writer and broadcaster. Born in Portlaoise in 1963, he lives in North Dublin, not far from Bull Island. He has published many books of poetry and prose, including *New and Selected Poems* (2005), *The Next Life* (2012), the humorous prose memoir *The Invisible Prison* (2009), and the popular writers' handbook *The Portable Creative Writing Workshop* (revised, 2013). He has edited numerous anthologies of poetry and prose and is a former presenter of *The Poetry Programme* and *The Enchanted Way* on RTÉ Radio 1. Awards include the Patrick Kavanagh Award for Poetry and the US-based Lawrence O'Shaughnessy Award for Poetry. He is a member of Aosdána, the Irish affiliation of creative artists. For a selection of his poetry films and other work, see www.patboran.com.